Barbara Kunz

KIND WORDS, CRUISE MISSILES, AND EVERYTHING IN BETWEEN

The Use of Power Resources in U.S. Policies towards Poland, Ukraine, and Belarus 1989–2008

With a foreword by William Hill

ibidem-Verlag
Stuttgart

Bibliografische Information der Deutschen Nationalbibliothek
Die Deutsche Nationalbibliothek verzeichnet diese Publikation in der Deutschen Nationalbibliografie; detaillierte bibliografische Daten sind im Internet über http://dnb.d-nb.de abrufbar.

Bibliographic information published by the Deutsche Nationalbibliothek
Die Deutsche Nationalbibliothek lists this publication in the Deutsche Nationalbibliografie; detailed bibliographic data are available in the Internet at http://dnb.d-nb.de.

∞
Gedruckt auf alterungsbeständigem, säurefreien Papier
Printed on acid-free paper

ISSN: 1614-3515

ISBN-13: 978-3-8382-1065-0

© *ibidem*-Verlag
Stuttgart 2017

Alle Rechte vorbehalten

Das Werk einschließlich aller seiner Teile ist urheberrechtlich geschützt. Jede Verwertung außerhalb der engen Grenzen des Urheberrechtsgesetzes ist ohne Zustimmung des Verlages unzulässig und strafbar. Dies gilt insbesondere für Vervielfältigungen, Übersetzungen, Mikroverfilmungen und elektronische Speicherformen sowie die Einspeicherung und Verarbeitung in elektronischen Systemen.

All rights part of this publication may be reproduced, stored in or introduced into a retrieval system, or transmitted, in any form, or by any means (electronic, mechanical, photocopying, recording or otherwise) without the prior written permission of the publisher. Any person who does any unauthorized act in relation to this publication may be liable to criminal prosecution and civil claims for damages.

Printed in the EU

Preface

During the Cold War American political leaders and government representatives advanced an unchanging policy toward the Soviet Bloc, calling for complete independence of these states from Moscow and observance of basic human rights and fundamental freedoms within them. As the Warsaw Pact and then the Soviet Union disintegrated in sudden, dramatic, and largely peaceful fashion from 1989 to late 1991, American leaders were faced with a dilemma as rare in international affairs as it was welcome: how to help fashion and put into the practice the institutional, political, and economic details of the independence and freedom won by the peoples of Eastern Europe and the Soviet Union after half a century of struggle. Although thinkers such as Francis Fukuyama heralded the momentous events in Europe as "the end of history," in truth for the nations of the Warsaw Pact and the former Soviet republics their independent national histories were recommencing after enforced interludes of decades, and for some, centuries.

Barbara Kunz's study, *Kind Words, Cruise Missiles, and Everything in Between*, describes and analyzes the efforts of American political leaders and diplomats during the first two decades after the end of the Cold War to develop and implement policies and courses of action that would help realize these lofty goals in three of the independent states which emerged from the end of the Soviet era: Poland, Ukraine, and Belarus. As an American diplomat and practitioner focusing on Europe and the former Soviet space during most of this period, the issues, policies, and events treated in this volume are intensely familiar, and reading about them evokes many memories and sensations, from satisfaction with successes to regrets over failures, omissions, and unexpected reverses. Since at least the adoption of the Helsinki Final Act, American representatives had been pushing for an end to the division of Europe into two hostile camps, calling for "a Europe whole and free." The dramatic events of 1989-1991 gave us a breathtaking opportunity to realize our wildest dreams for the future of Europe. At the same time, the epochal changes in Europe imposed a necessity for political vision and policy innovation comparable to that shown by post-World war II American and European leaders.

As the author indicates in her introduction, there is considerable doubt whether post-Cold War American presidents and administrations have had a consistent vision or grand strategy for Europe—indeed, whether they have had any real European strategy or policy at all. In my opinion, derived considerably from my own experience as an American diplomat and practitioner during this period and involvement in many of the policy debates and initiatives, there have been several crucial common elements in basic principles of the approach of all U.S. administrations to the region from 1989 to the present. First of all, the George H.W. Bush administration decided that the U.S. would remain physically present and actively involved in European security and defense affairs, a decision which has been reaffirmed and continued by each subsequent American administration (until the present one, for which at this writing the jury seems to be still out). This decision was neither preordained nor inevitable, and has had a formative influence on post-Cold War European history.

Second, Washington has insisted that all of the Warsaw Pact states and former Soviet republics should enjoy complete independence and sovereignty, without external limitations on their choice of geopolitical orientation or security arrangements. Growing out of opposition to the forced participation of the Soviet satellites in the Warsaw Pact, this basic principle provided one of the important intellectual underpinnings for the policies of NATO and EU expansion. Third, with respect to the internal political, economic, and social systems and arrangements within these states, both Republicans and Democrats in Washington generally expected that they would all undergo transitions from Soviet-style authoritarian political systems and command economies to open, pluralist, democratic polities and market economies.

There may have been important differences in the details of their analyses and approaches, but most of my colleagues inside and outside of government in the U.S. seemed to expect that such a transition was simply the natural order of things. This was, after all, the era of Samuel Huntington's *Third Wave* and the ascendance of the Washington consensus. Democratization and marketization were integral features of the intellectual and political context within which American policies were formed, including and in particular with respect to countries in this region. As one follows the arguments in this volume, one might conclude that perceived progress in pursuit of these two general principles of the American approach was one particularly important criterion in the determination made by U.S. administrations that a particular country or administration was friendly, undecided, or non-friendly.

Barbara Kunz's study delves into the specific details and reasons why, for U.S. policymakers and diplomats from 1989 to 2008, Poland was an overwhelmingly friendly country, Ukraine an undecided interlocutor, and Belarus after 1994 pretty clearly a non-friend. My own assessments agree emphatically with these characterizations, although I have reached my own conclusions more through observation and experience, and not the more rigorous analysis contained in this study. Irrespective of this difference, this volume addresses the same basic question that we American practitioners faced when dealing with non-communist Poland and newly independent Ukraine and Belarus: why did we get very different results in three countries which started in 1989–1991 from very similar circumstances? Why were we unable to apply largely similar policies and actions to each country and achieve similar results? From my own personal experience, I can attest that in the early 1990s (at the least) these questions were decidedly not just academic.

From 1989 on Poland was in most respects a pleasant surprise for American officials. Under both President Walesa and Kwasniewski, the land of the liberum veto achieved a commendable degree of political pluralism, freedom, and stability, while the Balcerowicz reforms seemed to produce the greatest progress toward a market economy in the region. The large Polish diaspora in the United States provided considerable domestic political support for the policy of NATO enlargement, while Polish representatives worked particularly closely with their American colleagues to make an enlarged Alliance a reality. In the 2000s Warsaw was at the forefront of "new Europe" standing with Washington in Afghanistan and Iraq. Differences between the two countries seemed minor, and policy visions and collaboration were closely aligned.

In contrast, for American practitioners Ukraine always seemed somewhere "in between." After the false start of President George H.W. Bush's "chicken Kiev" speech, American support for Ukraine's independence, sovereignty, and territorial integrity was unwavering. At times Washington asked Kiev to do things it found difficult or unpleasant in pursuit of larger political goals, such as giving up its nuclear weapons and delivery systems to Russia or accepting more flexibility for internal Russian troop deployments in the 1996 CFE Flank Agreement. On the other hand, the U.S. supported Ukraine on the status of Crimea and the presence of Russian military forces there, and played a leading role in fashioning Ukraine's "distinctive partnership" with NATO. In the 2000s, Washington offered strong support for the Orange revolution and Ukraine's bid for NATO membership.

American officials, in my personal experience, were most frustrated with Ukraine's seeming unwillingness or inability to make needed domestic political and economic reforms to build a stronger market economy, combat corruption, and promote political stability. Widespread disillusionment with the Kuchma administration over the Gongadze murder and Kolchuga radar sale epitomizes the frequent and recurring disappointment experienced by American officials who perceived their Ukrainian counterparts to be continually failing to live up to their own promises to reform. It has been a widespread American perception that Ukraine is a country which we would like to help, but whose officials will not follow through and help themselves.

Belarus is clearly another story altogether. Washington's relations with Minsk began optimistically, and the U.S. was successful in getting the nuclear weapons and delivery systems located in Belarus moved to Russia. However, the election of Luskashenka in 1994 effectively ended all cooperation between the U.S. and Belarus, and relations between the two deteriorated with extreme rapidity. By 1996 American officials were already talking about imposing sanctions on Belarus. The disappearance and killing of political opponents and opposition leaders in the late 1990s and widespread violations of electoral norms and basic human rights had made Belarus largely a pariah by 2000. Occasional attempts during the 2000s from one side or the other to alter this situation or improve relations generally foundered. For example, one U.S offer to lift a number of sanctions failed when Luskashenka apparently could not bring himself to free one prisoner originally promised by Minsk as part of the deal. In spite of, or perhaps at times because of such attempts, there has been basically no real change over some two decades in the U.S. perception of and attitude toward Belarus and Luskashenka.

What did we U.S. officials do to promote desirable change and manage relations with each of these countries after 1989? Barbara Kunz relates and analyzes many of those actions in this volume. Without giving away that narrative, I note that in my recollection we often asked ourselves both "What can we do?" and "What should we do?" For the first question, we frequently reviewed the instruments of state power at our disposal, to be employed in coercive or cooperative fashions. To the second question, there were usually many domestic and international political factors that needed to be taken into consideration in addition to the state of our relations with and estimation of the country in question. The answers we found were often interconnected, and—in particular for the latter question—rarely obvious.

Kind Words, Cruise Missiles, and Everything in Between provides a theory-based, analytic, detailed examination and explanation of how and why American officials addressed and answered such questions with respect to Poland, Ukraine, and Belarus in the first two decades after the Cold War. In so doing, this book also provides insights into the more fundamental bases of international relations and the behavior of states, questions which are of fundamental importance to practitioners, but which our operational duties rarely allow us time to contemplate. Both the substance of international politics and the particular period, events, and countries examined in this volume are both important in their own right and of great, continuing personal interest. This book thus provides both a welcome exercise in historical memory and at the same time a deeper understanding of international relations theory and practice, an uncommon and impressive combination.

William H. Hill
Washington, DC
June 2017

William Hill is a retired U.S. diplomat. He served in the USSR, Eastern Europe, and Washington in the Department of State, Department of Defense, and US Information Agency. He also served two terms between 1999–2006 as Head of the OSCE Mission to Moldova, and from 2007–2017 has been a Professor of National Security Strategy at the National War College in Washington DC. The views expressed here are his own.

Contents

Preface 5

Contents 11

Abbreviations 15

I   Introduction 17
    I.1   The background 18
        I.1.1   Preserving the unipolar moment 27
        I.1.2   On the ground: the U.S. in Central and Eastern Europe 33
    I.2   Empirical objectives 37

II   The theoretical framework and methodology 41
    II.1   Introduction and research questions 41
        II.1.1   Neoclassical realism: an introduction 46
        II.1.2   Elite perceptions: of more than just the system? 49
    II.2   Non-friends, friends and undecided states 56
        II.2.1   Non-friends 57
        II.2.2   Friends 62
        II.2.3   Concluding remarks: undecided states 65
    II.3   Two types of power resources
        and foreign policy tools 66
        II.3.1   Power in political realism 67
        II.3.2   Positive and negative power: the relevance of base values 72
        II.3.3   Negative power and its bases 78
        II.3.4   Positive power and its bases 79
        II.3.5   Power resources and foreign policy tools 82
    II.4   Linking states' friend / non-friend /
        undecided status to power 87
    II.5   Concluding remarks on the theoretical framework 89
    II.6   Methodological considerations 90
        II.6.1   The cases 92
        II.6.2   Sources 95
        II.6.3   Research design: Comparative case studies 95

    II.6.4 Three steps in addressing the sources 97

III U.S. Foreign Policies Towards Poland 103

  III.1 Introduction 104

  III.2 Laying the foundations: the U.S. and Solidarność 107

    III.2.1 Accompanying Poland
          to de facto independence 1989–1991 107
    III.2.2 Foreign Policy Tools in Solidarność-times 111

  III.3 An emerging new best friend in Europe:
         the second Gulf War and NATO enlargement 113

    III.3.1 Euro-Atlantic integration or: Overcoming Yalta 113
    III.3.2 Foreign policy tools 1991 to 2000 118

  III.4 The heydays and their aftermath: 2001 onwards 120

    III.4.1 State Tourism: Bush, Kwaśniewski and the Iraq war 121
    III.4.2 Foreign policy tools 2001 to 2005 128

  III.5 After Kwaśniewski: 2005 onwards 129

    III.5.1 The double Kaczyński era 130
    III.5.2 Donald Tusk, the conclusion of the Missile Defence
          Agreement — and still no visa waiver programme 133
    III.5.3 Foreign policy tools after Kwaśniewski 137

  III.6 Conclusions on U.S. foreign policies
         towards Poland 1989–2008 140

IV U.S. Foreign Policies Towards Ukraine 145

  IV.1 Introduction:
         America's recognition of Ukraine's independence 146

  IV.2 The early years: Moscow-centrism and a focus
         on nuclear non-proliferation 1991 to 1994 148

    IV.2.1 Solving the nuclear question 148
    IV.2.2 The Lisbon Protocol and Ukraine's accession
          to the NPT as a nuclear-free state 150
    IV.2.3 Foreign Policy Tools in solving the nuclear question 158

  IV.3 Conventional non-proliferation: Ukraine's accession to
         the MTCR, Bushehr and the Satellite Deal 1994 to 1998 160

    IV.3.1 Getting Ukraine to join the MTCR 161

IV.3.2 The Policy of issue linkage: non-proliferation,
nuclear power plants and satellites 165
IV.3.3 Foreign Policy Tools in making Ukraine join the MTCR ... 167

IV.4 Euro-Atlantic integration: Ukraine
in its wider context 1994 to 2004 169

IV.4.1 The U.S.-Ukrainian honeymoon: broadening relations 169
IV.4.2 Setbacks and frustration 174
IV.4.3 Multilateralising Ukraine's transformation:
Ukraine and NATO 179
IV.4.4 Foreign Policy Tools in promoting Ukraine's
Euro-Atlantic integration 183

IV.5 After the Orange Revolution:
diminished U.S. interest 2004 to 2008 186

IV.5.1 Few illusions left:
the Orange Revolution and its aftermath 186
IV.5.2 Foreign policy tools 2004 to 2008 193

IV.6 Conclusions on U.S. foreign policies towards Ukraine 195

V U.S. Foreign Policies Towards Belarus 199

V.1 Introduction: At odds with the West 200

V.2 Belarus and the US: the early years 202

V.2.1 Belarus:
The unproblematic answer to the nuclear question 202
V.2.2 Foreign policy tools in early U.S.-Belarusian relations 204

V.3 Lukashenka and "Selective Engagement" with Minsk 205

V.3.1 Rigged elections and referenda: Deteriorating relations 205
V.3.2 The Belarus Democracy Act 209
V.3.3 Political Prisoners, Sanctions and *Personae Non Gratae* 212
V.3.4 "Selective engagement" and foreign policy tools 214

V.4 The wider context: Belarus in international politics 216

V.4.1 The Bush II era: Belarus as a rogue state? 216
V.4.2 Belarus and Euro-Atlantic Integration 219
V.4.3 The wider context and foreign policy tools 222

V.5 Conclusions on U.S. foreign policies
towards Belarus 1991–2008 223

VI Conclusions 229

VI.1 Returning to the research questions 229

VI.2 Empirical findings: U.S. post-Cold War policies towards Poland, Ukraine and Belarus 231

VI.3 Implications for theory building: linking status to power 237

VI.3.1 Friends, non-friends and undecided states: an element of the missing link 237
VI.3.2 A category of its own: undecided states 239
VI.3.3 Positive and negative power as means to shape and control the environment 241

VI.4 Final remarks 244

Annex 247

High-level contacts between the U.S. and Poland, Ukraine and Belarus 247

References 251

Primary Sources 251

Speeches, Press Releases and Briefings 251
Background Notes 258
Treaties, Laws, Reports and Official Strategies 261
Websites 262

Books and Articles 263

Media Sources 274

Abbreviations

CIS	Community of Independent States
CSCE	Conference on Security and Cooperation in Europe
EAPC	Euro-Atlantic Partnership Council
EBRD	European Bank for Reconstruction and Development
EC	European Community (formerly Communities)
ENP	European Neighbourhood Policy
EU	European Union
FRG	Federal Republic of Germany
GDR	German Democratic Republic
GMF	German Marshall Fund of the United States
ICBM	Intercontinental Ballistic Missile
IMF	International Monetary Fund
MAP	Membership Action Plan
MTCR	Missile Technology Control Regime
NATO	North Atlantic Treaty Organisation
NPT	Non-Proliferation Treaty
NUC	NATO-Ukraine Commission
OSCE	Organisation for Security and Cooperation in Europe
PAUCI	Polish-American-Ukrainian Cooperation Initiative
PfP	Partnership for Peace
START	Strategic Arms Reduction Treaty
TACIS	Technical Aid to the Community of Independent States
UN	United Nations
USAID	United States Agency for International Development
USSR	Union of Soviet Socialist Republics
WMD	Weapons of Mass Destruction
WTO	World Trade Organisation

I Introduction

> The purpose of foreign policy is to influence the policies and actions of other nations in a way that serves your interests and values. The tools available include everything from kind words to cruise missiles. Mixing them properly and with sufficient patience is the art of diplomacy.
>
> Madeleine Albright

When the red flag on the Kremlin was hauled down for the last time in late December 1991, the United States attained a power matched by no other country. From that point in time onwards, U.S. grand strategy no longer consisted of checking a rival superpower within a bipolar international system, rather in preserving the unipolar moment and expanding its power position. This consistently was the goal of American administrations during the post-Cold War era. In pursuing that objective, it is yet remarkable that foreign policies led by the United States differed to the extent they did, even under circumstances that were largely identical. This observation indeed runs counter to expectations derived from fundamental (neoclassical) realist tenets: while the U.S. quest for (preserved) primacy confirms realist core assumptions, differences in foreign policy output under similar circumstances are puzzling. Realism is based on the assumption that it is first and foremost the environment that determines states' behaviour.[1] For that reason, policy design processes taking place under similar circumstances—both at the systemic *and* domestic levels—should essentially be expected to result in similar policies. These expectations notwithstanding, this is obviously not the case as far as United States policies towards Central and Eastern Europe in the post-Cold War era are concerned. Under the exact same circumstances of unipolarity, the exact same state conducted entirely different policies towards three neighbouring countries with about the same degree of relative power as compared to Washington and highly similar historical

---

1   Jennifer Sterling-Folker (1997) 'Realist Environment, Liberal Process, and Domestic Level Variables', *International Studies Quarterly* 41(1), p. 4.

legacies. These differences become apparent when analysing the United States' foreign policy output in terms of the foreign policy tools applied, based upon different types of power resources at Washington's disposal. This study, by means of an analysis of U.S. approaches to Poland, Ukraine and Belarus in the years 1989 to 2008, intends to provide an explanation of that puzzle. These almost twenty years cover the final years of the Bush senior administration as well as the complete Clinton and Bush junior administrations. They thus also include the formative years for post-Cold War security affairs on the European continent, from the fall of the Berlin wall to NATO's Bucharest summit at which Ukraine was denied membership in the Alliance. And while the literature on U.S. approaches to Russia in the same time-span is by now abundant, there are very few studies dealing with Washington's policies towards the countries 'in between' — that is, these other nations that had to (re)draft their security policies from scratch after the Soviet Union's demise.

The present study is divided into two major parts. The first part sets out to introduce the theoretical framework and the methodological considerations that form the basis of this study in chapter II. Readers not interested in these aspects may simply skip this part. The second — empirical — part contains the three case study chapters devoted to Poland (chapter III), Ukraine (chapter IV) and Belarus (chapter V). Each section in these empirical chapters ends with an analysis of the respective country's friend / non-friend / undecided status and the foreign policy tools employed. Finally, a concluding chapter (VI) sums up the findings of this study and discusses open questions and further avenues for research.

I.1 The background

Much of the Cold War had been fought, yet mostly virtually, in the heart of Europe, with the boundary between the two blocs going right through Berlin. When the Wall fell on 9 November 1989 after earlier unrest throughout the continent's Eastern part, it consequently was in the same region that changes were most palpable.

The end of the Cold War posed unique challenges and opportunities for many Central and Eastern European countries. Some, like the Baltic states, Ukraine and Belarus, were former Soviet republics and, as such, had very little experience as independent states. Others, such as Poland or Hungary, could look back on centuries of nationhood and, to some extent, statehood preserved throughout the Cold War, albeit as Soviet satellite states. Despite different legacies, all of Central and Eastern Europe hence faced similar challenges: besides the transformation of both the political and economic systems, the newly *de jure* or *de facto* independent states had to find their places within the international system and start maintaining relations with other states.

Repercussions were, however, not limited to the region as such. Given the United States' global ambitions, the disappearance of the Soviet Union as its main competitor also implied that Washington had to come up with updated European policies. In a speech addressing the Berlin Press Club in December 1989, then U.S. Secretary of State James Baker set out to define the four key features of the new European architecture as conceived by Washington: the North Atlantic Treaty Organisation (NATO), the European Community (EC), the Conference on Security and Cooperation in Europe (CSCE) and a continued American role in Europe.[2] In February of the following year, he identified four major challenges Central and Eastern European countries were facing:

> First, the spirit of revolution must move from the streets into the government. […] Second, the spirit of the new Europe needs to be reflected in security arrangements that remove the threat of military aggression or intimidation and promote the peaceful settlement of disputes. […] Third, the spirit of economic reform needs to move forward to allow free men and women to enjoy economic liberty—including the rights to private ownership and to work alone or collectively in markets where prices are set by individual choices, not centralized diktat. […] Following from these three challenges, I suggest there may also be a fourth: Some of the new democracies of the region may determine that they can better support and sustain their common

---

2   U.S. Department of State (1989) 'Speech to the Berlin Press Club', address by Secretary James Baker III, 12 December. Reprinted in: *Berlin Speeches: Secretary of State James A. Baker*, Washington D.C.: U.S.US Information Agency, 1991.

effort if they do so in concert, perhaps through some form of regional cooperation.[3]

And as President George H. W. Bush outlined two months later with respect to his country's role within that context,

> [t]he United States should remain a European power in the broadest sense — politically, militarily, and economically. And, as part of our global responsibilities, the foundation for America's peaceful engagement in Europe has been — and will continue to be — NATO.[4]

The way ahead was thus clearly laid out for U.S. foreign policy: America was to remain engaged in Europe, a reunified Germany was to remain part of NATO, and the independence of the newly free Central European states was to be preserved as being in the United States' national interest.

International post-Cold War politics began with a focus on the very same Central European country that had been responsible for most of the 20th Century's conflict and instability in the region: Germany. An often-overlooked aspect of U.S. policy towards Central Europe is the successful handling of Germany's reunification by the first Bush administration, notably the united country's continued membership in NATO. Initially neither desired nor supported by the French and British, and opposed by Gorbachev, it must be considered a success for U.S. diplomacy. A prudent approach by West German Chancellor Kohl — once he had overcome his reluctance to recognising Poland's Western border — certainly helped, but the U.S. stance was decisive in reaching what was to be known as the 2+4-agreement among the two Germanys and the four World War II allies. The 2+4-treaty, signed in Moscow in September 1990, set

---

3   U.S. Department of State (1990) 'From Revolution to Democracy: Central and Eastern Europe in the New Europe', address by Secretary James Baker III at Charles University, Czechoslovakia, 7 February. Cf. *U.S. Department of State Dispatch* 1(1), 3 September 1990.
4   The White House, Office of the Press Secretary (1990) 'NATO and the U.S. commitment to Europe', address by President Bush at the Oklahoma State University Commencement, Stillwater, Oklahoma, 4 May. Cf. *U.S. Department of State Dispatch* 1(1), 3 September 1990.

forth the framework for the external aspects of Germany's reunification. By obliging Germany to conclude an agreement with Poland,[5] the treaty thus not only solved the German question, but also a crucial aspect of the Polish question, a prerequisite for stability in Europe.[6] Furthermore, the way the unification was handled implied that it — technically — was nothing more but the German Democratic Republic's accession to the territory governed by West Germany's constitution, thereby permitting institutional continuity for Western Europe's most populous state and, in extension, for Europe as a whole. This clearly was the scenario favoured by the United States:

> The European Community and NATO represent the will of free peoples cooperating on both sides of the Atlantic to assure democracy, peace, and prosperity. That is why we and so many Europeans, including the Germans, believe that the new Germany should be a full member of a vigorous NATO alliance.[7]

The United States' handling of the breakdown of the Soviet Union, and especially the German reunification, laid the foundations for future developments in Central Europe. Yet, during the early 1990s, U.S. policies towards Central and Eastern Europe were in essence a

---

5   Cf. *Vertrag über die abschließende Regelung in bezug auf Deutschland vom 12. September 1990*, Artikel 1(2). Poland and Germany signed the required treaty on 14 November 1990, hence only weeks after the reunification on 3 October. Cf. *Vertrag zwischen der Bundesrepublik Deutschland und der Republik Polen über die Bestätigung der zwischen ihnen bestehenden Grenze*. Another important aspect of the 2+4-treaty is that Germany renounces all nuclear, biological or chemical weapons.

6   Contrary to what is suggested by the headline 'Federal Republic of Germany will Cease to Exist' in the vol. 1 no. 6 (8 October 1990) issue of the *U.S. Department of State Dispatch*, the United States' successfully solving the German question did yet not lead to the disappearance of Germany altogether (online archives accessed 17 October 2007). As of late 2010, the Federal Republic of Germany is still alive and well.
    For a detailed account on U.S. policies and the German reunification, cf. Philip Zelikow and Condoleezza Rice (1997) *Germany Unified and Europe Transformed. A Study in Statecraft*, 2nd edition, Cambridge: Harvard University Press.

7   Secretary James Baker (1990) 'Statement before the Senate Foreign Relations Committee', Washington D.C., 12 June.

continuation of Cold War policies, focused on preserving the existing Euro-Atlantic institutions, further expanding the West and eliminating existing threats.[8] Among those threats figured first of all the risk of political chaos due to a power vacuum in Central Europe. On numerous occasions, members of the administration therefore emphasised the necessity of continued American engagement in Europe by explaining it with the United States' national interest.[9] These considerations may well be translated into the language of political realism by stating that the American sphere of influence was not only to be preserved, but to be expanded.

The motto of the early post-Cold War days was "A Europe Whole and Free", an expression coined by Tomáš Masaryk, endorsed decades later by George H.W. Bush. It essentially implied the inclusion of the former Soviet satellite states or Republics into the Euro-Atlantic institutional architecture. The subsequent 1990s were a period propitious to U.S. engagement in Europe. Few major crises tied up American resources elsewhere, thus allowing for a focus on Europe. Partly — if not mainly — due to the absence of other priorities, Central Europe gradually became a major issue on America's foreign policy agenda. The region received attention from *le tout Washington* — think tanks, researchers and policy makers alike — informing the talk of the town for quite a number of years. The debate on NATO enlargement was tone setting, initially

---

8   Among the most problematic heritages from the Soviet Union was the presence of nuclear weapons in the newly independent states of Kazakhstan, Ukraine and Belarus, which understandably caused headaches in Washington. Related questions dominated much of the bilateral agendas throughout the early years of the respective countries' independence, until the Cooperative Threat Reduction Act, based on a law sponsored by senators Sam Nunn (D, Georgia) and Richard Lugar (R, Indiana) in 1992, the Nunn-Lugar programme and other measures with the same objective successfully dealt with the issue. As a result, none of the states mentioned above today possesses nuclear weapons (see below).

9   For an especially compelling argument to that effect, cf. for example James Baker III (1990) 'The Common European Interest: America and the New Politics Among Nations', address before the National Committee on American Foreign Policy, upon receiving the 7th Annual Hans J. Morgenthau Memorial Award, New York, 14 May. Cf. U.S. *Department of State Dispatch* 1(1), 3 September 1990.

pushed by two policy entrepreneurs, National Security Advisor Anthony Lake and Assistant Secretary of State Richard Holbrooke, who 'drove enlargement not through a series of decision meetings but through presidential language'.[10] They had the support of several enlargement proponents in the research community, nonetheless at the RAND Corporation. RAND's Ronald D. Asmus was later to become a major figure himself in the enlargement process. The personal ties of Madeleine Albright, the second Clinton administration's Secretary of State, to Central Europe certainly figured into U.S. efforts to make NATO enlargement happen as well.[11] From a Central European perspective, joining the Alliance meant more than simply membership in a security organisation. Besides the obvious desire for security guaranteed through NATO's collective provisions, overcoming the historical injustice of Yalta and returning to the West was certainly perceived as being equally important. The NATO-flag waving daily outside the Presidential palace in Warsaw once membership was attained, a phenomenon unheard of in the "old" member states' capitals where the flag is hardly ever seen, may serve as an illustration of this symbolic value.

After the breakdown and accession to *de jure* and *de facto* independence of the Central and East European nations, a complete remodelling of the institutional structures of a Europe "whole and free" has thus never really been on the agenda. The pattern of Washington's approach to Germany's reunification was to be repeated on several occasions: Central and Eastern European policies were much less about creating a "new order" than about consolidating the old order with new members. The few truly pan-European institutions such as the Conference on Security and Cooperation in Europe (CSCE, renamed Organisation for Security and Cooperation in Europe, OSCE, in 1995) and the Council of Europe played, if any, a marginal role. Although widely present in statements and declarations from the beginning of the decade, the CSCE / OSCE seems to gradually vanish from policy makers'

---

10 James Goldgeier (1999) *Not Whether But When. The U.S. Decision to Enlarge NATO*, Washington D.C.: Brookings Institution Press, p. 153.
11 Cf. Madeleine K. Albright (2003) *Madam Secretary*, New York: Miramax.

minds during the 1990s — not least since Russia lost its interest in the organisation as it began to insist on democratic principles with more and more firmness. The institutions that mattered were the European Community (European Union since 1993) and NATO. In that sense, post-Cold War policies in Europe are better understood as an update of membership in Western institutions than as the construction of a "Common House Europe". This, at the same time, implies the continued relevance of old geopolitical patterns, thinking in terms of spheres of influence and consequently the United States' involvement in European politics. Under these circumstances, opportunities for the U.S. to exert influence in Europe were numerous among the former Soviet Republics and Warsaw Pact states, from the Visegrád-countries to Central Asia. Many of these states came to play an important role in defining the new geostrategic structure of post-Cold War Europe. Russian power being in decline during the 1990s, their choice was between joining an expanding West or ending up in an emerging grey zone in the middle of Europe, dividing the continent into a pattern of the West, the rest and Russia. For most Central European nations, the priority undoubtedly lay on joining the West. A strong American presence in Europe notwithstanding, it is thus wrong to mainly portray Central and East European post-Cold War security policy as yet another instance of U.S. "imperialism".[12] This view overlooks the fact that the target states of that imperialism were more than eager to join the American "empire", even at a time when the U.S. itself had not made up its mind to welcome them. U.S. strategies towards the Visegrád countries during the 1990s are an excellent example of "Empire by invitation"[13]. Given the efforts made by numerous states to convince Washington to enlarge NATO, one can hardly speak of unilateralist imperialism on the United States' part.

---

12 Cf. for instance Ronald Hatto and Odette Tomescu (2007) *Les Etats-Unis et la "nouvelle Europe". La stratégie américaine en Europe centrale et orientale,* Paris: Ceri Autrement.
13 Cf. Geir Lundestad (1986) 'Empire by Invitation? The United States and Western Europe, 1945-1952', *Journal of Peace Research* 23(3).

Post-Cold War security affairs in Central and Eastern Europe are however no unequivocal success story. Although NATO membership was extended to encompass an additional twelve countries in three enlargement rounds (1999, 2004 and 2009), some states remain in a grey zone between East and West—some voluntarily so, others less. Not all former Warsaw Pact states succeeded in their transition to democracy, with various degrees of underachievement. Once the first and second rounds of NATO enlargement had taken place, however, American interest in Central Europe diminished considerably. Not only did the project of expanding the West seem to be concluded, with only a number of unlikely, if not hopeless, candidates left outside, other issues similarly began to occupy the upper parts of the agenda. This lack of interest is likely to be linked to Washington running out of ideas, but, more importantly, the emergence of other issues and the redefinition of U.S. priorities when George W. Bush succeeded Bill Clinton. Gradually, attention was shifted elsewhere, a process that naturally was enhanced by the definition of a terrorist threat emanating from the Middle East. By the end of the Bush II administration's first term, the "War on Terror" was the single dominating issue, with Central Europe receiving very little attention by the foreign policy establishment in the U.S. capital, not to mention the general public. With the elimination of concrete threats to U.S. security in the region and only a bunch of rather unlikely membership candidates left outside the Euro-Atlantic framework, U.S. interests diminished as well. Seen from a European perspective, the United States of America nevertheless remains the most relevant actor in European security affairs well into the 21st century.

Yet, it is often overlooked that there hardly was any unified "European strategy" on the United States' part. As late as in December 1993, two years after the demise of the Soviet Union, designated Deputy Secretary of State Strobe Talbott declared that the U.S. had a Russian policy, but no European policy.[14] In 1995 and with respect to NATO enlargement, Zbigniew Brzezinski complained that

> [i]t is not carping criticism to point out that, so far, the Clinton administration has projected neither a strategic vision nor a clear sense of direction on a matter of such salience to Europe's future as enlarging NATO.[15]

More than a decade later, things had arguably not changed much. As Janusz Bugajski contended,

> in terms of grand strategy, the "Newly Independent States" or the "Black Sea Region" have proved to be elusive concepts containing widely diverging countries that have mirrored bureaucratic divisions in regional responsibility within the U.S. foreign policy apparatus.[16]

U.S. foreign policy "towards Europe" is thus often endowed with a consistency it does not deserve. Not only was there hardly any coherent regional strategy, even different government organisations sometimes had different approaches to specific matters, regardless of the tenant of the White House. Even in times of European integration, transatlantic relations are to a much larger extent a matter between Washington and the respective capitals than a matter between Washington and "Brussels". For that reason, transatlantic relations and American policies towards Europe continue to be best understood in bilateral terms since national governments remain the key interlocutors for American administrations. This also means that although strategic objectives may be defined on a more abstract, "European" level, they have to be attained bilaterally. In other words, post-Cold War U.S. policies towards Central and Eastern Europe were in fact a set of — more or less coherent — policies towards every single state in the region.

---

14   Cf. Ronald D. Asmus (2002) *Opening NATO's door. How the Alliance Remade Itself for a New Era*, New York: Columbia University Press, p. xxx. See also: Asle Toje (2008) *America, the EU and Strategic Culture. Renegotiating the Transatlantic Bargain*, London: Routledge and Mike Winnerstig (2000) *A World Reformed? The United States and European Security from Reagan to Clinton*, Stockholm: Stockholm Studies in Politics.
15   Zbigniew Brzezinski (1995) 'A Plan for Europe', *Foreign Affairs* 74(1), p. 27.
16   Janusz Bugajski (2007) *The Eastern Dimension of America's New European Allies*, Washington D.C.: U.S. Army War College, p. 42.

I.1.1 Preserving the unipolar moment

Although the academic debate on the accurate description of the post-Cold War international system has never been settled, there is a wide consensus among scholars and observers that the United States played the dominant role in that system throughout the period covered in this study. Former French minister of foreign affairs Hubert Védrine qualified the U.S. as 'hyperpuissance'[17], whilst academic accounts of the nature of the post-Cold War international system range from 'uni-multipolarity' (Huntington) to pure unipolarity (Krauthammer and others). Samuel Huntington defines a uni-multipolar system as one with one superpower and several major powers:

> The settlement of key international issues requires action by the single superpower, but always with some combination of other major states; the single superpower can, however, veto action on key issues by combinations of other states.[18]

The one state, which according to Huntington occupies the role of the single superpower in the international system as of 2005, was the United States. Other authors put even more emphasis on unipolarity. For Charles Krauthammer, in 2002, '[t]he unipolar moment has become the unipolar era.'[19] A realistic interpretation of the term must lead to the conclusion that the situation is as unipolar as it can get, since '[…] those denying unipolarity can do so only by applying a ridiculous standard: that America be able to achieve all

---

17 Speech reprinted in: Hubert Védrine (2003) *Face à l'hyper-puissance. Textes et discours 1995–2003*, Paris: Fayard.
18 Samuel Huntington (2005) 'The Lonely Superpower', in: G. John Ikenberry (ed.) *American Foreign Policy. Theoretical Essays*, 5th edition, Princeton: Pearson Longman, p. 540 (originally published in: *Foreign Affairs* 78(2), March / April 1999).
19 Charles Krauthammer (2005) 'The Unipolar Moment Revisited', in: G. John Ikenberry (ed.) *American Foreign Policy. Theoretical Essays*, 5th edition, Princeton: Pearson Longman, p. 562 (originally published in *The National Interest*, vol. 70, Winter 2002).

its goals everywhere all by itself. This is a standard not for unipolarity but for divinity.'[20] Krauthammer continues by stating that the United States'

> principal aim is to maintain the stability and relative tranquility of the current international system by enforcing, maintaining and extending the current peace. The form of realism that I am arguing for—call it the new unilateralism—is clear in its determination to self-consciously and confidently deploy American power in pursuit of those global ends.[21]

The conclusion one may draw from Huntington, Krauthammer and others is that although there is disagreement as to the degree of the United States' (pre-)dominance, there nevertheless is agreement on its superpower status, at least as far as the last decade of the 20th and the first of the 21st century is concerned. During the 1990s and into the first years of the next decade, Washington did indeed enjoy unparalleled might within the international system, matched by no other state.

Realist logic dictates that it would be in the interest of the United States to seek to prolong this unipolar moment since

> [i]n a unipolar world, security threats to the United States are minimized, and foreign policy autonomy is maximized. According to realist logic, any great power should prefer to be a unipolar power, regardless of whether or not it possesses expansionist ambitions. For the state at the top, unipolarity is preferable to being a great power facing either the concentrated hostility and threat of a bipolar world or the uncertainty and risk of miscalculation inherent in a multipolar world.[22]

The ambition to prolong the unipolar moment was manifest throughout the three post-Cold War administrations covered in this study. Preventing the emergence of rivals to American-dominated unipolarity was on the agenda since the fall of the Soviet Union. Thus, as Michael Mastanduno noted, '[…] U.S. officials have in fact followed a consistent strategy in pursuit of a clear objective—the preservation of America's pre-eminent global position.'[23] Given the

---

20 Charles Krauthammer (2005) 'The Unipolar Moment Revisited', p. 551.
21 Charles Krauthammer (2005) 'The Unipolar Moment Revisited', p. 560.
22 Michael Mastanduno (1997) 'Preserving the Unipolar Moment. Realist Theories and U.S. Grand Strategy after the Cold War', *International Strategy* 21(4), p. 60.
23 Michael Mastanduno (1997) 'Preserving the Unipolar Moment', p. 51.

apparent U.S. resolution to preserve unipolarity, it seems fair to conclude that realist tenets apply in explaining and understanding American foreign policy in the years after the bipolar order's breakdown.

During the early years of the post-Cold War era, still under Bush I in 1991, the so-called Dobbins démarche was supposed to make clear to Europeans with ambitions for a European security policy that 'no "ganging up" against the United States would be tolerated'.[24] In 1992, the Pentagon's *Draft Defense Planning Guidance for the Fiscal Years 1994-1999* was leaked to the press, a document stating that '[o]ur strategy must now refocus on precluding the emergence of any potential future global competitor.'[25] As Zbigniew Brzezinski argued, '[t]he zone of U.S. predominance was to expand eastward in Europe and be firmly consolidated in the Middle East. The document postulated a view heavily influenced by traditional balance-of-power politics while bluntly asserting American global military superiority'.[26]

Although the rhetoric was different during the Clinton years, a substantial change in Grand Strategy never occurred. There is (especially in European public debate) a tendency to see the foreign policy of the Clinton years as "more multilateral" and thus "better" than the foreign policy pursued by the post-Cold War Republican administrations. However, a closer look at the matter reveals that Clinton can hardly be seen as an aficionado of multilateralism. Rather, following Barry R. Posen and Andrew L. Ross who propose

---

24 For a short account of Dobbins' démarche, cf. Geir Lundestad (1998) *'Empire' by Integration. The United States and European Integration, 1945-1997*, Oxford: Oxford University Press, p. 115.
25 Quoted from Robert Jervis (1993) 'International Primacy: Is the Game Worth the Candle?', *International Security* 17(4), p. 54.
26 Zbigniew Brzezinski (2007) *Second Chance. Three Presidents and the Crisis of American Superpower*, New York: Basic Books, p. 80. It is interesting to note that 'the document planted the intellectual seeds for the policy of unilateralist preemption and prevention that emerged a decade later. By then the authors of the working draft, who were midlevel officials in 1992, had reappeared as senior Defense Department and NSC officials, while its principal sponsor, Secretary of Defense Cheney, resurfaced in 2001 as the vice president of the United States.' (ibid.)

five different 'Grand Strategy visions', Clinton's Grand Strategy is one of 'Selective (but Cooperative) Primacy'. (Other options being Neo-Isolationism, Selective Engagement, Cooperative Security and Primacy, each based on different 'analytical anchors', namely various strands of International Relations Theory.[27] These visions should be understood as ideal types, unlikely to be observable in their "pure" forms in reality.) In line with Posen and Ross, Madeleine Albright uses the term of 'assertive multilateralism'[28], which emphasises American leadership. Stephen M. Walt consequently notes that

> President Clinton's handling of international institutions and multilateralism illustrates the central irony in his handling of foreign policy, namely, the degree to which he departed from his initial idealism and embraced realpolitik. [...] Clinton may cloak U.S. policy in the rhetoric of "world order" and general global interests, but its defining essence remains the unilateral exercise of sovereign power.[29]

Even during the Clinton administrations, often perceived by nostalgic Europeans as a better time in transatlantic relations than the subsequent George W. Bush administrations, American Grand Strategy was thus focused on primacy: multilateralism was not there to please the Europeans, but as a tool in U.S. Grand Strategy.

During the George W. Bush presidencies and ten years after the *Defense Planning Guidance* draft's leaking, the 2002 version of the National Security Strategy (NSS) was less explicit. A 'balance of power' and 'other great powers' were mentioned throughout the document. It was only in the military realm that the NSS explicitly claimed a dominant role for the United States, stating that the U.S. must 'dissuade future military competition'.[30] By 2006, however, in

---

27 Barry R. Posen and Andrew L. Ross (1997) 'Competing Visions for U.S. Grand Strategy', *International Security* 21(3), p. 6. On the analytical anchors, cf. p. 4: defensive realism, 'traditional balance of power realism', liberalism and unilateralism respectively.
28 Madeleine Albright, *Madam Secretary*, p. 223.
29 Stephen M. Walt (2000) 'Two Cheers For Clinton's Foreign Policy', *Foreign Affairs* 79(2), p.78.
30 National Security Strategy 2002, p. 29.

the updated version of the National Security Strategy, George W. Bush's conclusion in the foreword simply was that 'America must continue to lead'.[31] The idea of American leadership then reappeared throughout the whole text. "Leadership" might not sound as striking as "preclusion of potential competitors", but with a little imagination, the message is still very clear: the United States aspired to be the single superpower in a unipolar world. This is Robert Jervis's assessment of Bush's foreign policies, where he sees unipolarity as one of four elements of what he calls the Bush-doctrine: 'The final element of the doctrine [...] is the establishment of American hegemony, primacy, or empire.'[32] George W. Bush himself expressed similar ideas among others in his speech at West Point in June 2002.[33]

This Grand Strategy is sometimes perceived as new or something that has come about after the end of the Cold War, culminating under the Bush-administration. Yet, upon closer examination, the "unilateralist turn" in American foreign policy seems to be exaggerated. David Skidmore argues that U.S. foreign policy has never been genuinely multilateralist, but was characterised by "hegemony" already in the aftermath of World War II:

> While the U.S. invested in the creation of international institutions, postwar administrations only loosely subjected themselves to the constraint of institutional rules and procedures. In other words, the U.S.-sponsored institutional order was designed to bind the behaviour of other states, but not that of the U.S. itself. This strategic approach to constructing international order is hegemonic rather than multilateralist.[34]

---

31 National Security Strategy 2006.
32 Robert Jervis (2005) 'Understanding the Bush Doctrine', in: G. John Ikenberry (ed.) *American Foreign Policy. Theoretical Essays*, 5th edition, Princeton: Pearson Longman, p. 583 (originally published in: *Political Science Quarterly*, 118(3), fall 2003).
33 The White House, Office of the Press Secretary (2002) 'President Bush Delivers Graduation Speech at West Point. Remarks by the President at 2002 Graduation Exercise of the United States Military Academy', West Point, New York, 1 June.
34 David Skidmore (2005) 'Understanding the Unilateralist Turn in U.S. Foreign Policy', *Foreign Policy Analysis*, 1(2), p. 209.

Since the end of the Cold War, the hegemonic order has been shifting towards an even more pronounced unilateralism on the United States' part. The U.S. thus never led a truly multilateralist foreign policy, but sought to build a hegemonic order, which

> rested upon what Ikenberry [...] has referred to as an "institutional bargain" between the U.S. and its key allies. Outside the Communist world, most states voluntarily acquiesced to an American-shaped set of international rules and institutions that considerably narrowed their own policy autonomy.[35]

Indeed, G. John Ikenberry argues that 'American foreign policy after 1945 produced two post-war settlements'. One settlement was what he calls the 'containment order', a reaction to the 'deteriorating relations with the Soviet Union'; the second one is the 'liberal democratic order', which comprised the Western industrial democracies.[36] Ikenberry proceeds by stating that '[t]he two settlements had distinct political visions and intellectual rationales [...].'[37] In other words, Ikenberry's appraisal of the post-World War II order confirms the assumption that foreign policy making—even in its most abstract form, formulated as Grand Strategy—is largely determined by the intended recipient. Both the containment order and the liberal democratic order are thus subordinate strategies to the Grand Strategy of dominance, a means to the end rather than an end in itself. In sum, the United States has thus been pursuing grand strategy objectives consistent with realist assumptions throughout past decades. Basing a study on the idea that it would be the United States' overall ambition to maintain unipolarity is consequently a point of departure that receives ample support from a large body of literature.

This assumption naturally has ramifications. For Michael Mastanduno, given that prolonging the unipolar moment is 'the centerpiece' of U.S. grand strategy, 'we should anticipate that the

---

[35] David Skidmore (2005) 'Understanding the Unilateralist Turn in U.S. Foreign Policy', p. 209.

[36] G. John Ikenberry (2005) 'America's Liberal Grand Strategy', in: id. (ed.) *American Foreign Policy. Theoretical Essays*, p. 273.

[37] G. John Ikenberry (2005) 'America's Liberal Grand Strategy', p. 273.

United States will adopt policies of reassurance toward status quo states, policies of confrontation toward revisionist states, and policies of engagement or integration toward undecided states'.[38] This, however, is an approach to be applied on the ground, within the context of the web of bilateral relationships Washington maintains with other countries.

I.1.2   On the ground: the U.S. in Central and Eastern Europe

The dissolution of the Warsaw Pact equalled the retreat of the Soviet Union, later on Russia, from important parts of European security affairs (at least temporarily). The non-dissolution of NATO, on the other hand, meant that the United States remained a crucial actor in the same field and even increased its significance. For most of the western half of the continent, radical reorientation in security matters did not appear on the agenda. For the majority of the former Eastern bloc states, in turn, security was a highly prioritised issue during the 1990s. Afraid of ending up in a grey zone, squeezed between the West and an unpredictable Russia, many ex-Warsaw Pact states sought rapprochement with Western institutions. Given that NATO continued to set the tone in security matters, this intended rapprochement often focused more on the Alliance than on the European Community (European Union from 1993 onwards). Since European security continued to be so closely linked with the United States, a fact confirmed by the war in former Yugoslavia, American influence remained potentially strong. The United States was largely considered to be the key to integration into Western institutions. NATO membership was therefore the first priority in a number of Central European capitals – a matter of fact illustrated, for instance, by the Baltic states directly establishing a highly efficient lobbying network in Washington, whilst no comparable activity took place in Brussels. Washington's early post-Cold War policies towards Europe were in that sense a continuation of Cold War approaches, aiming at expanding the West.

In cruder geopolitical terms, what was (and, as the Russian annexation of Crimea in 2014 vividly illustrates, continues to be) at

---

38   Michael Mastanduno (1997) 'Preserving the Unipolar Moment', p. 63.

stake in Central and Eastern Europe after the dissolution of the Soviet Union was the redistribution of spheres of influence, essentially between the United States (and, by extension, Western Europe) and Russia. In 1997, former United States National Security Advisor Zbigniew Brzezinski summarised his ideas about U.S. policy towards Europe in the following words:

> In brief, for the United States, Eurasian geostrategy involves the purposeful management of geostrategically dynamic states and the careful handling of geopolitically catalytic states, in keeping with the twin interests of America in the short term preservation of its unique global power and in the long-run transformation of it into the increasingly institutionalized global cooperation. To put it in a terminology that hearkens back to the more brutal age of ancient empires, the three grand imperatives of imperial geostrategy are to prevent collusion and maintain security dependence among the vassals, to keep tributaries pliant and protected, and to keep the barbarians from coming together.[39]

Translated into more modern language and with respect to Europe, the U.S. thus had to keep NATO alive and relevant and prevent the Europeans from coming together as a unified power as well as any other state from becoming a great power in its own right. A strong American presence in Central and Eastern Europe could thus not only serve the local national interest, but even long term U.S. interests, allowing the U.S. to position itself as the "indispensable nation", to use Madeleine Albright's dictum. The United States certainly wanted an "international Europe", that is, a Europe interested in playing a global role, but it has to play that role alongside the United States.[40] Attitudes on the other side of the Atlantic thus evolved considerably since Dobbins' demarche with respect to European efforts directed at joining forces: from outright reject to open calls for more European defense cooperation, Washington in effect

---

39 Zbigniew Brzezinski (1997) *The Grand Chessboard. American Primacy and its geostrategic Imperatives*, New York: Basic Books, p. 40.
40 Cf. Robert E. Zoellick, Counselor of the State Department (1990) 'A New Europe in a New Age: Insular, Itinerant or International? Prospects for an Alliance of Values', address before the American-European Community Association's International Conference on US / EC Relations, Annapolis, MD, 21 September, U.S. *Department of State Dispatch* 1(4), 24 September 1990.

made a U-turn over the past two decades. Fears of a European balancing move have given way to much more favorable. At NATO's 2008 Bucharest summit, then U.S. President George W. Bush admitted that the European Security and Defense Policy (the Common Security and Defense Policy's predecessor) was both "useful and necessary."[41] This did, however, not alter the fundamental principles of U.S. approaches to Europe.

In determining U.S. approaches to Central and Eastern Europe, values no doubt mattered.[42] Yet, values are intrinsically linked to strategic aspects; friendship among states is never solely a matter of affinity and affection. The promotion of democracy and free market economy is thus not only an objective in its own right, but an agenda that moreover serves security interests. Politics being driven by interest, interests remain the most powerful explanatory variables even with regard to foreign aid and assistance. Consistent with this assumption, the U.S. administration transmitted an act to Congress in 1991 with the objective of regaining 'foreign assistance as an effective and well-integrated instrument of foreign policy' and restoring

> the President's authority to use this instrument as it was originally intended, as a flexible cost-effective means to advance our national interest, rather than permitting it to remain hostage to narrow special interests protected by heavily earmarked accounts.[43]

When values coincide with interests, this is for the benefit of all concerned parties, as especially the Polish case will illustrate. At the same time, domestic features being the main defining aspect of a

---

41 Andrew Duff (2008) 'Behold a European foreign policy', *Financial Times*, 9 April 2008.
42 Cf. for instance George H.W. Bush's programmatic speech on 'A Europe Whole and Free' in Mainz in the early summer of 1989: The White House, Office of the Press Secretary (1989) 'A Europe Whole and Free. Remarks to the Citizens in Mainz by President George Bush', Rheingoldhalle, Mainz, 31 May. The Clinton administration's focus on democracy promotion and George W. Bush's 'Freedom Agenda' are also proof of this concern.
43 Cf. U.S. Department of State (1991) 'Fact Sheet International Cooperation Act of 1991: Background', *U.S. Department of State Dispatch* 2(16), 22 April.

state's belonging to the West, transition towards democracy and free market economy also served a geopolitical purpose from 1990 onwards, as officials would point out:

> A successful transition to democracy and free markets in Eastern Europe would serve U.S. national interests in important ways: It would mean that the turn away from communism has become irreversible, and it would help ensure that the region will attain some stability and not once again become a power vacuum or an unstable theater of tension and rivalries. We, therefore, have every incentive to assist the Central and East European nations in their time of need — and we are doing just that.[44]

Assistance for Central and Eastern Europe was subsequently to be based on four objectives, namely:

> First, progress toward political pluralism, based on free and fair elections and an end to the monopoly of the communist party;
> Second, progress toward economic reform, based on the emergence of a market-oriented economy with a substantial private sector;
> Third, enhanced respect for internationally recognized human rights, including the right to emigrate, and to speak and travel freely; and
> Fourth, a willingness on the part of each of these countries to build a friendly relationship with the United States.[45]

Notably the fourth of these may well be interpreted as motivated by the desire to expand the American sphere of influence. In the empirical chapters below, these U.S. objectives and corresponding policy approaches shall be examined in greater detail, within their respective bilateral settings.

Within the context of Central and East European politics sketched above, Poland, Ukraine and Belarus each hold a different position as seen from Washington. Poland today is an official ally

---

44 Kenneth E. Juster, Senior Advisor to the Deputy Secretary of State (1990) 'Remarks from a conference sponsored by the RAND Corporation on Supporting East European Democracy and Free Markets', Santa Monica, CA, 21 September. Cf. U.S. *Department of State Dispatch* 1(8), 22 September 1990. These objectives were to be reiterated by President George H. W. Bush in his State of the Union Address on 14 February 1991.

45 Kenneth E. Juster, Senior Advisor to the Deputy Secretary of State (1990) 'Remarks from a conference sponsored by the RAND Corporation on Supporting East European Democracy and Free Markets'.

of the U.S. in NATO and was a member of the "coalition of the willing" in Iraq until 2008. Bilateral relations with Ukraine, in turn, were subject to ups and downs during the 1990s, justifying the categorisation of "undecided state". As far as Belarus is concerned, the official U.S. description of its policies towards the country is the rather diplomatic euphemism of "selective engagement"; the country qualifies as an "unfriendly state".

All three countries are potentially 'geostrategically dynamic and geopolitically catalytic' (to use Zbigniew Brzezinski's words). None of them is a key player in its own right, but developments involving them cannot be excluded from having major consequences on a much larger scale. The importance of the respective countries to the U.S. is thus not necessarily constant, and certainly not absolute. "Washington" as a conglomerate of government agencies, think tanks, interest groups and the like is subject to the ebb and flow of fashionable subjects. Poland, Ukraine and Belarus as objects for U.S. policies are no exception to that rule. There are of course a great number of people working on and with the respective countries on a permanent basis. However, fashion trends are also clearly observable. At this point in history, Ukraine receives by far the most attention, certainly due to its "at the crossroads" status — which by nature also implies that there is a certain chance "to do something". The very feeling of potentially being able to "make a difference" certainly explains the relatively high proportion of interest for Ukraine. Poland, in turn, is something like a victim of its own success. Considered "set" and firmly integrated within Euro-Atlantic institutions, the country is no longer considered a major problem. Well into the twenty-first century, Washington is not interested in Poland as such, but in Poland as a (potential) close ally, as the negotiations on a Polish site for the second Bush administration's planned missile defence system illustrate.

I.2 Empirical objectives

Needless to say, in light of the events unfolding in Eastern Europe in recent years, better understanding of the role played by the United States is of general interest. This study's primary empirical objective consists in analysing U.S. post-Cold War policies towards Poland, Ukraine and Belarus within the overall context of the United States' management of unipolarity up until 2008. Somewhat surprisingly, this remains an under-researched area despite the fact that much can be learned from it. Little attention indeed has so far been paid to the United States as an actor in Central and Eastern Europe, despite considerable scholarly interest in transition processes in the region and the enlargement processes of NATO and the European Union. With its empirical chapters, this study aims to fill that gap. It intends to analyse the role the United States played in transforming the political landscape of Central and Eastern Europe, how Washington built its relations with the countries in question and how it exerted power in order to obtain outcomes it desired and promoted. In that sense, this study is no study of these transformation processes *per se*, but primarily a study of the so-called only remaining superpower and its policies. Poland, Ukraine and Belarus are most informative cases to study to that end, since their relations with the United States were entirely redefined with the demise of the Soviet Union. In other words, Washington's relations with these countries are one of the rare occasions where bilateral relationships can be studied 'from scratch'.[46] That region therefore was of special relevance, since, for the first time ever or in decades, relations with those states could be built without considerable interference from Moscow. This makes it a most appropriate object for a study like this one, although other regions might be of higher strategic relevance. Looking at how Washington behaves in an 'Area Not of Essential Interest to the United States'[47] is perhaps

---

46 A few caveats to that assertion are naturally in order, especially in the Polish case. Still, given that no independent Ukrainian or Belarusian state existed prior to 1991 and given that Poland was unable to freely decide on its relationship with the U.S. after it became part of the Soviet sphere of influence, the argument may be considered valid to a very large extent.

47 See Geir Lundestad (1978) *The American Non-policy Towards Eastern Europe, 1943–47. The Universalism in an Area Not of Essential Interest to the United States*, Oslo: Universitetsforlaget.

more illustrative than following its actions in (potential) crises, offering insights potentially not to be gained from a study on U.S. approaches towards the 'usual suspects' such as China, India or Iran.

The end of the Cold War did not only mean victory for the United States, but also the necessity to define a 'new world order' — to use the terms George Bush Sr. borrowed from Mikhail Gorbachev — including the role the United States was to play under the new global circumstances. This was nonetheless the case in Europe, where the dissolution of the Soviet Union and the disappearance of the Warsaw Pact had the most imminent effects and were the most palpable illustration that a "new order" had actually emerged. Realist logic dictates that it would be in Washington's interest to play a hegemonic role in that new order, an assumption confirmed by the fact that preserving unipolarity was the declared U.S. Grand Strategy for all post-Cold War administrations analysed in the present study. Grand Strategy objectives however being achieved through foreign policy, the United States' management of unipolarity in its respective bilateral relationships is a matter of highest relevance for students of International Relations. How Washington went about managing and preserving unipolarity "on the ground" in its bilateral relations with three Central and East European nations is thus the main empirical focus of the present study: by what means did the United States attempt to exert influence over Poland, Ukraine and Belarus in the years from 1989 to 2008? These means are conceptualised as foreign policy tools, expressions of the United States' exertion of power. This study being a realist study, the rationale for U.S. foreign policy is taken for granted, assuming that foreign policy tools are employed with the invariable long-term objective of promoting U.S. national interest. In other words, not the *why?* behind American foreign policy shall be the focus of this study, but the *how?* in terms of the means and instruments and the circumstances under which these means and instruments come to use. Under the circumstances of unipolarity, the United States should arguably have had the widest room for manoeuvre imaginable in order to control and shape its environment. Yet, as the empirical analysis below illustrate, the United States' ability to effectively obtain outcomes it desires from other states was clearly limited—an observation running counter to what could be expected given the country's superpower status.[48]

Understanding the United States is however not merely an objective in itself. The U.S. remains a most crucial actor in European security affairs, and Central and Eastern Europe is said to have a special place in U.S. *Europapolitik*. The so-called Pacific Pivot and the debate surrounded it seemed to mark the end of large-scale U.S. involvement in European affairs. Yet, almost two decades after the dissolution of the Warsaw Pact, NATO—the key driver of transatlantic relations—has not gone out of business but out of area. As events unfolded in Ukraine and after the annexation of Crimea, the Alliance and its collective defence pledges even went back to playing a key role for Western Europe's security. At least under Obama, the United States were at the heart of reassurance measures to Allies on the Eastern flank. And although times may be more difficult after Donald Trump's winning the presidential election, Allies eventually managed to agree that NATO was not 'obsolete'.

---

48 On that matter, see also Stephen G. Brooks and William C. Wohlforth (2008) *World Out Of Balance. International Relations and the Challenge of American Primacy*, Princeton: Princeton University Press.

II The theoretical framework and methodology

II.1 Introduction and research questions

The primary theoretical objective of the present study is to offer a theoretically grounded explanation of the above identified puzzle: why did the United States lead largely different foreign policies under circumstances where (neoclassical) realism would predict highly similar policies? According to Gideon Rose, it is one of the core tenets of neoclassical realism that states strive 'to control and shape their external environment'.[49] To that end, they conduct foreign policies. Foreign policies require states to translate their various power resources into concrete measures in order to exert power over other states. Neoclassical realism consequently considers state behaviour to be its *explanandum*, as opposed to neorealism which seeks to explain recurrent patterns of behaviour. For that reason, neoclassical realists 'favor beginning intellectually at the systemic level but then taking care to trace precisely how, in actual cases, relative power is translated and operationalized into the behavior of state actors.'[50] This is also the approach chosen in the present study. Starting at the systemic level, it assumes that preserving unipolarity and even expanding its power position will be the key objective of the United States. Washington's actual behaviour towards three specific countries from 1989 to 2008 is then the focus of the analysis in the chapters below.

In this study, state behaviour is understood as acts of foreign policy directed towards one or several other states. Many factors account for the design of foreign policy, as neoclassical realists posit that there is no direct transmission belt between power resources and the foreign policy implemented by a state. Rather, a number of intervening variables are conceivably at work. The two major fac-

---

49   Gideon Rose (1998) 'Neoclassical Realism and Theories of Foreign Policy', *World Politics* 51(1), p. 152.
50   Ibid., p. 166.

tors identified by the emerging neoclassical realist research tradition include elite perceptions of systemic factors and domestic constraints. It is around these two sets of intervening variables that the bulk of contemporary neoclassical realist scholarship is centred, as for instance the 2009 volume on *Neoclassical Realism, the State and Foreign Policy* illustrates.[51] Within that context, the present study is essentially concerned with the former and places perception factors at the centre of attention. In doing so, it however argues that the neoclassical realist perspective needs to be widened in comparison with existing scholarship dealing with elite perceptions.

Indeed, if assuming that all states seek to control and shape their external environment, that environment must matter beyond the fact that amorphous systemic constraints determine a state's room for manoeuvre. This environment, in turn, will be populated by a number of actors — i.e. states — which deserve attention. In other words, the "inhabitants" of that environment states attempt to control and shape should be considered most relevant. It is these inhabitants that are the addressees of any state's foreign policy. For that reason, the object or receiving part of states' foreign policies must necessarily be part of the equation, and the primarily bilateral dimension of state behaviour needs to be acknowledged to a greater extent. Most importantly, if explaining state behaviour is the key research objective, what states' "think" of their policy addressees seems highly relevant to the policy designing progress. In that sense, states' perceptions of other states need to enter the picture. This, however, is a path hitherto neglected in neoclassical realism as well as in the realist tradition more broadly.[52]

By offering a response to that lacuna, this study intends to provide an explanation of the above identified puzzle and, simultaneously, to contribute to theory development: it proposes a theoretical

---

51 For an introduction, see Steven E. Lobell, Norrin M. Ripsman and Jeffrey W. Taliaferro (eds.) (2009) *Neoclassical Realism, the State, and Foreign Policy*, Cambridge: Cambridge University Press. See also Randall L. Schweller (2006) *Unanswered Threats: Political Constraints on the Balance of Power*, Princeton: Princeton University Press.

52 As ever, there are notable exceptions to that claim, cf. chapter II below.

argument that allows for the inclusion of states' perceptions of other states into a framework designed to explain states' foreign policies. Although "perception" figures prominently in many contributions to realist research in International Relations[53], the notion has remained surprisingly underspecified and not been theoretically elaborated to a substantial degree. The present study, by basing the analysis on the concepts of friends / non-friends / undecided states consequently seeks to demonstrate that a hitherto neglected element of the so-called missing link between power resources and state behaviour should be part of neoclassical realist analyses and proposes a framework which allows doing so.

At the heart of this study is thus the assumption that state behaviour is unthinkable without a bilateral dimension. In the framework developed and applied below, conceptualising different types of bilateral relations consequently is important. As shall be argued, states may consider their fellow states as being friends, non-friends or undecided. How states perceive others, in turn, is highly likely to have a considerable impact on state behaviour. As shall be demonstrated below, these categories are compatible with both realist tenets in general and neoclassical realism in particular.

Dividing states into categories is, however, no end in itself. It is at this point a second assumption central to this study enters the picture, only underlining the relevance of states' perception of friend, non-friend or undecided attitudes. In order to control and shape their external environment, states exert power. Yet, the conditions for doing so will be highly dependent upon the actor which whom a state is dealing: a friend, a non-friend, or an undecided state. For that reason, this study will moreover rely on a distinction of positive and negative power resources, again divided into the two respective sub-categories of material and symbolic power resources. Power, in the present context, will essentially be understood in the Weberian sense: the capability to get one's will across within a social relationship, even against resistance. Positive power essentially works through incentives and potential gains, whereas

---

[53] Cf. chapter II below for a more detailed discussion of perception in realist approaches to international politics.

negative power is based upon coercion and potentially negative consequences. In leading foreign policies, states translate their power resources into foreign policy tools, which are attributable to one of these types. It is through looking at the foreign policy tools employed that the appraisal that foreign policies are "different" at all becomes possible.

The sections below on the theoretical framework are, however, not only intended to introduce the two sets of categories discussed above. They also set out to explain why a correlation between a state's perception of another state's friend / non-friend / undecided status and the kind of power resources it recurs to should be expected on theoretical grounds. In a first step, the ideal-typical categories of friendly, non-friendly and undecided states will be derived from the more traditional realist concepts of status quo vs. revisionist states. The subsequent section will then be devoted to discussing different types of power resources and the base values upon which they are built. These types of power resources shall thereafter be put in relation to the previously introduced categories of states. By linking the use of positive and negative resources to the recipient's perceived friend, non-friend or undecided status, this study aims to establish the relevance of perceptions of the "receiving part" of foreign policy in connection with the distinction of different types of power resources, positive and negative. Based on these reflections and in response to the research questions detailed, general assumptions on the exercise of power and hence states' ability to control and shape their external environment will eventually be offered in section II.5. This study thus hopes to overcome the impossibility of explaining dissimilar policies designed under identical systemic and domestic circumstances, by arguing that the target state's friend / non-friend / undecided status should be considered an element of the missing link between power resources and policy output in terms of foreign policy tools applied.

In order to solve the empirical puzzle identified at its outset, this study seeks to offer a theory-grounded explanation: why did the United States lead essentially different policies in a situation where realism would predict the contrary? In more theoretical terms, this study sets out to get at the linkage between foreign policy tools employed by a foreign policy emitting state and a target state's perceived friend / non-friend / undecided status. Reformulated as research questions serving as a guideline throughout the chapters, this study thus seeks to address the following issues:

- How does the type of power resources employed in foreign policy vary when friendly, unfriendly or undecided states are targeted?

More precisely:

- What vehicles for power, i.e.: foreign policy tools can states resort to in their attempts to influence?

Since these tools all are embodiments of specific types of power resources:

- What are these tools' underlying principles and base values?

A further question pertains to testing the assumption that the use of power is highly circumstantial, i.e. that there is a clear correlation between the friend / non-friend / undecided status of a specific state and the type of power resources underlying foreign policy tools:

- Is the assumption correct that foreign policy tools applied towards friends will be predominantly based on positive power resources; foreign policy tools applied towards non-friends will predominantly be based on negative power resources, whereas foreign policy tools applied towards undecided states will be based on both types of power resources?

In empirical terms, the analysis of U.S. policies towards Poland, Ukraine and Belarus is guided by the following question:

- Which tools (and thus: what kind of power resources?) does the United States use in its policies towards Poland, Ukraine and Belarus?

The results of the empirical analysis will allow for inferences in theoretical terms. Two final questions to be addressed in the concluding chapter therefore are:

- How fruitful is considering perceptions of states' friend / non-friend / undecided status an element of the neoclassical realist missing link?
- What assumptions on intra-state influence can be deduced from this study, nonetheless in view of state objectives defined as "controlling and shaping the external environment"?

II.1.1 Neoclassical realism: an introduction

More than merely a school of International Relations theory, political realism is in fact a rather coherent system of (perhaps somewhat pessimistic) beliefs. As it stands, realism is a predominantly American research programme. However, the realist tradition, and classical realism especially, is deeply rooted in all-Western history of thought. At the beginning of the twenty-first century, the school has split into a number of rivalling labels, each again divided into sub-labels most commonly referred to as classical realism, neorealism and, most recently, neoclassical realism.

Modern realism is a response to the events of the early 20th century and the insight that liberal approaches to international politics were unsuccessful in preventing disaster.[54] What all realists, regardless of the sub-paradigm to which they adhere, have in common is the conviction that the world has to be understood as it is, and not as it should be. Realist critique of Wilsonian idealism and liberal approaches is thus by no means due to contempt for their moral arguments. Rather, realists claim that a Wilsonian ethic of intention (or *Gesinnungsethik,* to use the terms of Max Weber[55]) is

---

54 Most prominently so is Edward H. Carr's (1981[1939]) *The Twenty Years' Crisis 1919–1932,* 2nd edition, London: Macmillan.
55 "Wir müssen uns klar machen, daß alles ethisch orientierte Handeln unter zwei voneinander grundverschiedenen, unaustragbar gegensätzlichen Maxmimen stehen kann: es kann ‚gesinnungsethisch' oder ‚verantwortungsethisch' sein.

counterproductive; statesmen cannot do the real world justice on the basis of *Wertrationalität*. Responsible leaders base their judgements on an ethic of responsibility (*Verantwortungsethik*). In that sense, the widespread reproach for "immorality" against realism is simply wrong. On the contrary, the writings of Hans J. Morgenthau and Raymond Aron comprise clear normative elements. Yet, given that states' striving for power cannot be overcome, the recognition of that fact must invariably constitute the point of departure of political thinking and acting. All realist branches share the view that states are the principal actors of international politics.

The term "neoclassical realism" was coined by Gideon Rose in his 1998 article in *World Politics*.[56] The label refers to an attempt at

---

Nicht daß Gesinnungsethik mit Verantwortungslosigkeit und Verantwortungsethik mit Gesinnungslosigkeit identisch wäre. Aber es ist ein abgrundtiefer Gegensatz, ob man unter der gesinnungsethischen Maxime handelt—reli- giös geredet -: ‚der Christ tut recht und stellt den Erfolg Gott anheim', oder unter der verantworungsethischen: daß man für die (voraussehbaren) Folgen seines Handelns aufzukommen hat." (Max Weber, *Politik als Beruf*, p. 329) My translation: 'We need to understand, that all ethically oriented action can be attributed to two essentially different and irreconcilable maxims: it can be ethical in terms of the ethic of intention or in terms of the ethic of responsibility. This is not to say that the ethic of intention is identical with irresponsibility or that the ethic of responsibility is identical with a lack of character and the absence of ethical direction. But it is a very profound difference whether someone acts under the maxim of the ethic of intention—to put it in religious terms—: "the Christian does good and attributes the success to God", or under the maxim of the ethic of responsibility: that one has to answer for the (foreseeable) consequences of one's acts.'

Related to these two types of ethics are the concepts of *Wertrationalität* and *Zweckrationalität*: Weber distinguishes between rationality based on values (*wertrational*) and rationality based ends to be achieved (*zweckrational*). Although both types of rationality are essentially different, they are not mutually exclusive.

Note that also Raymond Aron's *Paix et guerre entre les nations* (Paris: Calmann-Lévy, 2004 [1964]) contains a chapter on *En quête d'une morale: conviction et responsabilité* ('Quest for morality: conviction and responsibility'), though without explicit reference to Weber—besides the chapter's very title. Aron made moreover crucial contributions to Weber's reception in France (see e.g. *Les Étapes de la pensée sociologique*, 1967), a fact which also supports the idea of his thinking being influenced by the sociologist.

56 Cf. Gideon Rose (1998) 'Neoclassical Realism and Theories of Foreign Policy'. In his article, Rose contrasts Neoclassical Realism with a wide variety of realist

reasserting classical realism, incorporating insights gained since the emergence of neorealism and the subsequent debate between neorealists and their critics. As the chosen label brings out, neoclassical realists see themselves in line with the tradition of political realism. However, they part company with both classical realists and neorealists on a number of important points. They question the strict neorealist distinction between the unit and system levels, and consider foreign policy behaviour instead of recurrent patterns of behaviour to be their *explanandum*. At the same time, they acknowledge the structural realist assumption that a state's position within the international system is highly relevant and even decisive — although they claim that systemic factors need to be filtered domestically. In explaining foreign policy, neoclassical realists indeed 'point out that there is no immediate or perfect transmission belt linking material capabilities to foreign policy behavior'.[57]

Since the above named transmission belt must by definition be situated somewhere between capabilities and behaviour, neoclassical realists open up the black box of the state. The school thereby constitutes an attempt to reconcile the richness of classical realism with neorealism's analytical rigour. Most neoclassical realists lay stress on the link between domestic factors and international politics. The bulk of the research carried out under the label is therefore focused on what neoclassical realists call 'the missing link', that is, the relation between domestic and international politics.[58] In neoclassical realist scholarship, this missing link includes two sets of intervening variables: domestic constraints and elite perceptions, in

---

approaches to international politics, an exercise therefore not to be repeated in the chapters and sections below.

57 Gideon Rose (1998) 'Neoclassical Realism and Theories of Foreign Policy', p. 146.
58 Stephen M. Walt (2002) 'The Enduring Relevance of the Realist Tradition', in: Ira Katznelson and Helen Milner (eds.) *Political Science, State of the Discipline*, New York: W.W. Norton & Co, p. 211. See also Steven E. Lobell, Norrin M. Ripsman and Jeffrey W. Taliaferro (eds.) (2009) *Neoclassical Realism, the State, and Foreign Policy*.

various constellations and with shifting salience.[59] The remainder of this chapter shall be concerned with the latter type of intervening variables, namely elite perceptions.

II.1.2 Elite perceptions: of more than just the system?

"Perception" is perhaps not readily associated with realism. As a matter of fact, the notion has played (and continues to play) a more prominent role within other research paradigms, notably constructivism and Foreign Policy Analysis (FPA) and the latter's "cognitive" strand in particular.[60] Foreign Policy Analysis, according to the journal of the same name, is defined as follows:

> Foreign policy analysis, as a field of study, is characterized by its actor-specific focus. The underlying, often implicit argument is that the source of international politics and change in international politics is human beings, acting individually or in groups. In the simplest terms, foreign policy analysis is the study of the process, effects, causes or outputs of foreign policy decision-making in either a comparative or case-specific manner.[61]

Within this field, perception especially matters since the so-called "behaviouralist turn". A detailed overview of FPA literature dealing with "perception" would obviously be beyond the scope of this chapter. Among its most prominent representatives certainly is Robert Jervis, who, in *Perception and Misperception*, applies cognitive psychology to International Relations in order to explain foreign policy decision-making. Jervis, following the above described, actor-specific focus, asks:

---

59 Cf. 'Introduction: neoclassical realism, the state, and foreign policy' in Steven E. Lobell, Norrin M. Ripsman and Jeffrey W. Taliaferro (eds.) (2009) *Neoclassical Realism, the State, and Foreign Policy* for a general overview.

60 For a first introduction to these two fields, cf. the respective chapters in the *Handbook of International Relations* (edited by Walter Carlsnaes, Thomas Risse and Beth A. Simmons, London, Sage 2002): Emanuel Adler (2002) 'Constructivism and International Relations', pp. 95–118; Walter Carlsnaes 'Foreign Policy', pp. 331–349.

61 Cf. the publisher's homepage at http://www.wiley.com/bw/journal.asp?ref=1743-8586.

What are the causes and consequences of misperception? What kinds of perceptual errors commonly occur in decision-making? How are beliefs about politics and images of other actors formed and altered? How do decision-makers draw inferences from information, especially information that could be seen as contradicting their own vies?[62]

Cognitive social psychology is also at the heart of Yuen Foong Khong's *Analogies at War*[63]; other examples to be named include the works by Margaret G. Hermann[64] or the 1976 *Structure of Decision: The Cognitive Maps of Political Elites* edited by Robert Axelrod.[65]

Within constructivism, the argument brought forward is essentially that 'foreign policy is what states make of it'. The key idea consists in stating that foreign policy decisions are inevitably taken by individuals whose perception (or: social construction) of the world surrounding them ought to be considered a crucial factor in understanding and explaining their behaviour. This leads the analyst to what J. David Singer labelled 'The Level-Of-Analysis Problem in International Relations'.[66] Constructivists and others putting a major emphasis on "constructed realities" and policy makers' view of the world consequently prioritise the so-called first image at the expense of the second (i.e., nation states) and third images (i.e., the international system). Representatives of this approach are manifold, and literature abounds.[67] Alexander Wendt is widely

---

62 Robert Jervis (1976) *Perception and Misperception in International Politics*, Princeton: Princeton University Press, p. 3.
63 Yuen Foong Khong (1992) *Analogies at War: Korea, Munich, Dien Bien Phu and the Vietnam Decisions of 1965*, Princeton: Princeton University Press.
64 See for instance Margaret G. Hermann (1980) 'Explaining Foreign Policy Behavior Using Personal Characteristics of Political Leaders', *International Studies Quarterly* 24, pp. 7–46.
65 Robert Axelrod (ed.) (1976) *Structure of Decision: The Cognitive Maps of Political Elites*, Princeton: Princeton University Press.
66 J. David Singer (1961) 'The Level-Of-Analysis Problem in International Relations', *World Politics* 14(1), pp. 77–92.
67 An extensive review of that literature would naturally be far beyond the scope of the present study. For a general overview of "perception" approaches within the field of International Relations, cf. Vendulka Kubalkova (ed.) (2001) *Foreign Policy in a Constructed World*, New York: M.E. Sharpe, and in particular the second chapter: Steve Smith (2001) 'Foreign Policy Is What States Make Of It: Social Construction and International Relations Theory, pp. 38–55. See also: David

considered to be among the key figures of constructivism within the field of International Relations. His *Social Theory of International Politics* is meant to be a direct response to Kenneth Waltz' *Theory of International Politics* and hence a direct challenge to neorealism. While Waltz argues that anarchy determines state behaviour, Wendt argues that 'anarchy is what states make of it', based on the assumption '(1) that the structures of human association are determined primarily by shared ideas rather than material forces, and (2) that the identities and interests of purposive actors are constructed by these shared ideas rather than given by nature'.[68] Many others have followed (and also, though perhaps not necessarily under the constructivist label, preceded) Wendt. To give just one prominent example, the so-called Copenhagen School — notably researchers such as Barry Buzan, Ole Wæver and Jaap de Wilde — attempts to capture the social aspects of security by introducing the notion of "securitization".[69]

"Perception" undoubtedly has played an important role in a number of (neoclassical) realist contributions to international relations, even within neorealism. Neoclassical realists consider the state and its decision-makers to be the missing link between power resources and foreign policy output. For that reason, '[t]he first intervening variable they introduce is decision-makers' perceptions, through which systemic pressures must be filtered.'[70] It is in this sense Gideon Rose concludes that 'neoclassical realists occupy a middle ground between pure structural theorists and constructivists'.[71] As Brian Rathbun notes, it is however crucial to understand

---

Mendeloff and Mira Sucharov (2005) 'Perception and International Security', unpublished paper, presented at the Annual Meeting of the American Political Science Association, Washington D.C., 1–4 September 2005.

68 Alexander Wendt (1999) *Social Theory of International Politics*, Cambridge: Cambridge University Press, p.1.

69 Barry Buzan, Ole Wæver and Jaap de Wilde (1998) *Security: a new framework for analysis*, Boulder: Lynne Rienner Publishers.

70 Gideon Rose (1998) 'Neoclassical Realism and Theories of Foreign Policy', p. 157.

71 Ibid., p. 152.

that neoclassical realism 'problematizes perception, but not the objective nature of reality. States must often fall back on perception not because reality is socially constructed but rather because they lack complete information'.[72] Neoclassical realists are therefore still realists, acknowledging the strategic character of foreign policy under anarchy, being a means to an end and no end in itself.[73] It is for this reason that 'neoclassical realists believe that the *innenpolitikers'* [i.e. those scholars essentially interested in states' domestic levels] preferred independent variables must be relegated to second place analytically because, over the long run, a state's foreign policy cannot transcend the limits and opportunities thrown up by the international environment'.[74]

Neoclassical realists have achieved a number of highly interesting studies demonstrating that the way in which elites perceive the international system greatly matters for state behaviour.[75] The question that arises, however, is whether considering how elites perceive systemic factors (and the way in which they are filtered domestically) is sufficient in order to account for state behaviour. Moreover, these approaches are arguably characterised by a lack of theoretical elaboration, leaving the very notion of "perception" underspecified.

Among the most useful definitions of "perception" is the following:

---

[72] Brian Rathbun (2008) 'A Rose by Any Other Name: Neoclassical Realism as the Logical and Necessary Extension of Structural Realism', *Security Studies* 17(2), p. 315.

[73] Jessica Sterling-Folker (1997) 'Realist Environment, Liberal Process, and Domestic-Level Vraiables', p. 16.

[74] Gideon Rose (1998) 'Neoclassical Realism and Theories of Foreign Policy', p. 151.

[75] See for instance William Curti Wohlforth (1993) *The Elusive Balance: Power and Perceptions during the Cold War* (Ithaca: Cornell University Press); Aaron L. Friedberg (1988) *The Weary Titan: Britain and the Experience of Relative Decline, 1895–1905*, Princeton: Princeton University Press; Thomas J. Christensen (1996) *Useful Adversaries: Grand Strategy, Domestic Mobilization, and Sino-American Conflict, 1947–1958*, Princeton: Princeton University Press.

> *Perception* [...] means the gathering and interpreting of information against the background of [one's] own understandings of the world, the judgment of the situation as based on interests and the way in which an actor sees the state of interests and power in other systems (as for example states and international organisations).[76]

The notion of perception is highly relevant for the study of state pursuit of objectives. As Gideon Rose notes, research carried out under neoclassical realist premises is characterised by the idea that

> [i]nstead of assuming that states seek security, neoclassical realists assume that states respond to the uncertainties of international anarchy by seeking to control and shape their external environment. Regardless of the myriad ways that states may define their interests, this school argues, they are likely to want more rather than less external influence, and pursue such influence to the extent that they are able to do so.[77]

Indeed, if controlling and shaping their external environment is that for which states strive, it seems short-sighted to merely take an interest in states' perceptions of the international system in abstract terms such as the balance of power. Systemic factors certainly matter, but it would seem equally logical to assume that perceptions of the units populating that external environment play a central role as well in states' attempts at controlling and shaping it. This thought is all the more compelling in light of neoclassical realists' conception of foreign policy as their major research interest. Although the school begins 'with the fundamental assumption of neo-realists that the international system structures and constrains the policy choices of states',

---

[76] Alexander Siedschlag (2001) (ed.) *Realistische Perspektiven internationaler Politik*, Opladen: Leske & Budrich, p. 49 [emphasis in the original; my own translation in the text]: '*Perzeption* bezeichnet [...] die Aufnahme und Bewertung von Informationen vor dem Hintergrund eigener Weltverständnisse, die interessenbedingte Lagebeurteilung und die Art, in der ein Akteur die Interessen- und Machtlage in anderen Systemen (zum Beispiel Staaten und internationalen Organisationen) sieht.'

[77] Gideon Rose (1998) 'Neoclassical Realism and Theories of Foreign Policy', p. 152.

> [n]eoclassical realism shares classical realism's concern for the state and its relation to domestic society. It also defines its mission largely in terms of building theories of foreign policy, rather than theories of the system within which states interact. Nonetheless, neoclassical realists aspire to greater methodological sophistication than their classical realist predecessors.[78]

This focus on foreign policy implies that state interaction is of major importance. It consequently also presupposes an understanding of international politics as an essentially bi- or multilateral phenomenon. In short, in addition to perceptions of systemic factors, states' perceptions of each other should logically be relevant in order to explain their behaviour. This, however, is an observation neoclassical realists have not dealt with thus far. How such perceptions translate into more general attitudes towards other states — and in turn, how states believe others perceive them — seems crucial for any analyst seeking to explain foreign policy.[79] Hence, states arguably not only position themselves in relation to others with respect

---

78 Steven E. Lobell, Norrin M. Ripsman and Jeffrey W. Taliaferro (eds.) (2009) 'Introduction: neoclassical realism, the state, and foreign policy', *Neoclassical Realism, the State, and Foreign Policy*, p. 19.

79 For an excellent introduction to this matter within constructivism, cf. for instance Peter J. Katzenstein (ed.) (1996) *The Culture of National Security. Norms and Identity in World Politics*, New York: Columbia University Press). Moreover, the classical theorist of friendship and enmity as the basic pattern of the Political is of course Carl Schmitt: 'The specifically political distinction, on which the political acts and motives are based, is the distinction between *friend* and *enemy*.' (Carl Schmitt, *Der Begriff des Politischen*, Berlin: Duncker & Humblot, 1987, p. 26 [emphasis in the original]. 'Die spezifisch politische Unterscheidung, auf welche sich die politischen Handlungen und Motive zurückführen lassen, ist die Unterscheidung von *Freund* und *Feind*.' [my own translation]) However, Schmitt's categories of "friends" and "enemies" are not characterised in moral terms. It is important to understand that the essence of enmity does not consist in different "opinions" on religious, moral, economic, ethnic or any other issues, although 'every religious, moral, economical, ethnic or other opposition is transformed into a political opposition if it is strong enough to effectively group human beings as friends and enemies' (Ibid., p. 37, '[j]eder religiöse, moralische, ökonomische, ethnische oder andere Gegensatz verwandelt sich in einen politischen Gegensatz, wenn er stark genug ist, die Menschen nach Freund und Feind effektiv zu gruppieren.' [my own translation]). In other words, not differences *per se* are the reason for enmity, but a choice that is made, elevating the controversial to a rank that makes it political: it yields a distinction of friends and enemies on the basis of sides taken regarding that specific issue.

Schmitt's friend / enemy-scheme therefore comprises a considerable constructivist element. What makes an issue "political", i.e. leads one political entity to consider another political entity in terms of friendship or enmity, is to a large extent a matter of perception. Herein lies the close connection between Schmitt and more recent approaches in International Relations and especially the so-called Copenhagen School. Their analyses of "processes of securitization" do indeed not aim at finding out how social groups identify "enemies", but at understanding how something can come to be perceived as a threat (Cf. Barry Buzan, Ole Wæver, Jaap de Wilde (1998) *Security: A new framework for analysis*, Boulder: Lynne Rienner Publishers). That threat is then supposed to represent a danger to something else that has become a referent object of security. As noted above, the Copenhagen School approach involves perception as a key element. In both cases—Schmitt and the Copenhagen School –, what leads to the classification as an enemy or securitization respectively, is linked to a specific content in a policy or "threat". Enmity is therefore the consequence of an escalated disagreement in a specific issue, elevated to the level of being "political" (in Schmitt's understanding of the term). This elevation, in turn, is the result of a construction process. The answer to the question of what differentiates revisionism from enmity can be found in an approach based on Morgenthau's assertion that international politics is the realm in which interest is defined in terms of power. If one were to apply Schmitt's categories to this realm, it becomes evident that what has the potential to become "political" (again, in Schmitt's meaning) is anything related to power (or, in Copenhagen School terms: power as the referent object for security. For a similar argument, see furthermore Carr, *The Twenty Years' Crisis*, p. 97). In other words, disagreement on a wide array of issues—ranging from different opinions on the Kyoto protocol to "banana wars"—is nothing but disagreement, as long as it does not pertain to the crucial category of power (in terms of capabilities, influence and all a relational concept of power comprises, that is: power primarily defined as the capacity to exert influence on others). A disagreement, however, pertaining to the very matter of power has the potential to become "political". It is at this precise moment enmity turns revisionist: disagreement in one (or several) issue leads a state to question another state's position in the international system. It no longer accepts the other state's range of influence and ceases to consider that influence as legitimate. Not accepting a state's range of influence equals to not accepting this state's place in the international system.

For this very reason, even when following Schmitt's arguably "constructivist" approach, a state cannot be categorised as "revisionist" in absolute terms. Not only can its intentions never become manifest in any other way than through interaction with other states, the very content of enmity leading to revisionism may furthermore be subject to change over time.

to specific single issues. To quote Arnold Wolfers, state attitudes follow (historically conditioned) patterns of amity and enmity[80], or, in the words of Raymond Aron, 'all collective bodies find themselves amongst enemies, friends, neutrals and indifferents'.[81] States thus hold different statuses vis-à-vis each other. These statuses — friendly, unfriendly as well as the intermediate status of undecided states — play a major role in international politics. One may thus conclude that every state will have to deal with its very own set of "friends" and "non-friends" and possibly "undecided" states.[82] These attitudes constitute the bilateral context within which states design and implement their foreign policies. Taking the bilateral context into consideration, in turn, is key to explaining why states lead divergent foreign policies towards different countries under identical systemic conditions.

II.2 Non-friends, friends and undecided states

Non-friends, friends and undecided states are three ideal types which allow for conceptualising states' perceptions of each other. Although these or similar notions have found their way into classical realism (cf., for instance, Wolfers or Aron quoted above), the conceptual pair of revisionist or imperialist states vs. status quo states has gained greater currency in realist thinking. This section therefore sets out to derive the concepts of friends, non-friends and undecided states from these more common realist ideas. In light of the above discussed assumption that considering elite perceptions on systemic factors is insufficient, the subsequent paragraphs are intended to transpose these systemic notions to the level of bilateral

---

[80] Arnold Wolfers (1962) 'Power and Influence: The Means of Foreign Policy', pp. 103–116 in: *Discord and Collaboration. Essays on International Politics*, Baltimore: The Johns Hopkins University Press.

[81] Raymond Aron (2004) *Paix et guerre entre les nations*, p. 22 [my own translation in the text]: 'Toute collectivité se trouve au milieu d'ennemis, d'amis, de neutres et d'indifférents.'

[82] The terms "friend" and "enemy" are of course not used in Carl Schmitt's meaning (cf. Carl Schmitt (1987[1932]) *Der Begriff des Politischen*, Berlin: Duncker & Humblot), but rather as umbrella terms capturing predominant tendencies in bilateral relations.

relations in order to make them applicable to the analysis of foreign policy within bilateral contexts.

II.2.1 Non-friends

In the realist tradition, the most widely spread concept grasping enmity among states is the idea of the revisionist state. The distinction between status quo and revisionist powers is in fact at the very core of classical realism, first introduced by E.H. Carr in 1939. A revisionist state is a state discontent with its current position in the international system, striving to overthrow the status quo. The concept consequently requires a system perspective. Surprisingly enough, this approach is seldom questioned or expanded. However, for revisionism to have an effect, the revisionist state's fellow states have to take note of its revisionism: clandestine revisionism would remain unnoticed and thus without effect. For that reason, the foremost level at which revisionism has an impact is other states' domestic level, where it first of all needs to get noticed. This does not mean that a system-based perspective is wrong. What it does mean is that the exclusive focus on the system level is insufficient: revisionism is first and foremost a matter to be analysed at domestic levels.

For Morgenthau, whereas status quo policies aim at maintaining the 'distribution of power as it exists at a particular moment in history', the objective of imperialist policies (his term for what is here referred to as revisionism) is to overthrow that status quo.[83] There are, however, no permanent or essential criteria which allow states to perceive imperialism; 'the evaluation of imperialistic tendencies and, consequently, of the policies countering them is never definitive. Both policies and counterpolicies are ever subject to reevaluation and reformulation'.[84] Morgenthau distinguishes different types of imperialism, depending on its origins and cir-

---

83 Hans J. Morgenthau (2006 [1948]) *Politics Among Nations. The Struggle for Power and Peace*, 7th edition, New York: McGraw Hill, p. 54.
84 Ibid., p. 82.

cumstances, the goal always being preponderance (global, continental or local).[85] Most interestingly, imperialism may also be served by three different methods, namely military imperialism, economic imperialism and cultural imperialism. The latter is defined as the 'conquest or control of the minds of men as an instrument for changing the power relations between two nations.'[86] Whilst this variant of imperialism certainly is the most subtle and, in a certain sense, elegant one, it is also the variant that seldom works without recurring to one or both of the other two methods. Hence, '[t]he typical role cultural imperialism plays in modern times is subsidiary to the other methods. It softens up the enemy, it prepares the ground for military conquest or economic penetration.'[87]

Revisionist policies need to become manifest in some way allowing other states to react to them. Although the structure of the system may be the eventual target of revisionist policies ("preponderance"), the system can only be influenced via the states forming it. Revisionism in its manifestations and effects must therefore be understood as a foremost bi- and / or multilateral phenomenon, depending on the number of states involved. In Morgenthau's writings, it is obvious that revisionism is directed towards other states — with the objective of overthrowing the status quo — whilst the revisionist state still is considered to be a system-level problem. Morgenthau is very clear about the fact that revisionism *primarily* is a bilateral issue:

> This question concerns the character of the foreign policy pursued by another nation and, in consequence, the kind of foreign policy that ought to be adopted with regard to it.[88]

Thus for Morgenthau, it is not only important to analyse the sources of revisionist policies, but also their consequences where they appear for the very first time. What follows is that both the origins and the effects of revisionism are therefore to be analysed at the

---

85 Ibid., whole chapter 5.
86 Ibid., p. 69–74; definition of "cultural imperialism" on p. 71.
87 Ibid., p. 72.
88 Hans J. Morgenthau (2006 [1948]) *Politics Among Nations*, p. 74.

domestic levels of two or more states. In order to affect the system level, revisionist states can only have an impact via one or more other states' domestic level. This by no means implies that revisionism does not affect the system level, yet merely effects of revisionism will become manifest there. Causes for revisionism lie elsewhere, as do reactions to it. What is observable at the system level is in fact nothing more than the result of *successful* revisionism, leading to a change in the overall system structure. An analyst wanting to detect mere revisionist ambitions, anti-revisionist strategies and countered revisionism must therefore look at the level of inter-state relations.

System stability is highly dependent on the prevalence of status quo states, in line with Aristotle who argued that the number of citizens wishing to maintain the state must be superior to the number of those who do not want to do so.[89] One may therefore conclude that intentions emanating at the domestic level indeed play a crucial role in international politics. Despite the anarchical character of the international system, state behaviour cannot be inferred from systemic factors alone. Instead, there is something like a relatively free will of states, allowing for the existence of different intentions. Those intentions must not necessarily be "good"; the very meaning of the term realism obliges realists to consider the possibility of "bad" intentions. This is a point neorealism — strangely — misses. The world described by Waltz should logically be a rather stable one (one of the reasons being that balancing is far more common than bandwagoning), eventually arriving at a status of Pareto-optimality. Nevertheless, in the writings of Morgenthau and others,

> [e]xternal threats — potential, imagined, or real — drive the realist model. It is surprising, therefore, that revisionist states are scarcely mentioned by contemporary neorealists. Instead, neorealists discuss threats as if they came from nature (the hand of God), not from other states in the international system.[90]

---

89 Aristotle (1998 [ca. 340 BC]) *Politik*, München: DTV, p. 154 (Book IV, Chapter 12, 1296b15).
90 Randall L. Schweller (1996) 'Neorealism's status-quo bias: What security dilemma?', *Security Studies* 5(3), p. 115.

In other words, claiming that states seek maximum security instead of maximum power makes contemporary neorealists ignore the very states that activate the systems and behaviours they wish to explain.[91] It is this Randall Schweller calls the status quo bias of neorealism, arguing that its emphasis on threats is in reality illogical from its own neorealist perspective. Given the (logically necessary) trade-off between security and power maximisation in neorealist theory, no state should take an interest in acting with a goal of power maximisation. Yet, some states do engage in power maximising behaviour. Because states are considered to be "like units" and all pursuing the goal of security, neorealists cannot explain power maximising behaviour with domestic level variables — since those are considered irrelevant. The exclusive focus on the system level at the expense of the unit level can therefore not provide for satisfactory explanations of state behaviour. Aggressiveness is unlikely according to the tenets of neorealism and even counterproductive; yet, it obviously exists in the real world. The neorealist neglect of the revisionist state is thus illogical even when judged in its own right. In other words, neorealism has lost sight of the revisionist state, although it is variation in state motives that accounts for trouble in international politics. Treating states as "like units" means in fact exaggerating parsimony; in this very case, a high degree of theoretical abstraction comes at the price of overlooking crucial variables.

Contrary to neorealists and in line with classical realists, neoclassical realists like Randall L. Schweller believe that the revisionist state should have its place in International Relations theory. Schweller's critique of neorealism has its roots in the conviction that 'staying in place is not the primary goal of revisionist states. They want to increase, not just preserve, their core values and to improve their position in the system'.[92] In his definition,

---

91 Ibid., p. 91.
92 Randall L. Schweller (1994) 'Bandwagoning for Profit. Bringing the Revisionist State Back In', *International Security* 19(1), p. 87.

revisionist states value what they covet more than what they currently possess, although this ratio may vary considerably among their ranks; they will employ military force to change the status quo and to extend their values. For revisionist states, the gains from nonsecurity expansion exceed the cost of war. Needing preponderant power to overturn the status quo, dissatisfied states band together precisely when it appears that they will thus be stronger than the conservative side, for it is only then that they can expect to succeed in their expansionist aims.[93]

Schweller's perspective is, by necessity, a systemic perspective. He nevertheless includes a domestic-level variable by stating that within the system, balancing and bandwagoning are the two options states face, and their choice for either option will be dictated by their ambition to establish a balance of interest. States therefore do not engage in balancing power (or capabilities), but instead join the side with which they share an interest. This should logically include the possibility of states pursuing interests directed against other states.

Whilst the revisionist state is not an object of neorealist theorising, it occupies a prominent place in classical realism. Schweller deserves credit for bringing it 'back in' to neoclassical realism. His discussion of the revisionist state is nevertheless limited to localising revisionism's origins at the domestic level. What Schweller does not discuss are revisionism's effects other than in terms of its consequences for balance (of interests). Even Schweller does not deal with the bilateral aspects of revisionist policies. In other words, his approach takes the neoclassical realist idea of the missing link into account on one hand, without considering it on the other. Yet, revisionism is better understood as a phenomenon with roots *and effects* at domestic levels. A state discontent with its current position in the international system may consider itself to be so disadvantaged that it turns revisionist, i.e., that state aims to undermine or overthrow the existing order. However, there can be no cases of revisionism explicitly directed towards the system without ever affecting other states within that system. It is indeed impossible to detect revisionism directed towards the system without resorting to an analysis of

---

[93] Randall L. Schweller (1994) 'Bandwagoning for Profit', p. 105.

the revisionist state's policies towards other states.[94] Curiously, the revisionist state in traditional IR literature seems to be revisionist without being anybody's antagonist in the first place. Yet, revisionism is not logically conceivable without being directed against other states. The states most likely to react to revisionism are therefore the main supporters of the system. In unipolarity, antagonism towards the hegemon is tantamount to revisionism. However,

> changes in the power structure will not, in and of themselves, bring war about. Satisfied great powers are not likely to interpret advantages gained by satisfied lesser powers as threatening. Moreover, the powerful and satisfied do not start wars. Only if the great powers think that the changing system challenges their positions, or if they no longer like the way benefits are divided, should the shifts be deemed dangerous.[95]

Whether a great power will consider other states' acts as revisionist will largely depend on whether it judges those actions as jeopardising its own position within the system, nonetheless in terms of its ability to exert power. For that reason, it seems more appropriate to classify a state as an "enemy" or "non-friend" in relation to another state, instead of in absolute terms classifying it as "revisionist".

II.2.2 Friends

The conceptual opposite of the revisionist state traditionally is the so-called status quo state. A status quo state is a state satisfied with the current shape of the international system and its position within it, hence a state wishing to maintain the status quo. Nevertheless, if—as argued earlier—categorising states in absolute, systemic terms overlooks the bilateral dimension, qualifying specific states as "status quo powers" is as short-sighted as merely calling them "revisionist". Instead, status quo ambitions will translate in the same way as revisionist ambitions do, i.e., first and foremost bilaterally. For that reason, it is much more useful to focus on a state's

---

94 In that context, see also Robert Jervis (1976) *Perception and Misperception in International* Politics, especially Chapter 1, 'Perception and the Level of Analysis Problem'.
95 A.F.K. Organski and Jacek Kugler (1980) *The War Ledger*, Chicago: Chicago University Press, p. 23.

status quo attitudes towards other states when seeking to explain foreign policy behaviour.

The idea of states' "friends" exists in various conceptualisations and with various connotations. "Friendship" in International Relations is mostly understood as alignment, generally within the framework of balance-of-something theories. The analytical focus generally lies on the "friend" to be, with scholars aiming to explain 'how states choose their friends'.[96] For classical realist Hans J. Morgenthau, alliances are 'a necessary function of the balance of power operating within a multiple-state system'.[97] Alignment is considered a possible strategy to improve a state's relative power position; both through adding another state's power to its own power and through withholding that other state's power from an adversary. The classical realist approach to alliances is thus essentially similar to the neorealist view and shares a concern for the balance of power. Kenneth N. Waltz distinguishes two types of alignment behaviour, namely bandwagoning (i.e., alignment with the strongest) and balancing (i.e., alignment against the strongest) with neorealism predicting that balancing should be far more common.[98] Among the most important contributions to the field is Stephen M. Walt's 1987 *The Origins of Alliances*, which refines balance-of-power theory by proposing balance-of-threat theory, suggesting that 'states ally to balance against threats rather than against power alone'.[99] Here again, two very different hypotheses are conceivable: alignment as balancing behaviour and alignment as bandwagoning behaviour. Whilst balancing implies that two or more states become allies in order to restore the balance of power / threat disrupted by another state, bandwagoning implies that a state aligns with the source of the threat. In either case, alignment is considered a reactive type of behaviour, triggered by a (perceived) threat emanating from one or several other states. The perception of being in danger is thus at the origin of alliance formation in traditional conceptualisations. For

---

96 Stephen M. Walt (1987) *The Origins of Alliances*, p. 1.
97 Hans J. Morgenthau (2006), *Politics Among Nations*, p. 193.
98 Kenneth N. Waltz (1979) *Theory of International Politics*, Reading: Addison-Wesley, pp. 125-126 and 128.
99 Stephen M. Walt (1987) *The Origins of Alliances*, p. 5.

that reason and as far as the alliance itself is concerned, the focus also generally lies on the aligning state. How to attract allies is in turn rarely of interest. This, however, is an aspect that should be crucial for every state seeking to control and shape its external environment.

Neoclassical realist balance of interest-theory is helpful in overcoming the bias on the aligning state. Randall Schweller (1994) argues that balancing and bandwagoning should not be seen as concepts in polar opposition. For Schweller, Waltz, and especially Walt, use the term of "bandwagoning" in a meaning that comes 'very close to the concept of capitulation'. Schweller instead argues for the conventional use of the concept, defining 'a bandwagon as a candidate, side, or movement that attracts adherents or amasses power by its momentum'[100]. This use opens up for the possibility of bandwagoning by free choice, regardless of the existence of a threat (imminent or not). Instead, states are likely to bandwagon for reward, or they may 'bandwagon with the stronger side because they believe it represents "the wave of the future"'.[101] Although Walt argues that foreign aid is not likely to be 'the principal cause of alignment or a powerful instrument', he admits that military or economic aid is 'believed to give the suppliers significant leverage over recipients'.[102] The ability to give rewards and to appear as "the wave of the future" will thus increase a state's attractiveness and induce others to bandwagon with it. Consequently, that state's ability to control and shape its external environment will increase as well.

Nevertheless, appearing as the wave of the future is more than merely a PR coup. By stating that bandwagoning need not necessarily presuppose the existence of a threat, the whole decision by one state to bandwagon with another loses its urgency. A state wanting to attract bandwagons therefore needs good arguments in order to find allies. Thus,

---

[100] Randall L. Schweller (1994) 'Bandwagoning for Profit', p. 96.
[101] Ibid., p. 96.
[102] Stephen M. Walt (1987) *The Origins of Alliances*, p. 41.

> [a]lliance choices [...] are often motivated by opportunities for gain as well as danger, by appetite as well as fear. [...] When profit rather than security drives alliance choices, there is no reason to expect that states will be threatened or cajoled to climb aboard the bandwagon; they do so willingly. The bandwagon gains momentum through the promise of reward [...].[103]

In the balance of interest approach, interest is what determines how states choose their friends. It is thus through considering those interests that a state can make another state want to be its friend. A broader conceptualisation of "friendship" among states therefore seems appropriate. For Aristotle, a person might like another because he or she is good, useful or pleasant.[104] Thus, states do not necessarily choose friends because they have a mutual enemy or wish to balance against threats (though this may well be the case), they may also choose their friends on the basis of shared values or out of respect of another state's greatness.

It is for these reasons that the neoclassical classical focus on (under)balancing does not go far enough: its limitation to the study of alignment (or lack thereof in cases where neorealists would predict otherwise) cannot capture the entire spectrum of states' attempts at controlling and shaping their external environments. In the present study, the notion of "friendly states" or "friends" is therefore preferred to the concepts of "allies" or "status quo states".

II.2.3 Concluding remarks: undecided states

In international politics, this section has argued, states will be confronted with friends and non-friends among other states, i.e., they will face states with friendly and non-friendly dispositions. Because of the exclusively systemic perspective inevitably inherent to the more traditional realist notions of revisionist and status quo states, the terms "friends" and "non-friends" are preferred within the context of this study. A friend is hence a state comfortable with another state's position within the international system, a non-friend is a

---

103 Randall L. Schweller (1994) 'Bandwagoning for Profit', p. 79.
104 Cf. Book VIII in Aristotle (350 B.C.) *Nicomachean Ethics* (e.g. the German translation as *Die Nikomachische Ethik*, München: DTV, 2006).

state which is not. Friends will likely have shared outlooks on specific issues and have (mostly) congruent interests, whereas non-friends will rarely be in agreement.

The two ideal-typical categories of friends and non-friends of course leave room for intermediate attitudes, with states (thus far) unable or unwilling to make up their mind as to how to position themselves with respect to another state. These actors may be called undecided states. Undecided states will oscillate between friendly and unfriendly behaviour, sometimes qualify as valuable allies and sometimes induce trouble in a bilateral relationship. These basic attitudes or ideal-typical statuses will define the bilateral relationships between the states in question. What a state perceives another state to be in terms of that status will consequently have considerable impact on the type of foreign policy it will lead towards it. Depending on the kind of counterpart with which a state is faced in the international system, it will have to find ways and means in order to realise its objectives. In other words, it will have to adapt its foreign policy—namely, its exercise of power—to the circumstances at hand. The following sections therefore set out to discuss the notion of power and the means states have at their disposal when attempting to control and shape their external environment.

II.3 Two types of power resources and foreign policy tools

In realist theorising on international politics, power is a lynchpin notion. As Lobell, Ripsman and Taliaferro however contend, neoclassical realism has so far failed to come up with a convincing concept of power.[105] When attempting to come to terms with the no-

---

[105] Steven E. Lobell, Norrin M. Ripsman and Jeffrey W. Taliaferro (eds.) (2009) 'Conclusion: The state of neoclassical realism', *Neoclassical Realism, the State, and Foreign Policy*, p. 297. See furthermore David A. Baldwin (2002) 'Power and international relations', pp. 177-191 in: Walter Carlsnaes, Thomas Risse and Beth A. Simmons (eds.) *Handbook of International Relations*, London: Sage; Stefano Guzzini (2000) 'The Use and Misuse of Power Analysis in International Theory', in: Ronen Palan (ed.) *Global Political Economy: Contemporary Theories*, London: Routledge, pp. 53-66.

tion, it therefore seems appropriate to go back to the research programme's intellectual predecessors. And in light of neorealism's rather unsubtle practice of equating power with (measurable) capabilities, returning to Morgenthau and his fellow students of foreign policy and even thinkers beyond realism indeed appears to be the most promising venture — a venture not least in line with the neoclassical realist ambition to rekindle classical realist thinking. The train of thought explicated below will thus incorporate arguments by classical realists as well as ideas which do not (solely) belong to realist approaches to international politics. This is especially the case as far as the distinction between positive and negative power resources and the concept of foreign policy tools are concerned. Yet, as this study argues, incorporating these ideas and concepts allows for building an analytical framework which grasps important aspects of international politics and the so-called missing link. This move therefore allows for greater explanatory power in neoclassical realist approaches, not least when it comes to explaining dissimilar foreign policies implemented by one state under identical systemic conditions. As shall be argued, considering the bilateral relationship in question as a central factor in explaining state behaviour, analysts will indeed come closer to elucidating the missing link between material capabilities and foreign policy.

II.3.1 Power in political realism

'Of the gods we believe, and of men we know, that by a necessary law of their nature they rule wherever they can.' Thucydides' dictum on human nature is at the very core of Hans J. Morgenthau's (and others') understanding of international affairs. In analogy, states act according to the same premises in the anarchical international system. They defend their interests against other states (themselves aiming to defend *their* interests), and interest is defined in terms of power, as Morgenthau states in his Six Principles of Political Realism:

> We assume that statesmen think and act in terms of interest defined as power, and the evidence of history bears that assumption out.[106]

The concept of (national) interest as intended by Morgenthau is best defined in the (somewhat cumbersome) words of Arnold Bergstraesser:

> By interest, we mean the concern for the present and future of the living structure of the social and national body to be represented through foreign policy, with this concern lying at the basis of the formation of the political will. What, in a specific case, is regarded as being an interest is thus the result of concrete living conditions on the one hand and the intellectually determined ideas about the sense and goal of foreign policy on the other.[107]

Neoclassical realists are somewhat more specific in their definition of states' objectives, assuming that they seek to control and shape their external environment. At the same time, this neoclassical realist assumption may well be subsumed under the above quoted definition of "interests". Yet, no matter what exactly various strands of realism consider states' ultimate aim to be, power is a *conditio sine qua non* for its realisation. Power is indispensable and hence simultaneously a means and an object of interest, and can even become an end in itself.[108] Morgenthau, by declaring that states first and foremost strive for power aggrandisement, thus simply eliminates the distinction between means and end. For neoclassical realists, power clearly is a means to an end — but this does not preclude returning to Morgenthau and others in order to establish what the notion of power implies.

---

106 Hans J. Morgenthau (2006) *Politics Among Nations*, p. 5.
107 Arnold Bergstraesser (1963) 'Auswärtige Politik', in: Herders *Staatslexikon*, Freiburg, Band I, p. 761, quoted from: Gottfried-Karl Kindermann, (introduction to the German translation of Morgenthau's *Politics Among Nations*, 1963), p. 27. [my own translation in the text]: 'Unter Interesse wird verstanden die der Bildung des politischen Willens zugrunde liegende Sorge um Gegenwart und Zukunft der Daseinsstruktur des außenpolitisch vertretenen Volks- und Gesellschaftskörpers. Was also im Einzelfall als Interesse gilt, ist das Ergebnis konkreter Daseinslagen einerseits und geistig bestimmter Auffassungen von Sinn und Ziel der Außenpolitik andererseits.'
108 Cf. Hans J. Morgenthau (1946) *Scientific Man vs. Power Politics*, Chicago: University of Chicago Press.

Despite the notion's central position in his thinking, Morgenthau fails to provide a concise definition of power – and with good reasons: for Morgenthau, power cannot be quantified, since power becomes manifest in a psychological relation between one part exerting it and one part being the recipient of power. This is why, for Morgenthau, there simply cannot be any concise definition of power, setting its content once and for all:

> Its content and the manner of its use are determined by the political and cultural environment. Power may comprise anything that establishes and maintains the control of man over man. Thus power covers all social relationships which serve that end, from physical violence to the most subtle psychological ties by which one mind controls another. Power covers the domination of man by man, both when it is disciplined by moral ends and controlled by constitutional safeguards, as in Western democracies, and when it is that untamed and barbaric force which finds its laws in nothing but its own strength and sole justification in its aggrandizement.[109]

The lack of an absolute definition of "power" is a recurrent problem in classical and neoclassical realism, as well as in International Relations in general.[110] Rather unsurprisingly, realists have been criticised on these grounds. One may, however, also consider taking Morgenthau seriously instead of blaming him with failure. As becomes clear from the above quotation, for Morgenthau, power is not to be equated with capabilities (though capabilities may play a crucial role when power is to be exerted). While capabilities remain constant and measurable, power may indeed be considered an ever shifting phenomenon: the power relationship at hand needs to be taken into account and is the defining element of the circumstances under which power occurs. It is this which explains the observation that power resources and the degree to which a state can impose

---

109 Hans J. Morgenthau (2006) *Politics Among Nations*, p. 11.
110 For an overview of approaches to power in IR in general, cf. David A. Baldwin (2002) 'Power and International Relations'. For specifically realist conceptions, cf. Brian C. Schmidt (2007) 'Realist conceptions of power', pp. 43–64 in: Felix Berenskoetter and Michael C. Williams (eds.) *Power in World Politics*, London: Routledge.

itself must not necessarily be on par. Even as far as the most powerful state in the system is concerned — in terms of material capabilities — it may thus be concluded that

> [t]he capabilities of a hegemon or other pole may be unchallenged, but that does not obviate the need for studying whether the hegemon influences other actors in the desired direction.[111]

In other words, not only do capabilities matter, but also reasons which make power effective and what Morgenthau terms the 'cultural and political environment'.

At closer look, Morgenthau is not alone with this standpoint but in rather good company. His understanding of the phenomenon is indeed very similar to Max Weber's, who famously defined power as

> any capability [or: chance, probability][112] to impose one's own will in a social relationship, even against resistance, regardless of the basis on which this capability [or: chance, probability] rests.[113]

---

111 Jeremy Pressman (2009) 'Power without Influence', *International Security* 33(4), p. 150.
112 The correct translation of Weber's definition of "Macht" (power) is a tricky issue, not least when it comes to the word "Chance" that Weber employs in the German original of *Economy and Society*. "Chance" has been translated into English as, inter alia, "chance", "probability" or "capability". In this study, I shall translate "Chance" by capability — arguing that Weber by no means implied that "getting one's will across" may be a coincidence. Although this may indeed be a connotation of "Chance", Weber's approach to basic notions of sociology makes this interpretation rather unlikely. For detailed discussions on how Weber's definition of power ought to be translated into English, cf. Richard Swedberg (with the assistance of Ola Agevall) (2005) *The Max Weber dictionary: key words and central concepts* (Stanford: Stanford University Press), in particular the entry on power p. 205/6. See also Isidor Wallimann, Howard Rosenbaum, Nicholas Tatsis and George Zito (1980) 'Misreading Weber: The Concept of "Macht"', *Sociology* 12(2): pp. 261-275.
113 Max Weber (1947 [1922]) *Wirtschaft und Gesellschaft*, 3rd edition, Tübingen: Mohr, Part 1, Chapter I, § 16 [my own translation in the text]: '*Macht* bedeutet jede Chance, innerhalb einer sozialen Beziehung den eigenen Willen auch gegen Widerstreben durchzusetzen, gleichviel worauf diese Chance beruht.' This Weberian influence on Morgenthau is especially palpable in *Scientific Man vs. Power Politics*. See also Tarak Barkawi (1998) 'Strategy as a Vocation: Weber, Morgenthau and modern strategic studies', *Review of International Studies* 24(2)

Max Weber's definition clearly comprises the idea that this 'basis' on which 'power rests' can indeed vary, as he explains in subsequent paragraphs of *Economy and Society*. Classical realists other than Morgenthau hold similar views. Raymond Aron, for instance, defines power[114] as follows:

> In the most general sense, power [puissance] is the capacity to do, produce or destroy. I call power [puissance] on the international scene the capacity of a unit to impose its will on other units. In short, power [puissance] is nothing absolute but a human relation.[115]

What is implicit in all three above quoted definitions is a distinction between the very "essence" of power ("what *is* power?") and the reasons that make it work. And looking for that essence may indeed be the wrong path to choose—elsewhere in *Economy and Society*, Weber in fact calls the notion of power 'sociologically amorphous'.[116] Embracing the idea that the essence of power must ultimately escape definition may sound like pulling the rug out from under the discipline's feet and moreover seem scientifically unsatisfying. Authors like William Curti Wohlforth[117] have nevertheless demonstrated that an entire (realist) study may be built upon the idea that power is more or less indefinable unless it is contextualised. As this section has argued, such an approach is indeed not by

---

and of course Christoph Frei (1993) *Hans J. Morgenthau: eine intellektuelle Biographie*. Bern: Haupt.

114   It is worth noting that the term "power" may be translated in two different ways into French, a point Aron insists on. The English "power" (as well as the German *Macht* as used by Weber) may either be translated by *pouvoir* or *puissance*. The concept of relevance in the present context is *puissance*.

115   Raymond Aron 2004 [1962]) *Paix et guerre entre les nations*, p. 58 [my own translation in the text]: 'Au sens le plus général, la puissance est la capacité de faire, produire ou détruire. [...] J'appelle puissance sur la scène internationale la capacité d'une unité d'imposer sa volonté aux autres unités. En bref, la puissance n'est pas un absolu mais une relation humaine.'

116   Max Weber (1947) *Wirtschaft und Gesellschaft*, Teil 1, Kap. I, § 16.

117   Wohlforth explores American and Soviet perceptions of the global balance of power in the Cold War period, cf. William Curti Wohlforth (1993) *The Elusive Balance: Power and Perceptions during the Cold War*, especially p. 15.

definition alien to (classical) realism.[118] Rather, it carries opportunities missed when trying to operate with once-and-for-all-type definitions — not least that of being able to take contexts into account.

The notion of power that forms the basis of the following sections is thus that taken from Weber: power is the capability to get one's will across, while the sources or bases of that capability must still be specified depending on contextual factors. These power bases are the subject of the following sections. As far as other terms such as "influence" or domination are concerned, they are considered here to be essentially synonymous with the Weberian notion of "power".[119]

II.3.2 Positive and negative power: the relevance of base values

While, paraphrasing Weber, defining power as the capability to impose one's will is straightforward, explaining the 'basis on which this power rests' is more difficult. For Morgenthau, the effect of power

---

118 See also Barbara Kunz (2010) 'Hans J. Morgenthau's Political Realism, Max Weber and the Concept of Power', *Max Weber Studies*, forthcoming.

119 Indeed, Weber himself prefers studying domination rather than power: 'Rulership *(Herrschaft)* will be termed the chance that a command of a certain kind will be obeyed by a given group of people.' (Cf. Max Weber (1947) *Wirtschaft und Gesellschaft*, Teil 1, Kap. I, § 16. Quoted in Keith Tribe's translation, in Whimster (ed.) *The Essential Weber*, p. 355.) Weber's own definition of "Herrschaft" is consequently deemed to be sufficiently close to "power" in order use it interchangeably in the present context.

The use of "influence" by some scholars may lead the reader to disagree with the practice of equalling these notions. Other "classical" definitions of the concept, in turn, clearly allow for equalling power and influence. For Kalevi J. Holsti, for example, influence is 'essentially a means to an end. [...] States use influence primarily for achieving or defending other goals, which may include prestige, territory, souls, raw materials, security, or alliances'. Cf. Kalevi Holsti (1995) *International Politics. A Framework for Analysis,* 7th edition, Englewood Cliffs: Prentice Hall, p. 118.

derives from three sources: the expectation of benefits, the fear of disadvantages, and the respect or love for men or institutions. It may be exerted through orders, threats, the authority or charisma of a man or of an office, or a combination of any of these.[120]

The expectation of benefits, the fear of disadvantages: This difference is to be captured in the notions of "positive" and "negative" power resources.[121] What differentiates these two sources of power is, to borrow a term coined by Harold D. Lasswell and Abraham Kaplan, their base values, i.e. the condition or mechanism that makes the exercise of power effective:

> the "base value" of the influence refers to the causal condition of its exercise: that which gives the influence its effectiveness.[122]

Many scholars have obviously followed the path of categorising power, both before and after Lasswell and Kaplan.[123] The categorisation of power is thus as present in antique thinking as in Machiavelli's dictum that the prince benefits from both being respected and feared. John R.P. French and Bertram H. Raven distinguish five bases of social power: reward power, coercive power, legitimate power, referent power and expert power.[124] Robert A. Dahl[125] in turn distinguishes 'influence terms' ranging from persuasion to physical force. Within International Relations properly speaking,

---

120 Hans J. Morgenthau (2006) *Politics Among Nations*, p. 31.
121 These two categories are first and foremost built upon the French terms *pouvoir d'injonction* and *pouvoir d'influence*, (cf. Madeleine Grawitz and Jean Leca (eds.) (1985) *Traité de Science Politique*, Paris: Presses Universitaires de France). In order to avoid confusion, *pouvoir d'influence* is translated by "positive power", and thus, accordingly, *pouvoir d'injonction* by "negative power".
122 Harold D. Lasswell and Abraham Kaplan (1950) *Power and Society. A Framework for Political Enquiry*, New Haven: Yale University Press, p. 83; see also pp. 86-92.
123 For an exhaustive overview, cf. Karl Sandner (1990) *Prozesse der Macht. Zur Entstehung, Stabilisierung und Veränderung der Macht von Akteuren in Unternehmen*, Berlin: Springer, pp. 27 ff.
124 Cf. John R.P. French and Bertram H. Raven (1959) 'The bases of social power', pp. 150-167 in: D. Cartwright (ed.) *Studies in Social Power*, Ann Arbor: Michigan University Press.
125 Cf. Robert A. Dahl (1989) *Democracy and its Critics*. New Haven and London: Yale University Press.

Joseph S. Nye's distinction between "soft" and "hard power", now accepted even outside academia, is the most recent contribution in this respect[126], covering parts of the argument made here. Classical realist Arnold Wolfers discerns "influence" from "power" along the exact same lines as positive power is here discerned from negative power.[127] David A. Baldwin labels the conceptual pair 'positive / negative sanctions' in his various works, while James W. Davis reasons in terms of 'threat' vs. 'promise'.[128] Alexander L. George develops the 'carrot and stick approach' within the framework of 'coercive diplomacy'[129]. Similar approaches are moreover found in the writings of Thomas C. Schelling[130] and Jack H. Nagel[131] as well as in those of Hans J. Morgenthau himself. None of these works is yet explicitly based upon the concept of base values, and none obviously makes the claim to be a contribution to neoclassical realism.

Beyond the narrower confines of political science, Max Weber distinguishes three ideal types[132] of legitimate domination (*Herrschaft*), which can be rational, traditional or charismatic.[133] These types also illustrate the idea of different kinds of power, since they are built upon different base values: the rational type rests on the belief in the legality of the rules on which domination is based. The traditional type, in turn, rests on a belief in the sanctity of the traditions. The charismatic type, finally, rests on the extraordinary

---

126 Cf. Joseph S. Nye (2004) *Soft Power. The Means to Success in World Politics*, New York: Public Affairs. For further discussion of the concept of "soft power", cf. section II.3.4 below.
127 Arnold Wolfers (1962) 'Power and Influence: The Means of Foreign Policy'.
128 James W. Davis (2002) *Threats and Promises: The Pursuit of International Influence*, Baltimore: Johns Hopkins University Press.
129 Alexander L. George (1991) *Forceful Persuasion: Coercive Diplomacy as an Alternative to War*, Washington D.C.: United States Institute of Peace Press.
130 Thomas C. Schelling (1980) *The Strategy of Conflict*, Cambridge: Harvard University Press.
131 Jack H. Nagel (1975) *The Descriptive Analysis of Power*, New Haven: Yale University Press.
132 An ideal type is a theoretical – though non-normative – construct of an "ideal picture" of a phenomenon. It is based on the exaggeration of specific features, serving the purpose of representing the characteristics of the phenomenon portrayed. An ideal type is therefore not the same as a definition.
133 Max Weber (1947) *Wirtschaft und Gesellschaft*, Part 1, Chapter III, p. 122 ff.

devotion to the exceptional sanctity, heroic power or exemplarity of a person and the order he or she revealed and implemented. Those types apply to domination in a domestic context, which makes Weber state that domination (*Herrschaft*) 'normally' requires a staff in order to be implemented. Nevertheless, although parallels have to be drawn carefully, it is an incontestable fact that domination as a phenomenon also occurs in international politics. International politics takes place under circumstances characterised by the absence of a world government, hence anarchy. For this reason, domination does not necessarily take the same form in domestic and international politics. Instead, states may attempt to coerce each other into doing or not doing something, without being able to recur to any superior instance.[134] This does, not, however, alter the nature of the forces at play; anarchy merely has consequences on enforcement. Legitimacy (or perceptions thereof) will matter in international relations since it will be relevant for states' willingness to yield to other states' influence. Power exerted on the basis of perceived legitimacy is consequently essentially different from power exerted on the basis of coercion.

Contrary to approaches by, for instance, Joseph S. Nye or David A. Baldwin discussed below, base values thus explain why power works *as seen from the recipient's vantage point*. Very importantly, therefore, the idea of base values in Lasswell's and Kaplan's understanding necessarily implies attention devoted to the receiving end of a power relationship, since that 'which gives influence its effectiveness' should logically be located on that side. This is an essential difference as compared to Nye or Baldwin, who (implicitly) classifies power from the emitter's vantage point. Only conceiving the 'causal condition' as operative at the receiving end of an influence attempt, however, allows for establishing a logical link between different types of power resources and the recipient — for instance, friendly, unfriendly or undecided states. When merely

---

[134] The ultimate illustration of negative power based on coercion is the condition referred to as MAD, mutually assured destruction. By threatening to entirely destroy the adversary, the (potential) adversary is deterred from launching an attack.

considering the emitting part and classifying power as "hard", "soft" or anything else from this perspective, that linkage must necessarily remain ungrounded. Yet, a state will encounter friends and non-friends in international politics: states that do or do not support it — as well as, by necessity, states that are indifferent. In order to maintain or even expand its position within the international system, a state needs to be able to counter its enemies, to keep its friends and perhaps to convince undecided states to become its friends. In other words, states need to be able to exert power on all of their fellow states. Given those fellow states' different friend / non-friend / undecided statuses, however, the means to impose one's will must logically differ: different types of power resources will be applied, as the base values to which recipients will respond vary. Because power is applied in context, the reasons for success and failure in a state's attempts at getting its will across will therefore differ depending on the recipient and the factors to which that recipient is deemed to be receptive. In other words, the base value is that which, in Max Weber's definition of power explains the 'capability to impose one's own will in a social relationship, even against resistance, regardless of the basis on which this capability rests' and accounts for the effective and successful wielding of power. This is the reason why the terms of positive and negative power resources, distinguished on the grounds of their base values, shall be used in the present study instead of, for instance, recurring to the admittedly better established soft power / hard power dichotomy.

In its exercise, both positive and negative power may either be physical or symbolic. Physical power tools are easy to understand: they are aimed at a state's material assets, such as its infrastructure, its material wealth and the like. Those can be targeted as means in themselves (e.g., destroying industrial sites), or because of their strategic value (e.g., destroying communication networks in order to hamper the adversary's military planning). Symbolic power tools, in turn, target a state's reputation or prestige. Distinguishing the two is not as relevant as distinguishing positive and negative power resources. Nevertheless, the distinction between material and symbolic tools may tell the analyst something about states' commitment (simply because symbolic power resources are less expensive to use as they require less material resources), but also about the easiness with which it can exert power over others (namely, by recurring to "cheap" symbolic measures as opposed to expensive material ones).

The concept of 'prestige' is linked to Robert Gilpin's discussion of 'governance' of the international system as composed by three components: the distribution of power, the hierarchy of prestige among states and the rules of interaction in the system. Gilpin claims that in international relations, 'prestige' is 'the functional equivalent' of the role of authority in domestic politics.[135] His argument is based on Ralf Dahrendorf's definition of the term, itself very close to Weber's 'power'. For Dahrendorf, authority (or prestige, in Gilpin's terms) is the 'probability that a command with a given specific content will be obeyed by a given group of persons'.[136] Given the closeness to Weber, 'prestige' also contains a large amount of perception factors. Much is thus in the eyes of the beholder, although resources and material assets play an ever so important role:

> In short, numerous factors, including respect and common interest, underlie the prestige of a state and the legitimacy of its rule. Ultimately, however, the hierarchy of prestige in an international system rests on economic and military power. Prestige is the reputation for power, and military power in particular. Whereas power refers to the economic, military, and related capabilities of a state, prestige refers primarily to the perceptions of other states with respect to a state's capacities and its ability and willingness to exercise its power.[137]

What follows is that the power of a state should be expected to be highly dependent on the target of its foreign policies. For that reason, its material capabilities and power resources give rise to foreign policy tools, based on the two types of power described above. They do not, however, need to be material assets only: a state's reputation is as much a resource as its arsenal of nuclear weapons.

---

135 Robert Gilpin (1981) *War and Change in World Politics*, Cambridge: Cambridge University Press, pp. 29 ff.
136 Quoted ibid., p. 30.
137 Ibid., p. 31.

II.3.3 Negative power and its bases

When power is applied in international politics, this is thus as much a matter of its material as it is of its immaterial aspects.

Negative power is mainly on par with most traditional definitions of power, such as offered by Thomas Hobbes[138] or, on a different level even Michel Foucault[139] or Steven Lukes[140]. Negative power is the kind of power neorealists have in mind, which is essentially the ability to cause damage or, at least, the ability to threaten to do so based on credible grounds. In other words, negative power is based on coercion: if B does not do X, then punishment will follow. Negative power hence works through undesirable consequences for the receiving end, judging the harm caused by non-compliance too high a price to resist the emitter of the stipulation. The very last resort of negative power is war; either in its traditional form based on physical violence or in its more modern forms of cyber-attacks, withheld energy supplies or the like. Symbolic negative power primarily aims at undermining another state's prestige, discrediting the state in question and pushing it into a pariah position within the international system. Moreover, that state's leadership will be deprived of opportunities to demonstrate its greatness to its own population. A prerequisite for the successful use of symbolic negative power is of course a certain capital of prestige lying with the wielding state, recognised by other fellow states. "Shaming" a state will only work if the majority of states within the international system share the symbolic power wielding state's system of values. Regardless of the form negative power takes, its effect will always be short-termed, limited in scope and suffer from a lack of sustainability if not continuously applied. At best, negative power can force an adversary into compliance. Building rapport must logically remain beyond the capacities of negative power.

---

138 Cf. Thomas Hobbes (1998 [1660]) *Leviathan or the Matter, Forme and Power of a Commonwealth Ecclesiastical and Civil*, Oxford: Oxford University Press.
139 Cf. for instance Michel Foucault (1975) *Surveiller et Punir. Naissance de la Prison*, Paris: Gallimard.
140 Cf. Steven Lukes (2004 [1974]) *Power. A Radical View*, 2nd edition, London: Palgrave Macmillan.

II.3.4 Positive power and its bases

Positive power works through rewards and incentives, both material and symbolic. It offers its recipients added value in various forms: material or symbolic remuneration, such as money, membership, information or the prestige acquired thanks to "friendship" with a mighty great power. As such, it has been the objective of scholarly interest mainly within the relational power paradigm.[141]

What essentially qualifies positive power resources is that they never can be effective against the recipient's will.[142] Whereas material remuneration is obvious and quantifiable, symbolic remuneration is harder to grasp. Symbolic positive power is intrinsically linked to what Hans J. Morgenthau calls the "Policy of Prestige"[143], which he essentially sees applied to international diplomacy with its strict and complicated rules. Yet, 'however exaggerated and absurd its uses may have been at times, [the policy of prestige] is as intrinsic an element between nations as the desire for prestige is of the relations between individuals'.[144] It is exactly this desire for recognition that opens up for the use of prestige as an expression of power, since

> in both spheres [domestic and international], the desire for social recognition is a potent dynamic force determining the social relations and creating social institutions. The individual seeks confirmation on the part of his fellows, of the evaluation he puts on himself. It is only in the tribute others pay to his goodness, intelligence and power that he becomes fully aware of, and can fully enjoy, what he deems to be his superior qualities. [...] The image in the mirror of our fellows' minds (that is, our prestige), rather than the original, of which the image in the mirror may be but the distorted reflections, determines what we are as members of society.[145]

---

141 For a brief introduction, cf. David A. Baldwin (2002) 'Power and International Relations', p. 187.

142 It is important to not confound positive power with humanitarian aid. Thus, when for instance the United States sends food to North Korea or supports victims of the Chernobyl disaster, this is not necessarily in exercise of its power, but (perhaps) merely to save starving people.

143 Cf. Hans J. Morgenthau (2006) *Politics Among Nations*, pp. 83 ff.

144 Ibid., p. 83.

145 Ibid., p. 83/84.

In international politics, this means that states can confer prestige on each other, either by openly fearing other states and thus acknowledging their might or by demonstratively showing respect for their prestige in a more positive sense. If the argument is reversed, this implies that leading states within the international system nonetheless have the capacity to make important contributions to other states' reputation by enhancing their prestige.

Among the established approaches to positive power in International Relations, Joseph Nye's concept of "soft power" comes closest to being comparable to the meaning intended here. Soft power 'rests on the ability to shape the preferences of others', being 'not merely the same as influence [...] and more than just persuasion or the ability to move people by argument':[146]

> You can command me to change my preferences and do what you want by threatening me with force or economic sanctions. You can induce me to do what you want by using your economic power to pay me. You can restrict my preferences by setting the agenda in such a way that my more extravagant wishes seem too unrealistic to pursue. Or you can appeal to my sense of attraction, love or duty in our relationship and appeal to our shared values about the justness of contributing to those shared values and purposes. If I am persuaded to go along with your purposes without any explicit threat or exchange taking part—in short, if my behaviour is determined by an observable but intangible attraction—soft power is at work.[147]

Soft power in international politics is said to primarily rest on three resources, which are a country's culture, its political values and its foreign policies—'when they are seen as legitimate and having moral authority'.[148] Reputation does matter, as do other factors like the spreading of popular culture and languages. "Values", and even "shared values" are in fact at the core of soft power, determining what others think of a country. Yet, Nye's concept remains vague. Interestingly though, Nye insists on power being relational and context bound.[149] It is therefore surprising that his discussion of origins of "soft power" is limited to the emitting part in the relation

---

146 Joseph S. Nye (2004) *Soft Power. The Means to Success in World Politics*, p. 5.
147 Ibid., p. 6.
148 Ibid., p. 11.
149 Ibid., p. 16.

(and there, only vaguely). Indeed, Nye does not provide any explanations as far as why the receiving part would find the values etc. in question attractive: this, however, would seem to be a core question. Still, "soft power" being a means to an end of shaping and controlling the environment, the concept obviously comprises elements of realist theory, leading Nye to conclude that

> There is no contradiction between realism and soft power. Soft power is not a form of idealism or liberalism. It is simply a form of power, one way of getting desired outcomes.[150]

Besides legitimacy, another crucial aspect of positive power naturally is identity of interest, i.e., a situation in which A gets B to do X because B realises that it shares that interest with A. As Weber's definition of power as 'any capability to impose one's will in a social relationship, *even against resistance* [...]'[151] suggests, resistance against that will is by no means present in all attempts at exerting power but merely one of several conceivable reactions. In his third Principle of political realism, Morgenthau in turn quotes Thucydides with the words 'identity of interests is the surest of bonds whether between states or individuals'.[152] Yet, again explicitly relying on Weber, Morgenthau reiterates that interests are not set once and for all, but depend on 'the political and cultural context within which foreign policy is formulated'.[153] In other words, already the formulation of interests by states may be a matter of interest for other states. For that reason, aiming at influencing the definition of that state's interests (for instance regarding the choice to adhere to a certain sphere of influence) might very well be an objective for actors within the international system.

---

150 Joseph S. Nye (2005) 'Notes on a soft power research agenda', in: Felix Berenskoetter and Michael J. Williams (eds.) *Power in World Politics*, London: Routledge, p. 170.
151 Max Weber (1947) *Wirtschaft und Gesellschaft*, Part 1, Chapter I, § 16, p. 28 [my own translation in the text]: 'Macht bedeutet jede Chance, in einer sozialen Beziehung, den eigenen Willen auch gegen Widerstreben durchzusetzen, gleichviel, worauf diese Chance beruht'.
152 Hans J. Morgenthau (2006), *Politics Among Nations*, p. 10.
153 Ibid., p. 11.

II.3.5 Power resources and foreign policy tools

The exercise of power may take different forms, through means of positive and negative power resources translated into various foreign policy tools. Strangely, the instruments or means with which states exercise power — that is, foreign policy tools — are (with notable exceptions) a neglected phenomenon in the discipline of International Relations, a conclusion David A. Baldwin arrived at in 1985 and which is still valid today.[154] Granted, the notion is quasi-ubiquitous and appears in many contexts even beyond political science, for example when the European Union describes its European Neighbourhood Policy as a "policy tool". Its content largely seems to be considered self-evident, with few concise definitions provided however.[155]

Among the most interesting contributions to be found are those published prior to the bifurcation of International Relations and Foreign Policy Analysis into (allegedly) separate disciplines. However, these contributions still remain too unspecified for the present purpose. While there certainly is no reason to object to, for instance, Arnold Wolfers' claim that 'power and influence' are the 'means of foreign policy'[156], the vagueness of that statement remains problematic.

Turning to more recent Foreign Policy Analysis scholarship does, unfortunately, only seem promising at first glance. Terms such as "means of foreign policy" or "foreign policy instruments" are indeed not alien to that body of literature. The listing of foreign

---

154 David A. Baldwin (1985) *Economic Statecraft*, Princeton: Princeton University Press, p. 9.
155 To name examples where foreign policy instruments are central to the argument without being defined, see Daniel Deudney and G. John Ikenberry (1992) 'Who Won the Cold War?', *Foreign Policy,* no 87: pp. 123-128; Otto Wolff von Amerongen (1980) 'Economic Sanctions as a Foreign Policy Tool?', *International Security* 5 (2), pp. 159-167; or Hans Mouritzen (1995) 'The Nordic Model as a Foreign Policy Instrument: Its Rise and Fall', *Journal of Peace Research* 32(1), pp. 9-21.
156 Arnold Wolfers (1962) 'Power and Influence: The Means of Foreign Policy'.

policy tools recurring in most introductions to Foreign Policy Analysis enumerates diplomacy, military measures, economic statecraft and culture.[157]

Within the narrower boundaries of International Relations, the most elaborate and valuable contribution in that respect is certainly David A. Baldwin's typology of "statecraft". In his own words,

> [t]o study statecraft [...] is to consider the instruments used by policy makers in their attempts to exercise power [...].[158]

More precisely, Baldwin defines these various instruments in the following way:

> *Propaganda* refers to influence attempts relying primarily on the deliberate manipulation of verbal symbols.
> *Diplomacy* refers to influence attempts relying primarily on negotiation.
> *Economic statecraft* refers to influence attempts relying primarily on resources which have a reasonable resemblance of a market price in terms of money.
> *Military statecraft* refers to influence attempts relying primarily on violence, weapons or force.[159]

There are, however, two reasons to avoid Baldwin's classification of instruments in the present context. First, it is essentially based on functional distinctions. Although Baldwin in general distinguishes between positive and negative sanctions, his statecraft approach does not allow for a systematic study of base values and a recipient-based view of these. Rather, Baldwin's instruments of statecraft are categorised on the basis of policy fields, which may well comprise both positive and negative power tools in some cases (economic statecraft, diplomacy). In addition, his classification of "techniques

---

157 Christopher Hill (2003) *The Changing Politics of Foreign Policy*, London: Palgrave Macmillan, p. 134 ff.
158 David A. Baldwin (1985) *Economic Statecraft*, p. 9.
159 Ibid., p. 13/14 (italics in the original).
  As said earlier, classifications of power are naturally not exclusive to this study, but have been proposed by many scholars such as for instance Dahl (1989) or Nye (2004). A detailed discussion of all these classifications would however be beyond the scope of the present study.

of statecraft" leaves little room for specific base values such as the lust for prestige as a target of foreign policy, be it positively or negatively.[160] "Prestige" appears in connection with possible explanations for successful economic statecraft, when Baldwin states that it is 'conceivable, not to say likely, that the target state may care more about its moral standing in the international community than about the effect of such sanctions on its economic welfare' in the case of economic sanctions being imposed on a human rights offender.[161] Yet, although Baldwin explicitly mentions prestige as a power base, this study argues that it should occupy a more prominent position in the analytical framework beyond being a mere by-product of economic statecraft. In sum, Baldwin's approach — which, at the same time, is widely spread within Foreign Policy Analysis — thus leaves little room for base values as a central distinctive feature in classifying foreign policy tools. For that reason, a different approach shall be used in the present study: an approach which classifies foreign policy tools on the basis of their base values.

A second reason for proposing an approach dissimilar to Baldwin's is the fact that he hardly incorporates longer-term patterns of friendship and enmity going beyond the limited chronological scope of the case studied into his framework for analysis. Despite his assertion that '[t]he determination of whether A will actually succeed in influencing B […] is not entirely within A's control; it depends on B's value system'[162] his approach lacks the element of this very relationship between A and B being more than a punctual event occurring at a precise moment in time but rather a long-term phenomenon. The long-term patterns of a bilateral relation, however, are a very important factor in international politics.[163]

---

160 Cf. especially chapter 6 on 'Bargaining With Economic Statecraft', including reflections on symbolic *economic* statecraft (italics added).
161 David A. Baldwin (1985) *Economic Statecraft*, p. 135.
162 Ibid., p. 22.
163 There are, of course, studies focusing on power exerted within longer-term relationships in the spirit of social power approaches, cf. for instance Linus Hagström (2005) *Japan's China Policy. A relational Power Analysis*, London: Routledge. Yet, in the present study, only acts that qualify as "social action" in Max Weber's definition are considered to be acts of foreign policy (cf. *Wirtschaft*

A foreign policy tool is defined here as any measure to which a state resorts in order to obtain a specific behaviour from another state, including everything from kind words to cruise missiles. Foreign policy tools are thus attempts at exercising power, and the classification offered below is made on the basis of the base values at hand.

Positive and negative power resources will give rise to two essentially different, yet combinable, sets of foreign policy tools. A foreign policy tool may either offer incentives or threaten with punishment, i.e., it can either be based on positive or negative power. A foreign policy based on a combination of tools is naturally also possible, i.e., promising rewards in the case of compliance but threatening punishment in the case of non-compliance such as in 'coercive diplomacy' scenarios.[164] The more solid the basis for common objectives and interests is, the more likely the use of positive power instruments. Thus, a state can only be rewarded with something it (a) actually desires and (b) the rewarding state effectively can offer. Rewards may include a wide range of assets and advantages, ranging from such fundamentally necessary needs like "security" to measures increasing a state's prestige on the international scene. Rewards may be material like financial aid or radar stations, at least tangible in the form of military co-operation or consultation, or simply symbolic such as publicly declaring that a relationship is considered a "strategic partnership". Other examples of material positive power are economic and / or military aid and co-operation, possibly through integration in various organisations and alliances. Symbolic positive power may include various demonstrations of friendship and closeness, aimed at increasing the respective state's prestige, both internationally—vis-à-vis enemies—and at home, offering its leadership the opportunity to bask in the glory of state visits and the like.

---

und Gesellschaft, Part 1, Chapter II) and is not intended to be a contribution to the social power literature.

164 Cf. Alexander L. George, (1991) *Forceful Persuasion: Coercive Diplomacy as an Alternative to War*, Washington, D.C.: United States Institute of Peace Press.

Politics however being an art exercised under shifting circumstances, no definite "catalogue" of foreign policy tools can ever be established. There is no simple equation of *objective x + tool y = desired outcome*. In other words, specific moves may yield the anticipated result in one case and prove entirely useless in another. For instance, inviting a foreign head of state to a dinner at the White House may be considered a great honour in one country and an unreasonable demand in another, depending on the relationship those countries maintain with the United States. For that reason, there can neither be a parsimonious theory of influence, nor a list of foreign policy tools that will "work" under all circumstances. It is, however, possible to establish a (non-exhaustive) listing of conceivable foreign policy tools and the type of power to which they are attributable, based upon the base value they presumably target:

Table 1: Foreign policy tools attributable to positive and negative power resources

	Negative power resources: fear of damage	Positive power resources: hope for rewards
material	Military attack (as a measure of last resort) Embargos / trade restrictions Freezing assets	Aid and assistance in various forms (economic, military, technological) Contributing to material advantages through third parties
symbolic	Abandoning or limiting diplomatic relations Verbal politics such as denouncing statements Denying state visits, photo-ops etc., i.e. the prestige granted by the display of good relations Travel restrictions Vetoing membership in international organisations	Frequent high-level contacts Membership in organisations / promoting membership for specific states Ostentatiously displayed good relations (photo-ops, banquets…)

II.4 Linking states' friend / non-friend / undecided status to power

The two types of power resources discussed above imply a rather different toolkit of foreign policy measures. Which tool is adequate is highly dependent on the circumstances of its use: kind words may be appropriate in one case, whilst they may be totally inappropriate in another where indeed cruise missiles are the only means left. States, when designing their foreign policies, are most likely to be aware of such considerations. In other words, it is reasonable to expect a link between the kind of foreign policy tools employed and the target state's perceived friend / non-friend / undecided status.

For realists, foreign policy is essentially made by what Steven Lobell labels the 'foreign policy executive.'[165] When they design foreign policies, decision-makers within that foreign policy executive

---
165 Steven E. Lobell (2009) 'Threat assessment, the state, and foreign policy: a neoclassical realist model', in Steven E. Lobell, Norrin M. Ripsman and Jeffrey W.

need to make assessments of the international system and the external environment surrounding their state. Moreover, they have the task define the state's objectives and to identify and implement 'those long-range measures which would be appropriate to the accomplishment of that end.'[166] These decision-makers also assess — implicitly or explicitly — other states' friend / non-friend / undecided status. When subsequently designing foreign policies, this assessment arguably plays a crucial role.

Friends, non-friends and undecided states are indeed highly likely to be susceptible to very different base values. In the case of friends, it seems reasonable to expect that there will be some interests congruent to at least a certain degree. Friends will be interested in the prestige to be shown by foreign policy emitting states, and they will care about rewards to be offered. In short, friends are thus likely to be responsive to positive power. The foreign policy emitting state will also have an interest in mainly operating with positive power resources: this will allow it to maintain the friendship, potentially at rather low cost if mainly using positive symbolic power.

Non-friends, in turn, are unlikely to be responsive to positive power resources. There hardly is any basis of shared interests, and they do not see any prestige to be gained from friendly relations maintained with the emitting state. If that emitting state seeks to get its will across, it will therefore have to resort to negative power resources — at a potentially high cost in the case of material power, cheaper in the case of symbolic power.

Undecided states, finally, occupy a middle ground in terms of status and consequently also in terms of the base values to which they are deemed susceptible. Depending on which disposition is considered to preponderate, states may thus resort to both types of power resources in dealing with their undecided counterparts. Yet,

---

Taliaferro (eds.) *Neoclassical Realism, the State, and Foreign Policy*. See also Margaret G. Hermann and Charles F. Hermann (1989) 'Who Makes Foreign Policy Decisions and How: A Theoretical Framework', *International Studies Quarterly* 33(4): pp. 361-387.

166 Morton A. Kaplan (1952) 'An Introduction to the Strategy of Statecraft', *World Politics* 4(4), p. 553.

as it is in any state's interest to have more friends than non-friends, a prevalence of positive power tools is to be expected, owing to the likely intention to make the state in question become a friend.

II.5 Concluding remarks on the theoretical framework

The conclusion to be drawn from what has been argued in previous sections is that states' perceptions of the states they address in their foreign policies ought to be considered an element of the so-called missing link. Neoclassical realists contend that there is no direct transmission belt between capabilities and state behaviour and have thus far sought to elucidate that missing link by introducing domestic constraints and elite perceptions of systemic factors as intervening variables. This chapter has argued that elite perceptions of systemic factors are insufficient, since perceptions of fellow states should be equally important: if states seek to control and shape their external environment, that environment must matter beyond amorphous systemic conditions — rather, perceptions of the units that populate this external environment must be highly relevant. How states perceive other states should thus greatly impact — if not determine — the kind of policies they adopt with respect to them. More concretely, the external environment in which states operate will be populated by different types of states, as seen from one specific state's vantage point. Each state will thus encounter friends, non-friends and, logically, undecided states situated somewhere in between. All three of these categories of fellow states will have to be dealt with by any state seeking to control and shape its environment.

In order to control and shape their environment, states make use of their power resources by translating them into foreign policy tools. These tools are then applied in states' relations with other states. Foreign policy tools may be effective for different reasons related to various underlying base values, as they may be the expression of different types of power at work. Power, in the present context, is understood as the capability to get one's will across. Power can be either positive or negative, i.e. essentially working through offering incentives or based on coercion. Which type of power is deemed most effective and / or suitable will largely depend on the emitting state's power resources, its perceptions of the target state and that targeted state's perceived inclination to yield to influence attempts. In other words, the following simple conclusion may be drawn: it matters who the recipient of foreign policy is and how the emitting state perceives this recipient. Which type of power can be expected to prove effective is contingent on the recipient and the base values to which it is receptive. States are likely to be aware of considerations of this kind. For that reason, it may be expected that positive power resources will predominantly be applied towards friends, negative power resources towards non-friends whereas undecided states will be met with foreign policy tools making use of both types of power resources.

The target state of foreign policy and perceptions of its friend / non-friend / undecided status has, however, so far been neglected by (neoclassical) realist scholars. Other states, if at all, appear as belligerents, revisionist actors, allies or balancing counterparts. Yet, friend, non-friend and undecided attitudes should indeed be taken seriously, as they ought to be seen as an element of the "missing link" neoclassical realists identified between states' power resources and their foreign policy behaviour. Since skilful foreign policy makers should be expected to adapt their use of foreign policy tools to the target state's perceived status, friend, non-friend and undecided attitudes should be taken into consideration within a neoclassical realist framework intended to explain foreign policy. To illustrate this point, the empirical chapters below shall therefore deal with the three categories of states constituting (parts of) that environment, namely a friendly, an unfriendly and an undecided state — i.e. Poland, Belarus and Ukraine, respectively.

II.6 Methodological considerations

As outlined above, this study intends to provide a theoretically grounded explanation of the observation that one state, under identical systemic conditions, led different policies towards three countries within the same regional environment: under the exact same circumstances of unipolarity, the United States conducted entirely different policies towards Poland, Ukraine and Belarus, i.e. three neighbouring countries with about the same degree of relative power as compared to Washington and highly similar historical legacies. In that sense, the following case studies are analyses of a state's attempts at controlling and shaping its environment, namely U.S. policies towards Poland, Ukraine and Belarus in the years 1989/1991[167] to 2008, i.e. from the end of the Cold War to the end of the George W. Bush administration. These policies shall be analysed in terms of the foreign policy tools employed by the United States. Foreign policy tools are seen as attempts at exerting power, and, as argued in the previous chapter, each attributable to one type of power. They are moreover easily discernible in the sources on which the analysis is based. "Foreign policy tools" is thus the concept used in order to make "power" tangible, hence allowing for its submission to analysis. In doing so, the study intends to establish a correlation between perceptions of the respective bilateral relationship's quality in terms of friend / non-friend / undecided status and the foreign policy tools — and thus the kind of power — to which Washington resorted. The present study thereby sets out to make a contribution to closing the gap neoclassical realists identified as the missing link between states' power resources and their foreign policy output; perceptions of the target states' friend / non-friend / undecided status should be considered an element of that missing link.

The three cases or sets of bilateral relations analysed here are seen as three "classes of events". They are studied 'with the aim of developing theory (or "generic knowledge") regarding the causes of similarities or differences among instances (cases) of that class of events.'[168] Quoting Alexander L. George and Andrew Bennett, the theory building objective of this study therefore consists in bringing forward a hypothesis conceived as a "typological theory" and illustrating its applicability. A typological theory is a

---

167 The date of the outset of relations with the United States varies between the countries: both Belarus and Ukraine attained to independence in 1991, whereas Poland's emancipation from Soviet rule already began in 1989.

168 Alexander L. George and Andrew Bennett (2004) *Case Studies and Theory Development in the Social Sciences*, Cambridge: MIT Press, pp. 17–18.

theory that specifies independent variables, delineates them into the categories for which the researcher will measure the cases and their outcomes, and provides not only hypotheses on how these variables operate individually, but also contingent generalizations on how and under what conditions they behave in specific conjunctions or configurations to produce effects on specified dependent variables.[169]

In the present study, the primary underlying hypothesis is the assumption that the kind of power used in applying foreign policy tools is dependent on the friend / non-friend / undecided status a country is perceived to hold. As discussed above, it may indeed be expected that friendly states will (predominantly) be met with positive power tools, unfriendly states will (predominantly) be met with negative power tools, while both types of power are likely to be applied in dealing with undecided states.

II.6.1 The cases

The three cases to be studied in the following chapters are U.S. policies towards Poland, Ukraine and Belarus covering the timeframe from 1989 to 2008. What makes these cases particularly interesting to study is the fact that they offer the very rare occasion to analyse sets of bilateral contacts "from scratch", i.e. from the very outset of a relationship.

The policies at hand are seen as instances of America's management of unipolarity in the aftermath of the Cold War. These cases have been chosen on the basis of what Adam Przeworski and Henry Teune call the 'most similar systems design', meaning that they are similar in all respects except the independent variable, or, in their own words, 'background variables'.[170] All three countries indeed share very important features, such as geography, historical legacies or the need to undergo post-Communist reform. Poland, Ukraine and Belarus are three neighbouring countries and belonged to the Warsaw Pact and Soviet sphere of influence prior to 1989 / 90. Ukraine and Belarus were integral parts of the Soviet Union, while the People's Republic of Poland qualified as a satellite

---

169 Ibid., p. 235
170 Cf. Adam Przeworski and Henry Teune (1970) *The Logic of Comparative Social Inquiry*, Malabar: Krieger Publishing, pp. 31 ff.

state. All three countries had systems of state directed economy, and none had a democratic political system. Before the Soviet Union's demise, Ukraine and Belarus did not conduct foreign policy. Poland, in turn, could not maintain relationships with Western nations without interference from Moscow. In all these respects, they can thus be said to be highly similar. The one factor they do not share is the way Washington perceived their status vis-à-vis the United States throughout the two decades after the Cold War ended. In that sense, they are similar in all aspects except the latter.

Similar does, however, not mean identical. The three cases of Poland, Belarus and Ukraine do not lend themselves to comparisons in the strictest sense, as important differences among the countries need to be taken into account. For that reason, time spans covered in the following chapters will not be entirely congruent. Their accession to independent statehood, but also events that marked bilateral relations, turning points and missed occasions occurred at different moments as far as the three states are concerned. At first glance objective criteria of comparison such as institutional membership also need to be handled with care. The NATO to which Poland strove to accede during the 1990s is not the same NATO to which Ukraine (perhaps) has an option to join in the future. Instead of going out of business, the alliance has gone out of area and is now about to draft its fourth post-Cold War strategic concept. To a lesser extent, the same is valid for the European Union. Just like the countries in question, the world surrounding them has evolved. So has Russia. American policies towards Central and especially Eastern Europe have always been, at least to some extent, U.S. policy towards Russia. The degree to which this statement is true has varied over time, but it nevertheless remains a (tacit) constant in Washington's view on the region. This is especially valid for the Ukrainian case, given Ukraine's sympathy oscillating between Moscow and the West.

Three chapters are devoted to these classes of events, one for each country. Each of the three countries is taken to represent one of the categories introduced above: as shall be demonstrated, Poland represents a friend of the United States, Ukraine an undecided state, whereas Belarus is considered to be a non-friend — always from a U.S. vantage point. This status is determined on the basis of U.S. official statements on the country in question. In order to determine that status, it is analysed separately from the foreign policy tools the U.S. applied in the respective bilateral relationship (see below: section III.4.2 A Three-Step Approach in Addressing the Sources). For that reason, the empirical chapters below comprise two types of sections, i.e., descriptive and analytical ones — the former serving to determine the respective country's friend / non-friend / undecided status as seen from Washington, the latter to analyse the foreign policy tools identified. Each chapter devoted to one country includes any kind of action performed by the United States with respect to that country identifiable in the sources for the time span covered in this study. All instances in which the respective country appears in the sources have been included, meaning that no events have been left out. An overall summary of the foreign policy tools identified in U.S. approaches to Poland, Ukraine and Belarus will be offered in table 2 in the concluding chapter at the end of this study.

Lastly, the United States' position as the only remaining superpower has important implications. Its relationship with Central and Eastern Europe will invariably be asymmetric. For that reason, the cases are particularly well suited for the study of U.S. attempts at exerting power. The relationship between the American superpower and Central and European states is unlikely to be characterised by rivalry and the struggle for relative power.[171] None of the three target states in this study is a competitor for the United States' position within the international system. This arguably allows for a more undisguised study of U.S. attempts at controlling and shaping its external environment, given that the United States' room for manoeuvre will be less constrained, because its position is not at stake in each move it makes.

---

[171] There will of course be rivalry between the U.S. and other aspiring superpowers (read: Russia) over influence on the states in question. This is however not the focus of this study.

II.6.2 Sources

The empirical material that came to use consists above all of public U.S. documents containing information on United States policies towards Central and Eastern European countries, more precisely Poland, Ukraine and Belarus. Secondary literature constitutes another category of sources, be it scholarly work, reports by independent authors or media coverage. A number of research interviews furthermore provided valuable background information.

II.6.3 Research design: Comparative case studies

As Gideon Rose points out, 'analysts wanting to understand any particular case need to do justice to the full complexity of the causal chain linking relative material power and foreign policy outputs.'[172] The conclusion to be drawn for neoclassical realist research design is that it will heavily rely on in-depth case studies.

According to Alexander L. George and Andrew Bennett, the purpose of the case study approach is 'the detailed examination of an aspect of a historical episode to develop or test historical explanations that may be generalizable to other events'.[173] The strength of such an approach lies in its high conceptual validity in the sense that it allows the researcher to 'identify and measure the indicators that best represent the theoretical concepts [he / she] intends to measure'.[174] In addition, case studies facilitate the deriving of new hypotheses and the exploration of causal mechanisms.[175] Nevertheless, the case study approach is not free from limitations.[176] Most importantly, the case selection bias must be named, as well as the fact that scholars 'can make only tentative conclusions on *how much* gradations of a particular variable affect the outcome in a particular case or how much they generally contribute to the outcomes in a

---

[172] Gideon Rose (1998) 'Neoclassical Realism and Theories of Foreign Policy', p. 165.
[173] Alexander L. George and Andrew Bennett, *Case Studies and Theory Development in the Social Sciences*, p. 5.
[174] Ibid., p. 19.
[175] Ibid., pp. 20-21.
[176] Ibid., pp. 22 ff.

class or type of cases'.[177] Yet, those potential shortcomings are deemed acceptable for the present study: its ambition is to show that perceptions of a country's status vis-à-vis the U.S. as the one variable distinguishing the cases matters *at all,* degrees being of minor importance.

The research design applied in the present study is best described as a comparative case study, following Charles C. Ragin's ideas on conducting cross case analysis. Ragin distinguishes two ways of learning from multiple instances, namely a variable oriented approach (primarily concerned with correlations in a large number of cases) and a case oriented one, with the present study being based on the latter:

> The case oriented strategy addresses a relatively small number of cases in an in-depth manner, paying attention to each case as an interpretable whole. In essence, this strategy is an extension of the single case study to multiple cases with an eye toward configurations of similarities and differences. In this approach, in-depth knowledge provides the basis for constructing limited generalizations that hold for the cases studied.[178]

The chosen approach is thus a hybrid: more detailed and focused on the cases than a comparative study, but without the *sui-generis-*argument typically characterising a classical single case study. It allows for an in-depth analysis of the three cases, then leading to a comparison embedded in different circumstantial contexts.

In terms of theoretical objectives, this study aims at following the 'method of congruence' proposed by Alexander L. George and Andrew Bennett:

> The essential characteristic of the congruence method is that the investigator begins with a theory and then attempts to assess its ability to explain or predict the outcome in a particular case. The theory posits a relation between variance in the independent variable and variance in the dependent variable; it can be deductive or take the form of an empirical generalization. The analyst first ascertains the value of the independent variable in the case at

---

177 Ibid., p. 25.
178 Charles C. Ragin (2000) *Fuzzy-set Social Science,* Chicago: University of Chicago Press, p. 22.

hand and asks what prediction or expectation about the outcome of the dependent variable should follow from the theory.[179]

In the present context, the independent variable ascertained at first is the respective country's status towards the United States as perceived by Washington, determined on the basis of U.S. historical records of bilateral contacts from 1989 / 1991 until the end of the George W. Bush administration in late 2008. The "prediction" consists in stating that the type of power resources used by Washington should be linked to that status. Hence, in proving that states vary their practice of foreign policy depending on who the recipient of foreign policy is.

II.6.4 Three steps in addressing the sources

The methodological approach in this study is rather straightforward and is designed in three steps which may be summarised as follows:

1. determine Washington's perspective of a country's friend / non-friend / undecided status vis-à-vis the United States by retracing the evolution of its bilateral relationship with Washington
2. identify the foreign policy tools applied by the United States within the framework of that bilateral relationship and the type of power resources upon which they are built
3. establish the correlation between the country's perceived friend / non-friend / undecided status and the type of power resources underlying the foreign policy tools employed

The first step consists of determining the respective country's friend, non-friend or undecided status from Washington's perspective with the help of the sources discussed above. This is essentially achieved by retracing the evolution of U.S. views of Poland, Ukraine and Belarus from 1989 / 1991 onwards in order to depict

---

[179] Alexander L. George and Andrew Bennett, *Case Studies and Theory Development in the Social Science*, p. 181.

the background against which policy-makers in Washington made their decisions. The ambition can therefore not be and has not been to provide an exhaustive or "objective" account of three relationships. Rather, it is deliberately limited to providing a chronological, Washington-perspective account of the 'classes of events' of U.S. policies towards Poland, Ukraine and Belarus. The objective of these descriptive parts in the chapters below is to provide information which allows for the classification of countries as friends, non-friends and undecided states as seen from Washington. This classification is crucial in order to assess the base values to which the respective state should likely be receptive in accordance with the theoretical assumptions underlying this study. As these qualifications of specific statuses may vary over time, pertinent statements are continuously included throughout the following chapters, allowing the reader to understand the evolution in Washington's assessment of its relations with Poland, Ukraine and Belarus. These narrative sections thus contain appreciations and appraisals of the respective target country by U.S. (former) officials. The sources used are transcripts of background briefings, fact sheets (the so-called *Background Notes*) for the broader public as well as the research interviews carried out in Washington—i.e., sources which convey information which was not directly intended to address Poland, Ukraine or Belarus, but was meant to inform third actors (e.g., journalists) about the status quo in the respective bilateral relationship. These statements are therefore not to be confounded with foreign policy tools: foreign policy tools require a counterpart and are thus instances of social action in that they are directed towards that counterpart. They convey a message on expected or desired behaviour and consequently call for a reaction—if the foreign policy tool is employed successfully, that reaction will be in line with expectations and demands. Statements used in order to determine a country's friend / non-friend / undecided status, in turn, are merely descriptive, simply qualifying views held in Washington. In other words, statements do *not* qualify as state behaviour. Needless to say, even statements such as 'U.S.-Ukrainian relations are bad' made in a background briefing probably imply that the United States is hoping for Kyiv to change its behaviour. Moreover, in most cases, it is very likely that Ukrainian officials will eventually take note of these statements. Yet, they are not directly made addressing, for example, Ukraine, but made in a context primarily involving third parties: press statements, speeches by officials or (research) interviews. Because of their merely descriptive character and the context in which they are made, these statements are taken to be essentially different from foreign policy tools. For that reason, they allow for the classification of countries as perceived friends / non-friends / undecided states on a basis separate from the foreign policy tools discernable via an analysis of the bilateral relationship in question. Moreover, as the respective country chapters each cover a time span of roughly twenty years, long term tendencies become visible, thus justifying the classification of countries according to status, i.e. as "friends", "non-friends" and "undecided" as seen from a specific vantage point.

Very importantly, "friend", "non-friend" and "undecided state" shall thus not be used in the essential meaning of the term. Rather, absent better words, the three notions are intended to serve as umbrella terms, grasping a set of general tendencies in bilateral relations as perceived from a U.S. perspective (i.e., through U.S. material). Thus, Belarus must for instance not be seen as America's enemy in Carl Schmitt's understanding of the phenomenon. In the present context, Belarus being the United States' "non-friend" simply means that Minsk's general attitudes towards Washington are perceived as negative by the US, i.e. "unfriendly" and that this tendency is observable over a longer period. In order to be qualified as a friend, the opposite tendency must accordingly be observable, meaning that friendly attitudes characterise, for example, Poland's approach to the United States. In order to be considered an "undecided state", no definite trend must be observable. An undecided state is moving back and forth between being perceived as friendly and unfriendly, hence illustrating that the state in question seems not yet to have made up its mind as to its general attitudes towards another state. Most importantly, this classification is always made from another state's (i.e., the foreign policy emitting state's) vantage point.

In a second stage, the sources have been read explicitly looking for foreign policy tools applied in these U.S. foreign policies. This second round of analysis has been guided by the theoretical principles identified in the previous chapter: what specific tools are apparent, to what type of power are they attributable? Power, as is widely argued, is difficult (if not impossible) to operationalise. For that reason, this study will be dealing with foreign policy tools as an *expression of* power, as a vehicle for influence. The fundamental idea on which the operationalisation of the four types of power resources — material or symbolic positive power; material or symbolic negative power — described above rests is the assumption that each observable foreign policy tool will relate to one of these types of power. In other words, not power *per se* is considered to be observable, but the expression it takes when translated into a foreign policy tool.

A foreign policy tool is identifiable by asking the following question:

> what measure did state A recur to when it wanted state B to act in a specific way (as defined by A)?

In the present context, the question would thus read:

> what measure did the United States recur to when it wanted Poland / Ukraine / Belarus to act in a specific way (as defined by the United States)?

In other words, the use of foreign policy tools will occur in situations in which the behaviour of A [the US] is directed towards the behaviour of B [Poland, Ukraine, Belarus], with A formulating clear ideas of how B should behave. In order to detect foreign policy tools, the first step therefore consists of discovering demands of specific behaviour on the United States' part, followed by identifying actions Washington takes in order to obtain that behaviour. These demands are identified and accounted for with the help of quotations of U.S. official sources describing what Washington expected from Warsaw, Kyiv or Minsk.

In the third stage, the objective consists of establishing the correlation between the country's perceived friend / non-friend / undecided status and the type of power resources underlying the foreign policy tools employed. It is in this last step that conclusions on the simultaneous occurrence of perceived attitudes towards the United States and the use of certain foreign policy tools on Washington's part may be drawn. It will thus be possible to answer the question whether friends would predominantly be approached with positive power tools, non-friends with negative power tools and undecided states with a combination of both and the intention to make them become friends. Studying these patterns over a period of almost two decades will allow for generalisable conclusions on the theoretically derived assumptions on the interrelationship between friend / non-friend / undecided status.

Quite evidently, as far as the linkage between friend / non-friend / undecided statuses and types of power is concerned, there is a risk for circular causalities. A certain friend / non-friend / undecided status brings forward the use of specific foreign policy tools which, in turn, is likely to reinforce the tendencies underlying that status. Such a reinforcing effect may be impossible to deny. If this is the case, however, deteriorated relations will become apparent through an analysis of statements as discussed above; a methodologically neat distinction between statements and foreign policy tools consequently remains possible.

Finally, *why* states hold specific attitudes towards other states matters little in the present context. The construction of identities, discourses about friendship and enmity or the origins of affinities among nations: all this is beyond the scope of the present study. What matters is the observation that one state perceives another state as friendly, non-friendly or undecided and designs its foreign policies accordingly. While there certainly is a hen-and-egg problem, explaining what led to what is not an objective of this study and thus must not necessarily be elucidated for the point to be made. Most importantly, however, this study intends to analyse the foreign policy output of the United States in terms of foreign policy tools linked to Poland's, Ukraine's and Belarus's general attitudes towards Washington as seen *from a U.S. vantage point* — not why the respective countries hold the attitudes they do. U.S. perceptions of attitudes constitute the context within which the objects of interest in this study—foreign policy tools—are unilaterally applied. Whether these attitudes (partly) are a consequence of U.S. measures is not relevant for the empirical analyses carried out below.

III U.S. Foreign Policies Towards Poland

The end of the Cold War marks the end of a several centuries long period of foreign dominance for Poland, only interrupted by a brief — and chaotic — intermezzo in the aftermath of the First World War. Abandoned by its allies more than once and determined to no longer be the victim of an unfavourable geopolitical position, Warsaw has ever since been eager to avoid the mistakes of the past. The consensus in Poland was that the country's security first and foremost was to be achieved by seeking rapprochement with the United States of America and its outpost in Europe, NATO. Building a close relationship with Washington has hence been a top item on the Polish foreign policy agenda throughout the 1990s. For Washington, these Polish ambitions meant that it had gotten a new friend and ally upon which to rely. The friendship between these two countries became apparent especially during the years in which George W. Bush and Aleksander Kwaśniewski were presidents, i.e. in the years 2000 to 2005 when the rhetoric of deep friendship flourished and Poland joined the U.S. in invading Iraq. By the end of 2008, however, U.S.-Polish relations had cooled and Washington's soft power over Warsaw had faded.

The purpose of this chapter is twofold: to describe U.S. policies towards Poland from 1989 to 2008 as seen from a U.S. vantage point, with the objective of determining the country's friend / non-friend / undecided status and to analyse these policies in terms of the foreign policy tools employed by Washington. It is divided into five sections. Section III.1 sets out to provide a very brief introduction to Polish history. Section III.2 is devoted to the first months of Washington's relations with a free Poland and the Solidarność movement. It is followed by III.3 dealing with Poland as an emerging new best friend in 1990 / 1991 and onwards; section III.4 jumps to the year 2001 and the ensuing "War on Terror". Section III.5 then deals with the development of U.S.-Polish relations since Lech Kaczyński became president in 2005. Each of these sections ends with an analysis of foreign policy tools employed by Washington. The chapter is closed by concluding remarks in section III.6.

III.1 Introduction

Although it is commonplace to state that a country's present cannot be understood without its past, this is perhaps even more true in the Polish than in any other case.[180] Throughout its history, Poland has been everything from a Great Power to nothing at all, wiped from the map as the result of Great Power politics. French playwright Alfred Jarry thus famously declared that his *Ubu Roi* was set 'en Pologne, donc nulle part'[181] in his speech at the première of the play: after the third partition in 1795, there was no more Polish state for one hundred and twenty-three years, with the country divided between Tsarist Russia in the East, the Habsburg KuK-Monarchy in the South and Prussia in the West. It was only in the wake of World War I that the Polish state was re-established as a direct consequence of the thirteenth of President Wilson's Fourteen Points:

> XIII. An independent Polish state should be erected which should include the territories inhabited by indisputably Polish populations, which should be assured a free and secure access to the sea, and whose political and economic independence and territorial integrity should be guaranteed by international covenant.

Established after World War I, the Second Polish Republic lasted from 1918 until 1939 and went through rough times, including uprisings and a *coup d'État*. Nazi Germany invaded Poland on 1 September 1939, followed shortly thereafter by the Soviet Union on 17 September. The Ribbentrop-Molotov-Pact was realised, the country divided. The 1944 Warsaw Uprising was brutally crushed by the Germans, with the Red Army watching from the other side of the Wisła River. After the war, Poland was literally moved westwards as the Allies had agreed upon in the Potsdam treaty: the Curzon-

---

180 For a concise introduction to Polish history, cf. Norman Davies (2001) *Heart of Europe. The Past in Poland's Present*, 2nd edition, Oxford: Oxford University Press.
181 'in Poland, thus nowhere'.

line became its Eastern border, whilst the Oder-Neiße-line became its border in the West. As a consequence, millions of people were resettled by force, Poles from East of the Curzon-line to the "new" Poland, whereas Germans living on newly established Polish territories were expelled westwards.[182]

Poland found itself in the Soviet sphere of influence soon after the end of World War II. The *Polska Rzeczpospolita Ludowa* (Polish People's Republic) was founded in 1952 and joined the Warsaw Pact as a founding member in 1955. It is, however, worth noting that Poland in many respects resisted Communism. The Catholic Church as the longstanding guarantor of Polish nationhood and Pope John Paul II in particular famously played an important role, but also the fact that farming land always remained in private possession may serve as an illustration in point. After the German Democratic Republic in 1953, Hungary in 1956 and Czechoslovakia in 1968, Poland saw its own uproar against the Communist government in 1980. Under its leader Lech Wałęsa, the trade union Solidarność (Solidarity) gained importance to an extent that led it to challenge the regime. On 13 December 1981, General Jaruzelski therefore imposed martial law, putting a preliminary end to the Solidarność movement. The Reagan Administration's sharp protest against this step was met with deep sympathy among Poles; a Reagan statue was unveiled in Warsaw in 2011.

The transition to democracy took place on the occasion of several roundtable talks between the Communists and the opposition in the first months of 1989. In the first free elections agreed upon

---

182 The expulsion of Germans continues to be important in Polish-German relations until today, although most Germans would arguably claim that the debate in Poland is informed by hysteria. Tellingly, Erika Steinbach, former chairwoman of the *Bund der Vertriebenen* (representing expelled Germans and their descendants) played a prominent role in many political speeches, whereas she by no means can claim a role as an eminent figure in German politics. If at all, she is known in Germany as the single most troublesome element in Polish-German relations. Yet, the PiS party and others obviously managed and continue to manage the art of capitalising on deeply rooted fear of Germany among certain groups of the Polish public. These matters may serve as an illustration of historical legacies that continue to matter in contemporary Poland.

during these talks and held in June 1989, Solidarność won all the seats to be won democratically in the *Sejm*, the Polish parliament, as well as ninety-nine out of one hundred in the Senate. Tadeusz Mazowiecki became the first non-Communist prime minister of the post-war era and one year later, Lech Wałęsa was elected president. Aleksander Kwaśniewski followed him in 1995 and remained in office until 2005, when the late Lech Kaczyński became his successor.

The economic system was quickly (and critical voices add: brutally) transformed into a market economy according to the so-called Balcerowicz Plan, the very prototype of shock therapy.[183] After 1989, Poland's position in international politics moreover underwent dramatic change. Joining the West had been a Polish priority ever since Communism was overcome.[184] From being a Warsaw Pact-member and satellite state firmly rooted in the Eastern bloc, the country is today both an EU and NATO member (the latter perhaps more important even, from a Polish perspective). Poland has also been a key-US ally in the Iraq war from 2003 onwards, and a (sometimes arguably annoying) partner to the "big" EU states. Relations with the United States were good from 1989 onwards, not least according to the State Department:

> Poland and the United States have enjoyed warm bilateral relations since 1989. Every post-1989 Polish government has been a strong supporter of continued American military and economic presence in Europe. As well as supporting the Global War on Terror, Operation Enduring Freedom in Afghanistan, and coalition efforts in Iraq, Poland cooperates closely with

---

183 Leszek Balcerowicz was minister of finance 1989–1991 and again 1997–2000. His economic reforms radically transformed the Polish economy by means of a programme containing eleven different acts, touching all realms of economic life, from employment to foreign currency regulations. For an upshot assessment of Polish economic reform, cf. for instance Michael P. Keane and Eswar S. Prasad (2001) 'Poland: Inequality, Transfers, and Growth in Transition', in: *Finance and Development* 38(1) (published online at www.imf.org).

184 Cf. for instance Aleksander Kwaśniewski (1996) 'Poland and NATO', remarks at the XIIIth NATO Workshop on Political-Military Decision Making, Warsaw, 19 June. See also: Roman Kuźniar (2008) *Droga do wolności. Polityka zagraniczna III Rzeczpospolitej*, Warsaw: Wydawnictwo Naukowe Scholar; Jan Zielonka (1994) 'Les paradoxes de la politique étrangère polonaise', *Politique Étrangère* 59(1).

American diplomacy on such issues as democratization, nuclear proliferation, human rights, regional cooperation in central and eastern Europe, and UN reform.[185]

Yet, even U.S.-Polish relations since 1989 have been subject to ups and downs, as the following sections set out to illustrate.

III.2 Laying the foundations: the U.S. and Solidarność

III.2.1 Accompanying Poland to de facto independence 1989–1991

Outright Atlanticism is considered a '*sui-generis* paradigm of Polish security policy' by many observers.[186] Once reforms were underway, Warsaw almost immediately turned to Washington and attached great importance to the transatlantic link it now was free to shape without interference from Moscow. The United States responded by publicly welcoming Poland with open arms.

Not even yet elected president, Lech Wałęsa – in his capacity of Nobel Peace prize laureate and leader of Solidarność – was given the opportunity to address a joint meeting of Congress on 15 November 1989, an honour very rarely bestowed on foreign politicians.[187] Yet, President Bush senior's appreciation of the situation in Poland and of Wałęsa as a leader was not unreservedly positive, as Strobe Talbott – who had then been travelling with the President as a journalist during the autumn of 1989 – relates. On visit in Poland in July 1989, Bush is said to have expressed concern in private that too rapidly occurring changes might be 'too much' for the economy, which was one of the main reasons why he did not want to see Wałęsa replace Jaruzelski too quickly. Bush is also said to have felt

---

[185] U.S. Department of State (2007) 'Background Note: Poland', Washington D.C., March.
[186] Cf. Olaf Osica (2003) 'In Search of a New Role. Poland vis-à-vis Euro-Atlantic Relations', in: Marcin Zaborowski and David H. Dunn (eds.) *Poland. A New Power in Transatlantic Security*, London: Frank Cass, p. 23.
[187] This was only the fourth time in U.S. history that a non-head of state was given such an opportunity.

more at ease with the cultivated General than with the revolutionary electrician from Gdańsk's dockyards whose personality he ultimately did not understand.[188] According to Talbott, Bush's (secretly) favoured scenario was an orderly reform process under Jaruzelski's leadership, avoiding the incertitude associated with Wałęsa's potential accession to power. Allegedly, Bush even preferred to see the General run for the presidency—which Jaruzelski eventually did despite having refused earlier. Yet, his own doubts about Polish developments did not prevent Bush from once more expressing, on the tarmac right after Air Force One landed in Warsaw, the 'American nation's burning desire for a Europe whole and free'.[189]

President George H.W. Bush's more careful stance also becomes apparent in his statement during a press conference upon receiving the news of the Berlin Wall's fall on 9 November 1989. When asked that day whether he was 'elated', Bush replied

> I'm very pleased. And I've been very pleased with a lot of other developments. And, as I've told you, I think the United States part of this, which is not related to this development today particularly, is being handled in a proper fashion. And we'll have some that'll suggest more flamboyant courses of action for this country, and we're, I think, handling this properly with allies, staying in close touch in this dynamic change—try to help as development takes place, try to enhance reform, both political and economic.[190]

Poland's turning to Washington must also be understood against the backdrop of events in Europe itself. As Lech Wałęsa expressed in a discussion with Chancellor Helmut Kohl of West Germany in Warsaw on the afternoon of 9 November 1989, he was aware that Poland was in dire need of both political support and money. Yet, Wałęsa's fear was that the rapidly evolving developments in the

---

188 Michael R. Beschloss and Strobe Talbott (1993) *At the Highest Levels: The Inside Story of the End of the Cold War*, Boston: Little & Brown, p. 115.
189 Ibid., p. 116.
190 The White House, Office of the Press Secretary (1989) 'Remarks and a Question-and-Answer Session with Reporters on the Relaxation of East German Border Controls', Washington D.C., 9 November.

German Democratic Republic (GDR), which essentially leapfrogged Poland and Hungary on the reform trail, would lead Bonn and the Western world to entirely focus on East Germany. To reassure the Polish delegation, Kohl replied that it was not his policy to neglect Poland and that he was aware of the fact that, without Poland, the reform movement would not have gained momentum in the GDR.[191] Ironically, Wałęsa was proved right only hours later on the very same day. On the evening of 9 November 1989, Günter Schabowski, member of the GDR's *Politbüro*, explained in a news conference broadcast live on television that Eastern German citizens were 'as from now' free to leave the country without prior authorisation. Within hours, the Wall had fallen. As desirable as these events may have been also for Poland, their effect was to draw attention to Germany, away from Poland.

Despite competition for U.S. attention and support, Poland managed to engage Washington. On his July 1989 visit to Warsaw, Bush promised financial aid for economic reform, as well as grants in order to address environmental problems in the southern city of Cracow. Yet, Wałęsa expressed disappointment over sums he deemed insufficient, which eventually led Bush to almost double the amount during the autumn of 1989.[192] In his historic speech to Congress on 15 November 1989—six days after the Wall came down—Wałęsa advocated a "Marshall Plan" for Poland, accusing the United States of saying a lot but doing palpably less:

---

191 The German protocol of this meeting is published in: Hans Jürgen Küsters and Daniel Hofmann (eds.) (1998) *Dokumente zur Deutschlandpolitik. Deutsche Einheit: Sonderedition aus den Akten des Bundeskanzleramtes 1989/90*, Munich: Oldenbourg, document number 76, pp. 492–496.
192 Michael R. Beschloss and Strobe Talbott (1993) *At the Highest Levels: The Inside Story of the End of the Cold War*, p. 118.

> We have heard many beautiful words of encouragement. These are appreciated, but being a worker and a man of concrete work, I must tell you that the supply of words on the world market is plentiful but the demand is falling. Let deeds follow words now.[193]

Although a certain degree of co-operation between the U.S. and the Polish People's Republic already existed during Cold War times, the bulk of assistance programmes and common projects was created and implemented after 1989. Named by President George H. W. Bush in December 1989, Deputy Secretary of State Lawrence S. Eagleburger was in charge of coordinating American assistance to Eastern Europe within the framework of the so-called Support to Eastern Europe's Democracy Act, hence also to Poland.[194] Concrete measures included exchange and internship programmes for students, young entrepreneurs and professionals of all levels, cooperation on environmental issues, technical assistance in a variety of fields, training for journalists and support for free media. Special importance was attached to the development of business opportunities, through for instance university cooperation, training programmes for executives and English language courses.[195] Much of the early post-Cold War U.S.-Polish relations would subsequently be centred on aid and assistance for Poland with the objective of

---

193 A translated version of the speech was reprinted in: Neil A. Lewis (1989) 'Clamor in the East, Gratitude and a Request; In Talk to Congress, Walesa Urges A Marshall Plan to Revive Poland', *The New York Times*, 16 November.

194 Though backed and often initiated by the U.S. administration, specifically the State Department, the main actors in the fields described were non-governmental organisations. Both existing NGOs such as the Peace Corps, and newly created organisations played a role. For example, an International Media Fund was created in order to foster independent media in Central and Eastern Europe. Needless to say, also a number of private initiatives came to have non-negligible impact.

195 Details on these projects can be found in the various issues of the U.S. Department of State Dispatch, mainly in the sections titled 'Focus on Central and Eastern Europe'. Moreover, there is a wide field of literature dealing with NGO's activities and the reform processes in Central and Eastern Europe. See e.g. Sarah E. Mendelson and John K. Glenn (eds.) (2002) *The Power and Limits of NGOs. A Critical Look at Building Democracy in Europe and Eurasia*, New York: Columbia University Press.

preserving the thrust of political change and fostering economic reform. At an early stage, the United States started out by pursuing a quiet policy of support for Poland (as well as Czechoslovakia, Hungary, Yugoslavia and Romania) with a view to promoting democracy and free market economy. Among the measures taken internationally in order to consolidate the Polish economy, Washington helped Poland achieve a reduction of its debt to its government creditors among the Paris Club members. In addition, the United States successfully pushed for the country's accession to the International Monetary Fund (IMF) and the World Bank. Early on, Poland (along with Hungary and Yugoslavia) was granted *Most Favored Nation* status, which waived all U.S. trade restrictions for Polish goods. In October 1990, the U.S. sponsored a series of conferences on economics and business in Poland.[196] Interest in investment in Poland was generally rather high among American entrepreneurs, and the considerable number of Americans with Polish origins certainly mattered as well. Business links were therefore quickly established through channels such as the Polish-US Economic Council, an affiliate of the U.S. Chamber of Commerce. In order to support the development of a market economy in Poland, the Polish American Enterprise Fund was established in 1989 and became operative in May 1990. The Fund essentially provided loans and investments and developed a number of enterprises.[197]

III.2.2 Foreign Policy Tools in Solidarność-times

As the above sections illustrate, in these early years, U.S.-Polish relations were essentially an element of wider U.S. approaches to Central and Eastern Europe. With respect to the entire region, Washington attempted to build rapport in order to set the course for the future. In the period of time covered in the above section, the main U.S. objective with respect to Poland thus consisted in

---

196 Cf. 'Focus on Central and Eastern Europe 10/1/1990', in *U.S. Department of State Dispatch* 1(5), 1 October 1990.
197 For more information, cf. the Polish American Freedom Foundation's website at www.pafw.pl (the Foundation was launched by the Fund in 2000).

helping to set the country on the right track towards democratisation and economic reform. There is hardly any evidence in the sources analysed that the United States considered the country anything else but a friendly state; the very character of Polish-American relations had yet to emerge.

As expressed by then Polish leader Lech Wałęsa on several occasions, Poland was more than eager to receive U.S. support and follow American guidelines. In other words, all prerequisites for the use of positive power were fulfilled. The mechanisms underlying such power could thus work in the early years of U.S.-Polish relations: Poland saw itself in need of material support, and — more importantly — international recognition and prestige. The United States was the one actor that could best provide these goods, at least as seen from Warsaw. During the beginnings of U.S.-Polish post-Cold War relations, positive power tools were therefore the order of the day. In its policies towards Poland, Washington resorted to a large number of such measures, both material and symbolic.

Many of the material foreign policy tools were not specific to Poland, but were designed with respect to Central and Eastern Europe in general. This category includes all economic and environmental aid programmes, as well as cooperation in education and language training. More centred on Poland, however, was U.S. support for the country's accession to international financial institutions and the facilitation of trade. On the symbolic side, Washington voiced support for Solidarność early on; U.S. efforts in backing the movement then culminated in inviting Wałęsa to speak to Congress in 1989.

No negative power tools are evident in the sources covering the Solidarność era. At the same time, there are no observable instances in which Poland acted counter to U.S. interest, the use of negative power hence being superfluous. Given the United States' desire to promote democratisation and the transition to market economy, this is hardly surprising. By exclusively resorting to positive power tools, Washington was able to build rapport with the new leaders in Warsaw, helping to preserve and even enhance the thrust of developments in Poland. Against that background, there clearly is evidence that, as a friendly state, Poland was met with positive power tools in the years 1989 to 1991.

III.3 An emerging new best friend in Europe: the second Gulf War and NATO enlargement

III.3.1 Euro-Atlantic integration or: Overcoming Yalta

The second Gulf War, which ended in 1991 after the U.S. missions *Operation Desert Shield* and *Operation Desert Storm*, was the first major international political crisis after the end of the Cold War. Authorised by the United Nations, a U.S.-led coalition intervened in 1991 and eventually liberated Kuwait, which had previously been invaded by Iraqi troops. The war was a first occasion for Poland to demonstrate its support for U.S. policies and to cooperate with the United States, when the Polish secret service allegedly helped to get American agents out of Iraq. Support for the war was rather uncontroversial in Europe, where governments either participated in the interventions or at least helped finance them. However, the Gulf War was merely a short intermezzo for Central European security affairs. Although it confirmed the United States in its role as the guarantor of the "new world order", it did not have any structural repercussions in the region. The question of NATO enlargement, in turn, did.

Despite the early focus on financial aid in its relation with Washington, Poland quickly turned its attention towards the wider question of the country's (re)integration in the West. The 'West', in this context, meant the European Community, but, above all, the North Atlantic Treaty Organisation (NATO). The key issue that would consequently mark U.S.-Polish relations throughout the 1990s was NATO enlargement.[198] This is also the foremost foreign

---

198 NATO's enlargement has been the subject of an impressive number of scholarly works. How the decision to enlarge NATO has come about has extensively been dealt with in James M. Goldgeier (1999) *Not Whether But When* and especially Ronald D. Asmus (2002) *Opening NATO's Door. How the Alliance Remade Itself For A New Era.* More specifically on Poland: Jeffrey Simon (2004) *Poland and*

policy objective expressed in the August 1994 State Department Background Note on Poland:

> Poland's primary foreign policy goal is integration into Western security and economic institutions, above all NATO and the European Union (EU).[199]

From a Polish perspective, membership in the Alliance was a solution to many problems, putting an end to Poland's centuries-old security dilemma created by its geopolitical location. Polish aspirations to join NATO to a considerable extent had their roots in historical grievances. "Overcoming Yalta", the arbitrary division of Europe that so much was to Poland's disadvantage must be taken very seriously as a motive for joining the Alliance.[200] Some observers even go so far as to contend that '[s]ince the very outset, Poland has interpreted its membership in NATO more in categories of redressing historical injustice than for building new foreign policy foundations.'[201] Polish fears may not always be rational from a Western European point of view; yet, they have to be dealt with as matters of fact — including when they concern Germany.[202]

Polish ideas about NATO enlargement were, however, received with little enthusiasm; indeed, 'much of the American foreign policy establishment opposed it; most Europeans were lukewarm at best'.[203] Proponents of enlargement were at first found in

---

NATO. A Study in Civil-Military Relations (Oxford: Rowman & Littlefield). For that reason, no detailed account shall be provided here.

199 U.S. Department of State (1994) 'Background Note: Poland', Washington D.C., August.

200 For an excellent example of this (official) discourse, see Przemysław Grudzinski, Polish Ambassador to the United States 2000–2005 (2004) 'Poland's Accession to the European Union and Its Impact on United States-Polish Relations', *The Ambassadors Review,* fall 2004.

201 Olaf Osica (2003) 'In Search of a New Role. Poland vis-à-vis Euro Atlantic Relations',
p. 28.

202 For instance, more than a year after NATO-accession, new versions of the Polish National Security Strategy and the Defence Doctrine stipulated that threats could come 'from all directions' — thus including the West, that is, Germany. Cf. Olaf Osica (2003) 'In Search of a New Role. Poland vis-à-vis Euro-Atlantic Relations', p. 28.

203 Ronald D. Asmus (2002) *Opening NATO's Door,* p. xxiv.

the potential candidate countries themselves only. In order to enhance their chances and to pool efforts, Poland, Hungary and Czechoslovakia formed the Visegrád-Group in March 1991, commonly referred to as the V3 (renamed V4 after Czechoslovakia split into the Czech Republic and Slovakia in 1993). Among the V3's declared objectives was Euro-Atlantic integration, and it was on these issues the Group had the most impact. Yet, its members would often be frustrated by the slow pace at which processes unfolded, having a hard time to make a case for their accession to the Alliance.

Progress was indeed slow, and measures taken to reassure the Central Europeans did not always have the intended effect. NATO's Partnership for Peace (PfP) for instance, introduced in 1994, was immediately dubbed "Partnership for Postponement", its critics arguing that all it did was to provide an alternative to full membership. Rhetoric to the contrary was not convincing in the East of Europe, despite President Clinton's announcing of the program as a 'great opportunity' which 'sets in motion a process that leads to the enlargement of NATO' at the Alliance's 1994 Brussels summit.[204] In his July 1994 visit to Poland, Clinton thus needed to reassure Poland that the U.S. indeed 'felt a responsibility to include them in a wider Europe "democratic and free, integrated and united".'[205] During the whole enlargement process, Poland was by far the most important among the candidates, the 'key nation'[206]. Largest in all respects – population, surface, economically and militarily – Poland simply played an important role in its region. Yet, despite all these factors, unconditional support for Polish aspirations at the expense of U.S. relations with Moscow had never been

---

204 The White House, Office of the Press Secretary (1994) 'Remarks By The President At Intervention for the North Atlantic Council Summit', NATO Headquarters, Brussels, 10 January.
205 Cf. Douglas Jehl (1994) 'Clinton Offers Poland Hope, But Little Aid', *The New York Times*, 8 July.
206 Joseph Fitchett (1995) 'Poland is the Key / Clinton and a Sense of History: Moving Cautiously On NATO Expansion Eastward', *The International Herald Tribune*, 29 May.

an option for Washington. For that very reason, the American approach to expanding NATO eventually resulted in the "dual track": pursuing enlargement *and* maintaining good relations with Russia. Unsurprisingly, Washington subsequently had to live with Polish (and other) reproaches of being too focused on Russia. Arguments such as Vice President Al Gore's that the impression that the U.S. had 'forgotten Central Europe' over its focus on Russia was not correct are unlikely to have been believed entirely in Warsaw.[207] Washington nevertheless undertook efforts to reassure the Poles. The bilateral relations were described in positive terms, and Polish leaders were given numerous opportunities to enjoy the pomp of high level visits.[208] U.S. reassurance to the Poles also included attempts at avoiding a narrowing down of the relationship to the single issue of NATO enlargement. Hence, in a visit to Poland in April 1993, Al Gore presented future prospects for the two countries' relations, which were received very positively by his hosts:

> As our relations develop, they will grow richer and more varied. They also will become, in diplomatic terms, "normal," meaning that they will become mature relations between democratic friends and partners. At any given moment, the United States and Poland together will be engaged on many issues at once--mostly in cooperation, sometimes working together to resolve difference as they arise. This is what good, developed relations between friends are all about: working together to move forward.[209]

Behind closed doors, the enlargement agenda was already more advanced than admitted in public. Nonetheless Clintonian personnel decisions may serve as an indicator, as noted by the *International Herald Tribune* in 1995:

---

[207] Cf. Al Gore, Vice President of the United States (1993) 'The Principles and Future of U.S.-Polish Relations', address delivered in Warsaw / Poland, 20 April, *U.S. Department of State Dispatch* 4(18), 3 May 1993.
[208] Cf. the overview in the annex.
[209] Al Gore, Vice President of the United States (1993) 'The Principles and Future of U.S.-Polish Relations', 20 April.

Mr. Holbrooke, after a brief tenure as ambassador to Germany, was brought back last year, insiders say, mainly to be a point man on enlargement, since the lead policymaker on Europe, Deputy Secretary of State Strobe Talbott, has the job of staying on good terms with the Russian leadership.[210]

The election of Aleksander Kwaśniewski to the Polish presidency in December 1995 renewed the thrust of Poland's efforts to join the Alliance. Poland, together with Hungary and the Czech Republic, was officially invited to join NATO on 8 July 1997 at the Madrid summit. Yet, preparation for membership represented a great challenge for the country, suffering from budget restraints, the need for military reform and modernisation.[211] Two years later, the three countries became members of the Alliance on 12 March 1999, an event overshadowed by the impending air campaign in Serbia.

Throughout the rest of the 1990s, Poland served as a loyal ally of the United States. No major problems affected the relationship. Examples of Poland's being an unconditional ally of the United States abound: 'Even on such controversial policies such as sanctions against Libya and the continuous bombing of Iraq, Poland's support is constant and uncritical.'[212] Poland has shown strong commitment to participate in military interventions: Bosnia, Macedonia, Kosovo, Afghanistan, and, of course, in Iraq in 2003.

Until 1995, Poland continued to be the largest recipient of U.S. assistance to Central and Eastern Europe. For debt relief alone, the United States has contributed more than 4,6 billion U.S. Dollars.[213] By the end of the decade, it was decided that half of the assets of the Polish American Enterprise Fund (see above) were to be used to establish the Polish American Freedom Foundation which

---

210 Joseph Fitchett (1995) 'Poland is the Key / Clinton and a Sense of History: Moving Cautiously on NATO Expansion Eastward'.
211 For a most detailed account, cf. Jeffrey Simon (2004) *Poland and NATO. A Study in Civil-Military Relations*, especially the section entitled 'NATO Integration Challenges' in Chapter 5 (pp. 92–97).
212 David H. Dunn (2003) 'Poland: America's New Model Ally', in Marcin Zaborowski and David H. Dunn (eds.) *Poland. A New Power in Transatlantic Security*, p. 66.
213 U.S. Department of State (1994) 'Background Note: Poland', Washington D.C., August.

started operating in May 2000. Leaving the exclusive focus on economic and entrepreneurial development behind, the new Fund's mission statement is defined in broader terms: 'The Foundation's goal is to support the development of civil society, democracy and market economy in Poland, including efforts to equalize opportunities for personal and social development, as well as to support the transformation processes in other countries of Central and Eastern Europe.'[214] It is thus fully in line with the Clinton administration's focus on democracy promotion.

III.3.2 Foreign policy tools 1991 to 2000

Poland qualifies as a friend from a Washington vantage point in the years 1991 to 2000. The relationship between Warsaw and Washington went on without strain or irritation. The State Department's Background Notes on Poland issued during these years consequently depict the relationship as 'deep', in 1994 expressing the hope for 'continued close cooperation'.[215] The June 2000 version of the Background Note moreover contends that

> The United States and Poland have enjoyed warm bilateral relations since 1989. Every post-1989 Polish government has been a strong supporter of continued American military and economic presence in Europe and has identified membership in NATO, the European Union and other Western security and economic structures as Poland's principal foreign policy priority. [...] [Poland] has done a superb job as the formal protector of American interests in Iraq since the Gulf War and cooperates closely with American diplomacy on such issues as nuclear proliferation, human rights, regional cooperation in central and eastern Europe, and United Nations reform.[216]

In light of the above characterisation of Polish-American relations, considering Poland a friend from a U.S. vantage point seems more than appropriate.

---

214 Cf. its website at www.pafw.pl.
215 U.S. Department of State (1994) 'Background Note: Poland', Washington D.C., August.
216 U.S. Department of State (2000) 'Background Note: Poland', Washington D.C., June.

Given the fact that Poland was perceived as a friend by Washington, it is hardly surprising that foreign policy tools based on positive material power are evident throughout the years 1991 to 2000. The tools appear both in a more general context, with an objective to maintain a good relationship, and on very specific matters as well:

- Continued economic and technical aid in a variety of fields: Poland continues to be the largest recipient of U.S. assistance in Central and Eastern Europe
- Military cooperation, especially within the framework of NATO-accession

Positive symbolic power is also a frequent phenomenon in U.S. policies towards Poland from 1991 to 2000:

- Most prominently, support for Poland's accession to NATO and Washington as the main driving force behind the enlargement project (complemented by positive material power used to the same end)

During the time span covered above, the United States continued to work towards democratisation and economic reform in Poland and provided support for the respective steps taken by Warsaw. In the years 1991 to 2000, Poland continued to define and consolidate its place within the international community. The United States came to play a major role within that context, as Warsaw considered it to be the main conveyor of international prestige. Put bluntly, the expectation could be summarised stating that being Washington's friend and ally would enhance Poland's standing in the world. Moreover, Washington became active in reshaping the European security landscape by becoming the driving force behind NATO enlargement from 1994 onwards. Poland, in turn, was consolidating its relationship with the United States and continued to seek close ties, first and foremost through NATO. Against this backdrop, the U.S. enjoyed an extremely high degree of prestige from a Polish perspective. On that basis, Washington had the possibility to exert a considerable amount of influence based on positive power resources. America's wielding of power over Warsaw could indeed easily rest on positive power bases, with no need for negative power tools. Yet again, as a friendly state, Poland was thus met with U.S. foreign policy tools based on positive power.

III.4 The heydays and their aftermath: 2001 onwards

Good relations during the Clinton years became seemingly even better during the Bush II administrations. All U.S. Department of State Background Notes issued during the years 2000 to 2009, twenty in number, detail that '[t]he United States and Poland have enjoyed warm bilateral relations since 1989'.[217] Moreover, it is noted that Poland and the U.S. cooperate closely on Iraqi matters, for instance underlining that

> [Poland] has supported the Global War on Terror, contributed to Operation Enduring Freedom in Afghanistan and been a leader in the coalition in Iraq, where it has deployed some 2,400 troops. Poland cooperates closely with American diplomacy on such issues as nuclear proliferation, human rights, regional cooperation in central and eastern Europe, and UN reform.[218]

The rhetoric of friendship blossomed during these years, and Poland officially became 'America's best friend' in 2003.[219] According to David Dunn, it is fair to say U.S. relations with Poland qualify for the status of "special relationship", comparable to U.S.-British or U.S.-Israel relations.[220] In hindsight, this statement needs to be relativised. Nevertheless, Poland undoubtedly played the role of an exemplary ally during the first years of the new millennium, at Washington's delight. Whilst the enlargement of NATO left its mark on U.S.-Polish relations under the Clinton administration, the defining aspect of Washington's relations with Warsaw during the

---

217 These are respectively the Background Note versions dated June 2000, April 2002; October 2003; May and November 2004; January, February, April, May, June, August, October and November 2005; August 2006; February, March, August and November 2007; June 2008 as well as January 2009.
218 U.S. Department of State (2005) 'Background Note: Poland', Washington D.C., January.
219 Cf. Kai-Olaf Lang (2003) *Amerikas bester Freund? Polens atlantizistisch-europäischer Kurs*, Berlin: SWP Aktuell, February.
220 David H. Dunn (2003) 'Poland: America's New Model Ally', p. 65.

Bush II administrations was September 11 and its aftermath. For Poland, the terrorist attacks on New York City and Washington D.C. and especially the resulting war in Iraq were an occasion to demonstrate unconditional solidarity with the United States, albeit with its own agenda in mind. Nevertheless, it would be unfair to state that Poland's only motive consisted in furthering its own interest. U.S. rhetoric on freeing Iraq most likely convinced more than one Polish decision-maker.

III.4.1 State Tourism: Bush, Kwaśniewski and the Iraq war

When George W. Bush came to power as the 43rd President of the United States, he opted to deliver his first major speech on U.S.-European relations in Warsaw.[221] For Polish president Aleksander Kwaśniewski, the symbolic significance of that decision was obvious:

> We are very honored that the first visit of the newly-elected President of the United States of America is taking place in Poland; we take it as a symbol but, at the same time, as the confirmation of friendly and allied relations that Poland and the United States have enjoyed for more than a hundred years and which have developed in the last decade very strongly, and that is a good reason for respect.[222]

During that visit, the presidents signed an Open Skies agreement.[223] More importantly, George W. Bush announced his support for the

---

221 Cf. The White House, Office of the Press Secretary (2001) 'Remarks by the President in Address to Faculty and Students of Warsaw University', Warsaw, 15 June.
222 The White House, Office of the Press Secretary (2001) 'Press Conference of President Bush and President of the Republic of Poland, Aleksander Kwasniewski', Presidential Palace, Warsaw, Poland, 15 June.
223 The White House, Office of the Press Secretary (2001) 'Statement by the Press Secretary: U.S. and Poland Sign Open Skies Agreement', Presidential Palace, Warsaw, Poland, 15 June. An Open Skies agreement abolishes limitations for airlines offering flights between the signing countries.

second transfer of a U.S. frigate to Poland.[224] In addition to this, another $20 million was to be transferred to the Polish-American Freedom Foundation.[225]

President Bush subsequently invited Kwaśniewski for a state visit—the highest level of official visits—to Washington, as was announced by George W. Bush's spokesman in June 2002:

> President Bush has invited Polish President Aleksander Kwasniewski to Washington for a state visit on July 17–18th. Poland has become a friend, partner and NATO ally of the United States, and is an ardent supporter in the war on terrorism. President Kwasniewski shares the President's vision of creating a Europe whole, free and at peace. Poland hosted the President and Mrs. Bush's visit to Warsaw in June of 2001.[226]

Although the announcement did not cause much interest (no single question pertaining to the visit or even Poland in general came up during the entire press briefing), this rhetoric nonetheless sets the tone for the language to be used during Kwaśniewski's visit, which only was the second state visit for the Bush 43 administration. In taking pathos-laden rhetoric—already well-established in U.S.-Polish relations—a step further, Presidents Bush and Kwaśniewski engaged in mutual praise during the visit. Bush declared that America was 'grateful' and called Poland a 'friend and ally, and a partner'. Kwaśniewski replied that he had arrived in Washington 'with readiness and joy you feel when you come to meet your best friend'. He added:

---

[224] The White House, Office of the Press Secretary (2001) 'President Bush Announces Support for Transfer of Frigate to Poland', Presidential Palace, Warsaw, Poland, 15 June. This "gift" nevertheless implied costs for Poland: training for the sailors and the obligation to buy Seahawk helicopters. Cf. Jeffrey Simon (2004) *Poland and NATO*, p. 107.

[225] The White House, Office of the Press Secretary (2001) 'U.S. To Transfer An Additional $20 Million to Polish American Freedom Foundation', Presidential Palace, Warsaw, Poland, 15 June.

[226] The White House, Office of the Press Secretary (2002) 'Press Briefing by Ari Fleischer', Washington D.C., 19 June.

> Our conviction and faith is that what we are doing is right, we are taking largely from the example of the United States. In its policy, we find confirmation that these values are not an empty slogan, but a living motto: substance of everyday life, and the only axis of good.[227]

Within the context of these visits, a number of cooperation agreements were signed, including a "US Poland Military Cooperation Initiative" which stipulated, among other objectives, that the countries would be '[w]orking together to modernize Poland's defense acquisition process'.[228] This initiative seems all the more interesting in light of the F-16 deal concluded in the aftermath of Kwaśniewski's visit (see below).

These state visits took place in the run-up to "Operation Iraqi Freedom" launched in March 2003. When America decided to go to war in Iraq, Poland was on its side as a prominent member of the so-called coalition of the willing. While it seems exaggerated to consider the Iraq crisis the ultimate proof of Poland's Atlanticism as opposed to its Europeanism (after all, there was no European position on the matter which Poland could have feasibly adopted), Warsaw chose America over Berlin and Paris. Washington rewarded Poland with its own occupation zone in Iraq. Perhaps not of crucial relevance from a military point of view, this move's symbolic value must not be underestimated. At least for a while, it gave Poland the impression that it truly mattered in international affairs. Washington understood the Polish need for recognition and respect and displayed willingness to satisfy Polish desires. The United States clearly benefited from Poland's distrust in its European allies, based on the centuries-old experience that neither Great Britain nor France had shown determination to be on its side in times of distress. Germany, in turn, was perceived as part of the problem by many in Warsaw (nonetheless in the Kaczyński circles), not as part

---

227 The White House, Office of the Press Secretary (2002) 'President Bush Welcomes President of Poland for State Visit', 17 July. During that same state visit, Kwaśniewski also was honoured through a state dinner — an event possibly related to the Bush Administration's determination to make Poland buy American instead of European fighter jets (see below).
228 Cf. The White House, Office of the Press Secretary (2002) 'Fact Sheet: U.S. Poland Military Cooperation Initiative', Washington D.C., July 17.

of the solution. Close alignment with the United States was the widely preferred remedy to Poland's security concerns. On the Iraq issue, Washington moreover spoke in a language Poles could understand and to which they could relate (as probably opposed to many in Western European countries).

Yet, given that the concrete threat against the country arguably was negligible and moreover several thousand kilometres away, Warsaw was not (only) primarily preoccupied by terrorism, but had ulterior motives of purely strategic nature. Defence analyst Wojciech Luckzack's assessment of the situation, as quoted in an interview with the BBC, was widely shared:

> A great success in Iraq will immediately launch Poland from the group of the not-so-significant countries in Europe, into the first league of the decision-makers.[229]

This position was also defended by officials, as then Polish ambassador in Washington Przemysław Grudzinski explained in 2004:

> Poland considers participation in this operation as an investment in international security. Our contribution to the operation in Iraq also sends a strong message that Poland is a trustworthy and reliable ally and takes its international obligations seriously.[230]

Against the background of a lingering sense in Poland of not being taken seriously by Berlin, Paris or London, Warsaw's ambitions to assert itself seem understandable. Yet, Polish consideration certainly rested on misjudgements on the leadership's part. When Marek Siwiec, an advisor to President Kwaśniewski, explained in an interview what he perceived as the value-added of Poland's going to war, he clearly failed to foretell reactions from Berlin, Paris and other states:

---

229 Nick Thorpe (2003) 'Why Poland Loves America', *BBC News Online,* 30 May.
230 Przemysław Grudzinski, (2004) 'Poland's Accession to the European Union and Its Impact on United States-Polish Relations'.

What we are bringing to the European community, this is the confidence of the United States. And this confidence is very much required to build future transatlantic relations — on one side the United States, on the second side United Europe.[231]

Yet, neither Berlin nor Paris saw any need for Poland to bring the confidence of the United States to Europe. Poland's and other Central European governments' decision to support and participate in the invasion of Iraq famously prompted French president Jacques Chirac to furiously declare that the new EU member states had 'missed a good occasion to be quiet'. Except for the war in Iraq itself, to many Europeans, Donald Rumsfeld is likely to be most remembered for coining the terms of "Old and New Europe". Whilst its unintended effect might have been the strengthening of "Old European" identity (then German Minister of Foreign Affairs Joschka Fischer, for instance, declared on the spot that he was proud to be an 'Old European, like Kant'), the statement nevertheless illustrated an undeniable fact: the continent was divided into two groups of states, one supporting the U.S. invasion of Iraq, one opposing it. The dividing line was not even equal to the geographic boundary between Western and Central Europe.[232] This fact notwithstanding, Warsaw's loyalty with the United States came at the price of palpably cooled relations with France and Germany (though differences over the Iraq war were not the only reason for this). In that sense, Washington hence proved more attractive than Berlin or Paris — and obviously more influential.

Complaints about Poland being "America's Trojan horse" were thus reasonably common phenomena during those years.[233] Poland

---

231 Quoted in: Nick Thorpe (2003) 'Why Poland Loves America'.
232 More Western Europeans than Central Europeans signed the so-called "Letter of the Eight". The subsequent "Letter of the Ten" or "Vilnius letter", a more direct declaration of support for U.S. policies, however, was signed by members of the Vilnius Group only, i.e. Estonia, Latvia, Lithuania, Slovakia, Slovenia, Croatia, Albania, Romania, the FYROM and Bulgaria.
233 This reproach is mainly — but not exclusively — to be found within the European left. A number of examples: Frank Unger (2007) 'Ein Trojanisches Pferd: Politisch Unkorrektes über mögliche US-Raketen in Polen und Tschechien', *Freitag*,

was said to serve as a facilitator of U.S. interests in Europe, be it in the realms of economy, security or policy. Though Poland, U.S. power could be projected into the region as a whole, both westwards and eastwards. Within the EU, Poland (as well as other Central European states) can play the role of 'tipping the scales'[234]. Eastwards, Poland is often more qualified to talk to neighbours such as Belarus and Ukraine. The more instrumental and outward-oriented the bilateral relation between Poland and the U.S. gets, the more the question arises to what extent Poland might be a medium for U.S. influence within European contexts. 'For America, Poland's willingness to take an independent, robust and strategic approach to international politics, is one which is refreshing and very welcome.'[235] In sum, many Europeans considered Poland's willingness to so closely follow the United States suspicious.

"Old European" annoyance over Poland was however not limited to events immediately pertaining to the Iraq war. On 27 December 2002, Poland announced its intent to purchase forty-eight Lockheed Martin F-16 aircraft at a total price of 3.5 billion U.S. dollars, a decision 'welcomed' by the United States embassy in Warsaw and qualified as 'the deal of the century' by U.S. ambassador in Warsaw Christopher A. Hill in an interview with the *New York Times*.[236] Armament deals tending to be somewhat opaque in nature, the information available in the Polish F-16 purchase remains sketchy. For this reason, the following account heavily relies on a

---

30 March; Gilbert Achcar (2003) 'Auxiliary Americans: Washington Watches Over EU and NATO expansion', *Le Monde Diplomatique* (English edition), January; Christian Schmidt-Heuer (2003) 'Die freundliche Übernahme. Vor dem EU-Referendum: Wie Polen zu einer amerikanischen Tochterfirma in Europa geworden ist', *Die Zeit*, 5 June. See also: Barbara Kunz (2008) 'Les relations polono-américaines depuis 1989: Varsovie, cheval de Troie des États-Unis en Europe?', *Le Courrier des Pays de l'Est*, Paris, April 2008 (no. 1066), pp. 62–70.

234 Cf. Wess Mitchell (2006) *Tipping the Scales. Why Central Europe Matters to the United States,* Washington D.C.: CEPA Working paper.

235 David H. Dunn (2003) 'Poland: America's New Model Ally', p. 66.

236 U.S. Embassy to Poland (2002) 'Poland Chooses the F16 Fighting Falcon', press release, 27 December; John Tagliabue (2003) 'Lockheed Wins Huge Sale to Poland With Complex Deal', *The New York Times,* 19 April.

research report by Barre R. Seguin from the George C. Marshall European Center for Security Studies[237], supplemented with official documents where available. What is known is that when Poland chose to buy the Lockheed F-16s, this equalled dismissing both the Swedish / British *Jas 39 Gripen* and the second European option by Dassault of France. The Swedish and French reaction was to argue that Poland had taken a 'political decision'.[238] It is rather likely that this assessment is correct and that the Polish decision was at least partly motivated by more political than military considerations — as is often the case with armament deals.[239] Several facts point into that direction.

What eventually seemed to tip the scales for the Lockheed offer was the offset deal to be signed in parallel with the airplane deal[240], in addition to extremely favourable financing conditions offered by the U.S. government. Thus, Poland received the largest ever loan granted, with a 15-year repayment term, even though these conditions were not covered by U.S. legislation. In other words, '[t]he Bush Administration needed to be creative to overcome limitations imposed by existing U.S. Government financing programs.'[241]

Nevertheless, the French and Swedish conditions were likely to be equally advantageous.[242] For that reason, it seems fair to believe that other aspects tipped the scale. As Seguin concludes, 'the

---

237 Cf. Barre R. Seguin (2007) 'Why did Poland Choose the F-16?', *Occasional Paper Series*, George C. Marshall European Center for Security Studies, Garmisch-Partenkirchen, no. 11, June.

238 Cf. for instance 'Polen har tagit ett politiskt beslut', *Dagens Nyheter*, 27 December 2002 / 'Le F-16 et l'Otan l'emportent en Pologne', *Air & Cosmos*, no. 1872, 10 January 2003.

239 History repeated itself when the Polish decision to buy American helicopters instead of French products caused a major diplomatic crisis between Paris and Warsaw in 2016.

240 For an overview, cf. Barre R. Seguin (2007) 'Why did Poland Choose the F-16?', p. 23.

241 Ibid., p. 16.

242 Ibid., p. 17.

sale is best framed through a political lens, with the Polish commitment in Iraq exchanged for U.S. investment in Poland'.[243] This assessment is based on a Polish source's saying that 'Lockheed Martin didn't win the contract, the U.S. government did, with pressure and support coming from the highest levels. They created a program that, politically and economically, it was very hard to say no to.'[244] The conclusion to be drawn from this is that the United States, backed by a vast arsenal of foreign policy tools, proved to have more influence on Polish decision making than European actors. If the assessment that Poland's opting for the American offer was predominantly motivated by political concerns is correct, this implies that a good relationship with Washington is what Warsaw values most. The statements by Polish officials quoted above may serve as an indicator that this assessment indeed is correct.

III.4.2 Foreign policy tools 2001 to 2005

An analysis of events that marked Polish-US relations in the years 2001 to 2005 unequivocally confirms State Department Background Notes: the United States and Poland indeed enjoyed warm bilateral relations in this period. For George W. Bush, in 2002, Poland is 'America's friend' and the sources covering the years 2001 to 2005 do not contain information giving reason for reassessment. Throughout that time span, Poland qualified as a friendly state from Washington's perspective—perhaps even as the friendliest state within the international system.

Given that Poland clearly qualified as a friend, like in previous periods in U.S.-Polish relations, the foreign policy tools employed in the years 2001 to 2005 were exclusively based on positive power. Positive material power tools have come to use in a number of important occasions, most prominently the fighter jet deal:

- Cooperation and aid, notably in the military field
- Offset deals and extremely favourable loan conditions for Poland's purchase of the F-16 fighter jets

---

243 Ibid., p. 27.
244 Quoted ibid., p. 28.

Still more importantly, positive symbolic power tools have been a recurrent theme after 2001 in U.S. policies towards Poland, a point in time when the Bush administration needed allies in its so-called War on Terror:

- A comparatively large number of high-level contacts (see overview in annex), as well as high quality high level contacts: Bush's first speech on Europe after his election held in Warsaw, President Kwaśniewski's state visit with great pomp
- Ostentatious (rhetorical) display of "friendship" on numerous occasions

Yet again, no evidence for negative power tools could be found in the source material.

During the years covered in this section, the United States' main objective regarding Poland has been to cultivate the friendship between the countries and to preserve Poland's willingness to serve as Washington's model ally. In the Bush-Kwaśniewski era, the Polish quest for prestige and international recognition continued. Seen from Warsaw, these were intrinsically linked to the country's relation with the United States. This once more allowed Washington to apply the positive power toolkit, nonetheless at a time when the Bush Administration was in need of friends and allies for its so-called War on Terror. Washington excelled at playing out the range of mainly symbolic measures for which Warsaw was hoping, catering to the Polish longing for recognition. The underlying mechanisms of positive power thus continued to work in U.S. policies towards Poland, once more illustrating the interrelationship between the country's status as a friend and the use of positive power on the United States' part.

III.5 After Kwaśniewski: 2005 onwards

To state that Polish-US relations are a perfect example of friendship among states seems to be a common place. It is, however, also a statement that overlooks certain aspects. In the years after 2005, U.S.-Polish relations have shifted in focus. Along with this shift came new sources of problems. At the outset entirely about Poland as such, the relationship gradually evolved into being more instrumental in the sense that the U.S. aims not merely at helping Poland, but rather wants Poland to be a reliable partner with shared concerns and ambitions. Recognising, not to mention accepting, this development has not been easy for Warsaw.

III.5.1 The double Kaczyński era

A few years on and into the Kaczyński era, the picture had changed since the heydays of close friendship between Poland and the United States and Warsaw's enthusiastic support of the War in Iraq. Certainly contributing to Washington's less favourable view on Poland was the political culture of the Kaczyński brothers, i.e. President Lech Kaczyński (in office from 2005 until his death in 2010) and Prime Minister Jarosław Kaczyński (2005-2007) of the PiS-party[245]. Unlike Aleksander Kwaśniewski, the Kaczyński government was indeed never considered a serious interlocutor by American officials.[246]

Much of the Polish dissatisfaction since about 2007 with the country's involvement in the Iraq war is not about the war itself, but the consequence of a deep disappointment over what the country got out of it in terms of an emboldened role in world politics, Poland's standing in Washington and financially. As early as 2004, then President Kwaśniewski expressed his frustration in an interview with the *International Herald Tribune*, taking a surprisingly critical stance towards the United States:

> "Of course, as a realistic politician I understand the situation," he said. "But as a man, a human being, a friend of America, I do not understand it. In my opinion, a big country should be open, and sometimes more flexible, more gracious."[247]

Among the major points of contention was (and continues to be as of 2017) the visa issue, an open question for a number of years on

---

245 "Prawo i Sprawiedliwość", i.e. "Law and Justice"
246 Author's interview with U.S. official, Washington D.C., autumn 2007.
247 Judy Dempsey (2004) 'Take flexible stance, Polish leader urges. A Plea from a Close Friend of U.S.', *The International Herald Tribune*, 2 September.

which the Iraq participation had absolutely no effect. Polish citizens are still required to obtain a visa to enter the United States. For Warsaw, the issue was always linked to Polish support in the Iraq and Afghanistan wars. This is for instance illustrated by a 2007 article by then Polish ambassador to the U.S. Janusz Reiter in the Washington Post, in which he argues that 'Poland has fought in Iraq from the very beginning of the operation and is also one of the biggest contributors to the mission in Afghanistan'.[248] In doing so, the ambassador is by no means engaging in horse trading. Rather, the U.S. Immigration and Nationality Act itself has been amended in 2006, stating that a country could become a so-called programme country if it—besides fulfilling other criteria such as EU membership and not compromising U.S. law enforcement interests—allocates 'the equivalent of, but not less than, a battalion (which consists of 300 to 1,000 military personnel) to Operation Iraqi Freedom or Operation Enduring Freedom to provide training, logistical or tactical support, or a military presence'.[249]

In addition to complaints about visa requirements, there was thus a general sense in Poland that the nation has been "betrayed", as Kwaśniewski's and Ambassador Reiter's remarks illustrate. American advocates of Polish positions even warned that the U.S. might "lose the new Europe" over an 'apparent lack of enthusiasm for increasing military aid' and its unwillingness to share post-war Iraqi reconstruction contracts'.[250] It therefore again appears that the "war on terror" never was the single rationale to go to war for Poland, but that participation in America's endeavours was (also) perceived as a means to an end, and not (only) as an end in itself, as an American observer notes:

---

[248] Janusz Reiter (2007) 'The visa barrier', *The Washington Post*, 29 August.
[249] Cf. Section 413 of the *Comprehensive Immigration Reform Act* of 2006.
[250] Wess Mitchell (2006) *Mending Fences. Repairing U.S.-Central European Relations after Iraq*, Washington D.C.: CEPA Working Paper, p. 6.

> For most Central European capitals, postwar contracts, military aid, and visas were valued as ends in themselves or as ways of offsetting the costs of participation in the war. But for policymakers in Poland, the significance of these concessions lay less in their intrinsic value and more in what Washington's willingness (or unwillingness) to grant them would say about the country's importance as a U.S. ally.[251]

Whether the relevant circles in Washington were aware of these Central European motives remains unclear (though it is unlikely they were not). It is, in any case, difficult to argue against the assessment that Poland's participation in the Iraq war has caused more damage than benefits. This is certainly true in terms of human lives, but also financially. Moreover, Warsaw's strategic considerations did not compute: Poland became neither "the new Britain" enjoying a "special relationship" with the U.S., nor did it become one of the key players in Europe. Washington never saw Poland as a country of the same order of importance as Russia or the EU-3, Great Britain, Germany and France. Despite the crisis in transatlantic relations caused by disagreement on the Iraq war, the so-called New Europe simply did not replace the Old Europe. The key players on the continent do not change as easily, and, more importantly, Washington's ability to define and make key players is limited. Despite obvious Polish ambitions, Poland thus remained a medium power within the EU (its Iraq engagement, and lateron its domestic situation, perhaps being more counterproductive than anything in the European context). As a U.S. official, who wished to remain unidentified, put it in 2007

> if the Under Secretary [of State] were to go to Europe, she'd first try to get appointments in London, Berlin, Paris, Moscow, then Kyiv, and then, if there is time left, one of the other capitals — perhaps Warsaw.[252]

The Kaczyński government's unsubtle attempts at loudly claiming benefits and great power status for Poland not only led to annoyance in Brussels and various European capitals, they were not ap-

---

251 Wess Mitchell (2006) *Mending Fences. Repairing U.S.-Central European Relations after Iraq*, Washington D.C.: CEPA Working Paper, p. 7.
252 Author's interview with U.S. official. Washington, autumn 2007.

preciated in Washington either. Especially repeated Polish demands for advantages in return for participation in the Iraq war upset Americans, rejecting an approach to foreign policy seen as essentially based on requests for *quid pro quos*. This, as officials pointed out, is not the way for instance Great Britain would behave. Rumour has it that then Minister of Defence Radosław Sikorski[253] — reminiscent of Wałęsa's demanding a Marshall plan for Poland in front of Congress — travelled to Washington with a list, detailing what Poland wanted to obtain from the Pentagon in 2006, at Washington's dislike. As a result of this and similar events, Polish-American relations suffered considerably. Given that Poland's standing in Europe did not benefit from the Kaczyński's policies either, their consequences were contrary to their intended effects. Not only did Polish-US relations reach a low point by 2007, even Warsaw's relationship with Berlin and other European capitals was at its worst since 1990. The Polish strategy of requesting to be respected and taken seriously has largely proved counterproductive.

III.5.2 Donald Tusk, the conclusion of the Missile Defence Agreement — and still no visa waiver programme

In the autumn of 2007, Prime Minister Jarosław Kaczyński lost the parliamentary elections to his liberal opponent, Donald Tusk. In his government declaration from November 2007, Tusk stressed the importance of the Weimar triangle while also insisting on the relevance of Poland's strategic partnership with the United States — which nevertheless equals a change of discourse on Warsaw's part. Strong ties with Washington notwithstanding, he planned the withdrawal of Polish troops from Iraq for 2008. Moreover, it had become more than evident that Poland no longer was a naturally willing partner in the Bush administration's endeavour to install a missile defence shield in Europe. Intended to protect the United States from ballistic missile attacks emanating from so-called rogue states, the plan consisted of establishing the system at two different sites

---

253 Sikorski went on to become foreign minister in Donald Tusk's cabinet, 2007–2014.

on the territories of the Czech Republic and Poland. Whereas agreements with the Czech Republic on a radar system to be based near Prague were signed in July 2008[254], negotiations with Poland were far from being concluded at this point. Rather, both parts at first proved unable to reach an agreement on the terms of the deal, with Poland holding concrete ideas on U.S. *quid pro quos*. Formal negotiations were opened in May 2007 in Warsaw, still under the Jarosław Kaczyński government, and continued from October 2007 onwards by the new liberal administration on the Polish part. In essence, Poland's leadership was dissatisfied with what the U.S. was ready to offer in return for a missile defence site on Polish territory. Arguing that stationing an American system on Polish soil would have negative consequences for Poland's security by increasing risks and threats, the government requested security guarantees and compensation.[255] During a news conference in July 2008, Prime Minister Donald Tusk hence once more declared — and in effect rejected the latest U.S. offer — that it was 'necessary to obtain an effect, which we would assess as augmenting Poland's security'.[256] On Warsaw's list was, besides 'real security guarantees', military aid worth several billions of dollars intended to help modernise the Polish air force. In the present context, "real security guarantees" meant the permanent stationing of a *Patriot* missile battery corresponding to Polish demands, whereas, according to media reports, the U.S. offer merely included temporary stationing for one year.[257] On the U.S. side, although this was never officially confirmed, the idea (read: threat) to base the system elsewhere — most frequently mentioned

---

254 Cf. 'Agreement between the Czech Republic and the United States of America on establishing a United States Ballistic Missile Radar Site in the Czech Republic', signed in Prague on 8 July 2008. See also U.S. Department of State (2008) 'Remarks by Secretary of State Condoleezza Rice With Czech Foreign Minister Karel Schwarzenberg at Ballistic Defense Agreement Signing Ceremony', Prague, 8 July.
255 Cf. Polish Prime Minister, Press Service (2008) 'Negotiations on the anti-missile shield continue', Press release, Warsaw, 4 July.
256 Ibid.
257 Cf. for instance Polskie Radio dla Zagranicy (2008) 'Keine Patriotraketen? Kein Abwehrsystem!', Warsaw, 8 July.

in that context was Lithuania—popped up in various press briefings.[258] This may well be seen as a subtle hint for Warsaw that the U.S. had alternatives, should no agreement be reached in its negotiations with the Polish government.

The United States and Poland eventually signed the "Agreement Between the Government of the United States of America and the Government of the Republic of Poland Concerning the Deployment of Ground-Based Ballistic Missile Defense Interceptors in the Territory of the Republic of Poland" on 20 August 2008.[259] During a press conference following the signing ceremony, President Kaczyński declared that

> today during my conversations with Madame Secretary [Rice], we have concluded that from the point of view of my country and from the point of view of the United States, the way of thinking about interests connected with the missile defense are very similar. So both sides have achieved their goals. This is a huge success of Poland. I think this is another stage in building the global position of the United States, the most powerful country in the world, which is where they're going to remain, the most powerful country for a long time still. So for this reason, this day of the 20th of August, 2008, is the date of success and the date of satisfaction for me.[260]

Condoleezza Rice replied that one of the messages conveyed by the agreement is that "it says strongly to the world what we already know, that Poland is one of America's greatest friends and allies".[261]

Signature of the agreement notwithstanding, it remained to be ratified by the *Sejm*, the Polish parliament. In an interview with the Polish Radio in October 2008, General Henry Obering (then Director of the U.S. Missile Defense Agency) expressed his concern over consequences of delays in ratification, arguing that

---

258 Cf. for instance Spokesman Sean McCormack's Briefings on both 2 and 3 July 2008 (U.S. Department of State, Office of the Spokesman (2008) 'Daily Press Briefing', Washington D.C., 2 July respectively 3 July).

259 Cf. U.S. Department of State, Office of the Spokesman (2008) 'Ballistic Missile Defense Agreement between the United States of America and the Republic of Poland', Media Note, Washington D.C., 20 August.

260 U.S. Department of State, Secretary Condoleezza Rice (2008) 'Remarks With Polish President Lech Kaczynski', Presidential Palace, Warsaw, Poland, 20 August.

261 Ibid.

> But more importantly, [the U.S. Congress] based [funding] on ratification of agreements, to be able to move ahead. If we get ratification by the end of this year, we still will not be able to put an interceptor in the ground in Poland until 2012. This money is contingent upon ratification and if we don't get that, that puts that money at risk and that's very problematic for U.S. as well. So I think that it's very important that we move ahead very strongly on the ratification for both the radar as well as the interceptor site.[262]

Yet signing the agreement on missile defence once again failed to pay off in terms of Poland's inclusion in the Visa Waiver Program. Regulations on visas for Polish citizens travelling to the United States remain in place. As late as October 2008, the Visa Waiver Program was extended to the Czech Republic, the three Baltic States, Hungary, Slovakia and South Korea, whereas Poland again missed out.[263] In reaction to this, a Polish diplomat was quoted in the *Washington Post* saying that '[t]here is a sense of disappointment on our part. [...] We hope the next administration will take up this issue as a top priority. We have signals from both [the Obama and McCain] campaigns that they will look at Poland's membership in the program favorably.'[264]

Otherwise, however, signing the agreement meant *quid pro quos* for Poland. On the same day the agreement was signed, the U.S. and Poland issued a "Declaration on Strategic Cooperation Between the United States and the Republic of Poland".[265] As is stipulated in the Declaration,

> The United States and Poland intend to expand air and missile defense cooperation. In this regard, we have agreed on an important new area of such cooperation involving the deployment of a U.S. Army Patriot air and missile defense battery in Poland. We intend to begin this cooperation next year and

---

262 Polskie Radio dla Zagranicy (2008) 'Missile Defense Agreements should be ratified as soon as possible', Warsaw, 31 October.
263 Cf. The White House, Office of the Press Secretary (2008) 'President Bush discusses the Visa Waiver Program', Washington D.C., 17 October.
264 Nicholas Kralev (2008), 'Poland excluded from visa-waiver list', *The Washington Post*, 18 October.
265 Cf. U.S. Department of State, Office of the Spokesman (2008) 'Text of the Declaration on Strategic Cooperation Between the United States and the Republic of Poland', Media Note, Washington D.C., 20 August.

to expand it with the aim of establishing by 2012 a garrison to support the U.S. Army Patriot battery.²⁶⁶

An important Polish demand had therefore been fulfilled. Moreover, the Declaration foresaw increased cooperation and consultation in the political-military field, namely the exchange of information as well as defence industrial research and technology cooperation. Perhaps even more lucrative is the fact that the U.S. and Poland agreed that

> the United States remains committed to assist Poland with the modernization of its Armed Forces, and recognizes that this assistance will strengthen Poland's contributions to NATO and facilitate strategic cooperation between our two countries.²⁶⁷

In sum, Poland did not give away its territory "for free" but did receive the promise of substantial return services for allowing the U.S. to build a missile defence site in the country. Yet, Poland was obviously not able to entirely dictate the nature of these return services, as its citizens' continued exclusion from the Visa Waver programme illustrates. The Bush administration's missile defence plans, in turn, were modified by the incoming Obama administration in 2009.²⁶⁸ The matter of ratifying the agreement thus became obsolete.

III.5.3 Foreign policy tools after Kwaśniewski

As may be concluded for U.S.-Polish relations from 2005 to 2008, Washington continued to perceive Warsaw as its friend, though no longer as its best friend. While Background Notes continued to call U.S.-Polish relations 'warm', reality was more differentiated. After Lech Kaczyński's accession to presidential power in Poland, the

---

266 Ibid.
267 U.S. Department of State, Office of the Spokesman (2008) 'Declaration on Strategic Cooperation Between the United States and the Republic of Poland', Media Note, Washington D.C., 20 August.
268 Cf. American Forces Press Service, Fred W. Baker III (2009) 'Obama Announces Changes for European Missile Defense', Washington D.C., 17 September.

days of intense Polish-US friendship, blossoming rhetoric and grandiose state visits were over. As former Polish president Aleksander Kwaśniewski concluded in an interview in September 2009, Poland's relevance to the United States had decreased.[269] Yet, although Poland may no longer have been America's best friend, it certainly continued to qualify as a friend as seen from Washington.

The period from 2005 to 2008 was characterised by a change of personnel on the Polish side, which eventually resulted in a less solid base for U.S. positive power in its approaches to Poland. Whereas the Kaczyńskis were simply not taken seriously in Washington, Donald Tusk's becoming prime minister marked a shift towards greater independence from Washington. Poland's prestige was no longer perceived as first and foremost being an outcome of the country's relationship with the United States. As a result, the mechanisms underlying especially symbolic positive power measures lost in effect. The reasons for these developments may be manifold, ranging from the implementation of what could be qualified as more mature Polish foreign policies by Donald Tusk and Radek Sikorski to a loss of American prestige worldwide as a consequence of George W. Bush's approach to international politics, especially in Iraq. Regardless of the reasons, however, the United States' ability to exert power over Poland on the basis of (symbolic) positive power resources diminished. With Warsaw less and less inclined to tie its own prestige to Washington's, the attractiveness of close friendship with the United States faded — possibly as the result of the incoming Tusk government's reassessment, but also due to changed parameters within the international system during the Bush administration.

The somewhat cooled relationship between the United States and Poland in the years 2005 to 2008 did, however, not translate into an increased number of negative power tools during the period — or even the use at all of such tools. Nevertheless, the number and volume of positive power measures such as high level contacts

---

269 Cf. the interview with the former Polish President: Jan Puhl (2009) 'Aus für Atomschild. Kwasniewski beruhigt die Polen', *Der Spiegel*, 20 September.

significantly decreased. The qualitative difference between this period and the previous one did not consist in an increased number of instances in which negative power tools have come in use, but the United States' diminishing willingness to engage in positive power measures, perks and gifts with respect to Warsaw. It would hence be erroneous to speak of worsened bilateral relations, as the more accurate epithet would be "less tight". This is illustrated by:

- In total eleven high level visits (involving heads of state or government, in either Poland or the United States) in the years 2002 to 2005, as compared to only three such visits since Lech Kaczyński's accession to the Polish presidency in 2006 and until the end of 2008.[270]

No foreign policy tools based on negative power are apparent in the sources. The United States' refusal to include Poland in the Visa Waiver programme does not qualify as a negative power tool. Power, to reiterate Max Weber's definition, would be a social action aimed at changing another actor's behaviour. Yet, by refusing to include Poland in the programme, Washington did not obviously intend to impact on the way Warsaw behaves (with regard to the U.S.). For that reason, the Visa Waiver issue must not be included in the list of U.S. foreign policy tools in the present context. What it does illustrate, however, is Poland's lack of leverage over Washington in order to obtain the results it wants. In that sense, the question is thus yet another indicator for the relationship's asymmetric nature.

In sum, also the findings for the years 2005 to 2008 confirm the assumptions that Poland, as a friendly state, would be met with foreign policy tools based on positive power.

---

270 See the overview in the annex.

III.6 Conclusions on U.S. foreign policies towards Poland 1989–2008

For almost two decades, from 1989 to 2008, Poland qualified as a friendly state from a Washington vantage point. The recurrent characterisation of bilateral relations as 'warm' ever since 1991 in all Background Notes issued after 1994 corroborates this conclusion – and comparing the Poland Notes to those on Belarus, for example, clearly shows that such friendly formulations are no matter of course; the U.S. State Department does not shy away from very directly describing bad relations as such. Although that friendship has been closer at some points than at others, the overall pattern of the bilateral relationship between Poland and the United States undoubtedly were one of amity. As the sections above illustrated, Polish-US relations were predominantly characterised by unity rather than conflict. Consequently, the principal task for Washington was rarely to convince Poland to change its mind but rather to sustain a high level of "friendship" among states. Using Zbigniew Brzezinski's terminology, U.S.-Polish relations were thus mainly a matter of maintaining 'security dependence among the vassals [and keeping] tributaries pliant and protected'.[271] In Washington's approaches to Warsaw, positive power tools were the instruments of choice in Washington's approach to Warsaw. This observation hence confirms the initial assumption that friends would be met with positive power.

As a matter of fact, Warsaw was exclusively the target of United States foreign policy tools based on positive power. Negative power tools apparently never came to use in the relationship. Between "kind words" and "cruise missiles", "kind words" would therefore be the defining feature of U.S.-Polish relations throughout most of the 1990s and during the first years of the new millennium. The United States being able to offer most of what Poland craved, it could in effect exert a considerable amount of power over Warsaw by using positive power tools: Membership in NATO (and, as

---

271 Zbigniew Brzezinski (1997) *The Grand Chessboard*, p. 40.

some would argue, even membership in the EU given the interconnectedness of both organisations' enlargement processes) would not have been possible without the support of the United States. The pomp and glamour in which Polish presidents could bask during various state visits is a courtesy Washington clearly does not reserve for everybody. If there were any perfect example of American "soft power" at work in recent times, Poland would be it. Washington excelled at catering to Poland's longing for recognition and respect, and resorted to a great many instruments from its symbol-heavy tool kit. State visits, public praise and declarations of friendship, its own sector in Iraq: on a symbolic level, Washington has indeed been very generous towards Warsaw. Especially during the Bush II-Kwaśniewski era, Polish-American relations were full of symbolism and talk about common history and values. To just give one example, both sides were quick to mention the common national hero Tadeusz Kościuszko (1746–1817), still present today in granite in the respective capitals. The troubles Warsaw and Washington encountered by the end of the Bush II administration (notably the visa issue) can hardly be seen as a "stick" scenario. Rather, it was Washington denying Warsaw any more carrots, with Warsaw trying to influence the U.S. administration and Congress to change their minds. In sum, Warsaw was thus a low-maintenance partner for Washington for many years.

With Poland's objectives largely coinciding with Washington's, the United States did not have to resort to any of the harder instruments at hand in its foreign policy toolkit. The objective of Polish foreign policy for many years consisted of increasing the country's prestige by coupling it with the prestige of the United States of America. In other words, by serving as Washington's model ally, Poland would achieve status in Europe and internationally — or so its leaders thought. Poland's decision makers seemingly perceived their interests to be the same as the United States', leaving Warsaw more than happy to let itself be influenced by the mighty U.S. At times, Warsaw's desire for a close relationship even outpaced Washington's, when the United States was less ready to fulfil Polish desires. NATO enlargement in particular may serve as an example, considering that Polish politicians pushed for membership long before the U.S. administration was willing to even think in that direction. In that sense, the flow of (attempted) influence was thus reversed: quite often, Warsaw tried to influence Washington rather than the other way around. Nevertheless, Poland remained at the receiving end of the relationship, making efforts in order to obtain something the United States could and would grant — or not. America's leverage over Poland was thus great, and essentially "by invitation" from Warsaw. Without the Polish willingness to be America's best friend, U.S. power would most likely have been much harder to exert.

Post-Iraq Polish-US relations nevertheless reached a historical low point (which, of course, needs to be seen relatively). The power of kind words on the United States' part was fading away. Poland's "new role" in transatlantic relations was largely overstated. Although Warsaw's support for the U.S. invasion in Iraq did temporarily increase Poland's standing in Washington, the geopolitical realities in Europe — and within the EU — remain unchanged. Poland might be (or rather, have been) "America's best friend", but that did not mean that it also was America's most important friend. Warsaw served as Washington's reliable partner in many respects, and Poland and the United States moreover shared a number of interests — including interests pertaining to the future of Europe. Most prominent among those shared interests was both capitals' eagerness to see Ukraine integrated in Euro-Atlantic structures. Yet, the United States' failure to deliver on Poland's most dearly wanted accommodation — i.e., inclusion in the visa waiver programme — put the relationship under strain. The general Polish inclination to accept most of what Washington requests, displayed for more than a decade, perhaps led to a tendency to take Poland for granted in the later years of the Bush II administration. This tendency became ever more apparent since Donald Tusk and Radek Sikorski took over the helms of Polish foreign policy.

There is little reason to assume that Washington would have considered the necessity or usefulness of eternally supporting Poland for simply altruistic reasons. The U.S. was looking for reliable partners, not recipients of aid. In that sense, the relationship between the two countries underwent a process of normalisation in the sense of being less and less "bilateral", i.e. the relationship was no longer without connexions to events in the surrounding world. U.S.-Polish relations being less about Poland itself meant a development towards cooperation on common agendas, that is, relations not (anymore) taking place in a Polish-American vacuum but within a regional and even global context. Consequently, the American focus was less on what Poland *needs*, and more about what it had to *offer* as a friendly state.

IV U.S. Foreign Policies Towards Ukraine

U.S.-Ukrainian relations evolved considerably over time and were characterised by a certain lack of continuity. During the early years of Ukrainian statehood, Washington mainly saw the country in terms of a non-proliferation problem and as a recipient of humanitarian aid. Despite a strong interest in economic reform and consolidation, the paramount U.S. objective consisted in solving the nuclear question. The nuclear weapons Ukraine had inherited from the USSR (a feature it shared with Belarus and Kazakhstan) would set the course for bilateral relations throughout the early 1990s. Once the nuclear problem more or less resolved, Washington began to focus on the non-proliferation of conventional weapons and the conversion of Ukraine's military industry. Subsequently, U.S. attention gradually shifted to more general aspects of economic reform and democracy; still valid to date as anchoring Ukraine in the West, this remains on the agenda, albeit with less intensive commitment than in the questions directly linked to security. The foreign policy tools Washington employed with respect to Kyiv reflect these changing patterns of U.S.-Ukrainian relations.

This chapter sets out to analyse U.S. Ukrainian policies in five sections, retracing the bilateral relationship as events were unfolding. After an introduction to the beginnings of U.S.-Ukrainian relations and the path to the United States' recognition of Ukraine's statehood (IV.1), section IV.2 is dedicated to nuclear non-proliferation. Section IV.3 deals with conventional non-proliferation and Ukraine's accession to the Missile Technology Control Regime (MTCR). The fourth section (IV.4) sets out to present U.S. policies and Ukraine in a wider European context with a special focus on NATO. Section IV.5 discusses events from the Orange Revolution to 2008. Each of these sections is concluded with an analysis of the foreign policy tools upon which Washington relied. Finally, VI.6 sums up these findings.

IV.1 Introduction: America's recognition of Ukraine's independence

U.S.-Ukrainian relations began with what has been dubbed 'the biggest foreign policy blunder' of the Bush senior presidency by William Safire of the New York Times.[272] In his so-called "Chicken Kiev speech" to the Supreme Soviet of Ukraine on 1 August 1991, only months before Ukraine declared its independence, George H. W. Bush expounded that

> freedom is not the same as independence. America will not support those who seek independence in order to replace a far-off tyranny with a local despotism. They will not aid those who promote a suicidal nationalism based upon ethnic hatred.[273]

Bush's message boils down to the statement that Washington would not support Ukrainian independence, meaning that Washington was not ready to challenge Moscow and stop considering the Soviet regime as its main interlocutor. From a Washington perspective, establishing diplomatic relations with Kyiv was tantamount to substantiating the *de facto*-end of the USSR, with Moscow unable to keep the Union together. Recognition of an independent Ukraine would thus have equalled a major reorientation of U.S. foreign policy, a step Washington was not yet ready to take. In that sense, the beginnings of U.S.-Ukrainian relations were therefore characterised by Washington's unwillingness to formulate a Ukraine-specific policy at all. Ukraine's status as a newly emerging actor was almost entirely overshadowed by the acceptance of a Soviet sphere of influence, a way of thinking Washington took a certain time to overcome.

Ukraine declared independence from the Soviet Union on 24 August 1991, only days after and in reaction to the attempted putsch against President Gorbachev in Moscow. A referendum on 1 December 1991 confirmed Ukrainians' desire for independence,

---

272 William Safire (1991) 'Ukraine Marches Out', *The New York Times*, 18 November.
273 The White House, Office of the Press Secretary (1991) 'Speech by President Bush to the Supreme Soviet of Ukraine', 1 August.

and Leonid Kravchuk was elected the first president of his country. Even after that referendum, President Kravchuk had difficulties convincing President Bush that the United States should grant diplomatic recognition to an independent Ukraine.[274] When Ukraine voted for independence, the United States did in fact not officially recognise the new state. Instead, the White House 'supported' Ukrainian aspirations and defined three priorities. Most prominent among them was Ukraine's 'adherence to democratic values and practices', including 'respect for borders'.[275] Washington eventually recognised independent Ukraine on 25 December 1991, when the step seemed unavoidable. The consulate in Kyiv reopened its doors as the American embassy to Ukraine in January 1992.

The United States' recognition of Ukraine's independence was a symptom of a more comprehensive, though incomplete, shift in American foreign policy. The issue obviously was a matter of relevance within the larger framework of U.S.-Soviet relations, hence considered in terms of geopolitics and not primarily in terms of democratic values and the like. Independent Ukraine was proof of the USSR's falling apart, and U.S.-Ukrainian relations consequently were a function of U.S.-Soviet relations. Only when Washington had taken a decision regarding its attitude towards Moscow did Ukraine itself enter the picture as a matter in its own right. This pattern would continue to characterise U.S.-Ukrainian relations for some time to come. Ironically, the first major issue between Washington and Kyiv would be a remnant of the Soviet Union, thus being in accordance with that assessment.

---

274 Cf. Clifford Krauss (1991) 'Ukraine Chef Faces Hurdles in Quest for U.S. Recognition', *The New York Times*, 30 September.
275 The White House, Office of the Press Secretary (1991) 'Ukrainians Vote for Independence', press release, Washington D.C., 2 December. Cf. *U.S. Department of State Dispatch* 2(49), 9 December 1991.

IV.2 The early years: Moscow-centrism and a focus on nuclear non-proliferation 1991 to 1994

IV.2.1 Solving the nuclear question

Independent Ukraine inherited a vast arsenal of conventional Soviet weapons. Most importantly, however, the country found itself with the world's third largest arsenal of nuclear arms on its territory, not to mention respective facilities and related know-how. Much of the Soviet expertise on missiles and space technology came in fact from Ukraine, where most of the USSR's intercontinental ballistic missiles (ICBMs) were developed and built. The city of Dnepropetrovsk had been the Soviet Union's rocket industry's centre, with facilities for development and factories: the *Yushnoye* engineering bureau and the *Yuzhmash* manufactures, at times employing more than fifty thousand people.[276] The challenges were hence considerable, and the first U.S. priority rather naturally consisted of solving the nuclear question. Yet, besides tackling the imminent risk of conventional and nuclear proliferation, the United States also faced a necessity to see the conversion of Ukraine's military industry into civilian production if demilitarisation was to be sustainable, so as to make sure that the weapons destroyed would not rapidly be outnumbered by a fresh supply.

Among the gloomier scenarios for the post-Cold War era was the risk of nuclear weapons in the hands of uncontrollable regimes and WMD proliferation spurred by economic decline in countries of origin. Not surprisingly, therefore, solving the nuclear question

---

276 For an introduction to weapons present in Ukraine as well as the Ukrainian aero-spatial industry, cf. the following official report: U.S. Congress, Office of Technology Assessment (1994) *Proliferation and the Former Soviet Union*, Washington D.C.: U.S. Government Printing Office, September. The biggest problem was the 43rd Rocket Army and 46th Bomber Army; the former was composed of 35,000 soldiers and had 257 intercontinental ballistic missiles and more than 1,300 nuclear warheads.
It is moreover interesting to note that many members of Ukraine's elite during the 1990s had strong connections with the Dnepropetrovsk region—including president Kuchma who served as *Yuzhmash*'s president for more than a decade during Soviet times.

received considerable attention and occupied most prominent positions on political agendas. The issue was also crucial in determining U.S. approaches to Ukraine. Indeed, only two days after the referendum on independence, and before even officially recognising the country's sovereignty, President Bush ordered his Secretary of State to travel to Kyiv in order to 'discuss with Ukrainian leaders the steps we would like to see Ukraine take to implement their desire to achieve a non-nuclear status and to ensure responsible security policies'.[277]

As far as the nuclear question was concerned, the U.S. objective first and foremost consisted of extending existing non-proliferation regimes to Ukraine, although the only legal successor state of the Soviet Union was the Russian Federation. In other words, Ukraine was under no legal obligation to respect the existing instruments that were agreed upon with the USSR. In the field of demilitarisation and non-proliferation, this concerned the START and Non-Proliferation (NPT) treaties, which to join and respect Kyiv had to be convinced. This would be the major endeavour in U.S. policies towards Ukraine during the first years of Ukrainian independence.

The American approach was backed up financially by the so-called Nunn-Lugar programme, which allowed Washington to not only ask for a solution to the nuclear question, but to actively contribute to that objective. "Nunn-Lugar", named for its sponsors, senators Sam Nunn (D, Georgia) and Richard Lugar (R, Indiana), was started on the basis of the Soviet Nuclear Threat Reduction Act of 1991, adopted on 12 December.[278] Ensuing President Gorbachev's request for assistance in dismantling the Soviet nuclear arsenal, President Bush senior had proposed 'United States cooperation on the storage, transportation, dismantling, and destruction of Soviet nuclear weapons'. The act identified three types of danger to nuclear safety and stability (cf. Section 211), namely

---

277 The White House, Office of the Press Secretary (1991) 'Ukrainians Vote for Independence', Washington D.C., 2 December.
278 United States Public Law 102-228.

> (A) ultimate disposition of nuclear weapons among the Soviet Union, its republics, and any successor entities that is not conducive to weapons safety or to international stability; (B) seizure, theft, sale, or use of nuclear weapons or components; and (C) transfers of weapons, weapons components, or weapons know-how outside of the territory of the Soviet Union, its republics, and any successor entities, that contribute to worldwide proliferation.

In its findings, Congress subsequently concludes

> that it is in the national security interests of the United States (A) to facilitate on a priority basis the transportation, storage, safeguarding, and destruction of nuclear and other weapons in the Soviet Union, its republics, and any successor entities, and (B) to assist in the prevention of weapons proliferation.

The programme was renamed "Cooperative Threat Reduction Program" in 1993. By 1997, 395,2 million $ had been allotted to projects with Ukraine.[279] In hindsight, few programmes have been as successful as Nunn-Lugar, which fully accomplished the goal of a nuclear-free Ukraine: On 30 May 1996, the last remaining strategic nuclear weapons present on Ukrainian soil were transferred to Russia. In October 2001, Ukraine's last SS-24 silo was destroyed at a ceremony on the site in Pervomaysk.

IV.2.2 The Lisbon Protocol and Ukraine's accession to the NPT as a nuclear-free state

The path to a nuclear-free Ukraine, however, was criss-crossed and the Ukrainian government's commitment to that objective was ambiguous at best. To quote a senior U.S. official, Ukraine's commitment to denuclearisation was in fact 'in a stall mode' for several years.[280]

Article 5 of the Treaty on the Commonwealth of Independent States (CIS), signed in December 1991, stated that Ukraine, Belarus and Kazakhstan were to transfer all nuclear weapons on their territory to Russia so as to become nuclear-free. By moreover signing

---

279 Cf. U.S. Department of Defense (1997) 'Cooperative Threat Reduction Assistance to Ukraine', Fact Sheet, Washington DC, 16 January.
280 The White House, Office of the Press Secretary (1994) 'Background Briefing by Senior Administration Officials', Washington D.C., 14 January.

the Lisbon Protocol[281] of START I on 23 May 1992, Ukraine formally agreed to become nuclear-free in a context beyond the CIS, involving the West. The Lisbon Protocol included measures, which were (1) the transfer of all nuclear weapons to Russia and (2) the accession to the Non-Proliferation Treaty, as a non-nuclear state and 'in the shortest time possible' (Art. V). Yet, despite its formal commitment, Ukraine's getting rid of its nuclear weapons was no smooth process, and enforcing the agreed provisions was *de facto* a task to be taken on by the United States.

U.S.-Ukrainian relations during the early 1990s (between 1991 and at least the autumn of 1993) thus were 'a pretty difficult relationship which was focused in very great part on almost exclusively how the nuclear issue in Ukraine would play itself out and how we would have a relationship with a country which had an ambiguous approach to that problem'.[282] On several occasions, the Ukrainian leadership would either not fulfil its commitments or even question reached agreements, sometimes changing its position by one hundred eighty degrees. Before signing the START I treaty, for instance, President Kravchuk had expressed doubts that the strategic weapon systems transferred to Russia were actually destroyed there and, for that reason, temporarily halted transports in mid-March 1992. Despite having signed the Lisbon Protocol, Ukraine thus did not show much enthusiasm for ratification (and respect) of START and the NPT.

Solving the issue of Ukraine's nuclear weapons hence proved complicated, nonetheless absent unanimity within the Ukrainian elite, as the situation was perceived in Washington:

---

281 The official name of the document is 'Protocol to the treaty between the United States of America and the Union of Soviet Socialist Republics on the Reduction and Limitation of Strategic and Offensive Arms', signed 23 May 1992 in Lisbon / Portugal by Belarus, Kazakhstan, the Russian Federation, Ukraine and the United States.

282 The White House, Office of the Press Secretary (1994) 'Background on Kravchuk Visit', press briefing, Washington D.C., 4 March.

> American officials say Ukrainian officials can be grouped into three camps. Those who favor the dismantling of the nuclear arsenal include President Leonid Kravchuk, Foreign Minister Anatoly Zlenko and Defense Minister Morozov. In another category are Ukrainians who favor holding on to the weapons for the time being so Kyiv can trade them for more generous economic aid and some sort of security assurances. In the third category are legislators and nationalists who want to hold on to the weapons at all costs.[283]

Secretary of Defence Les Aspin came to visit Kyiv in June 1993 in order to discuss the matter. Only months later, President Kravchuk himself—contrary to previous statements—declared that Ukraine might keep some of its nuclear weapons. Although he had agreed to dismantle the strategic warheads present on Ukrainian territory, he now claimed that his earlier pledges had not included forty-six SS-24 missiles.[284] On 18 November 1993, the Ukrainian parliament, the *Verkhovna Rada*, passed a first ratification of START I, yet based on specific conditions. The nuclear weapons present on the territory were nationalised with the adoption of its "Guidelines for the Foreign Policy of Ukraine", moreover declaring that Ukraine was not bound by Article V of the Lisbon Protocol, which sets forth that Ukraine should join the Non-Proliferation Treaty at the earliest time possible.[285] President Kravchuk declared that earlier agreements only applied to about fifty percent of the strategic missiles on Ukrainian soil and, moreover, disavowed the crucial article V of the Lisbon Protocol, which laid forth that Ukraine would accede to the NPT as a non-nuclear state. Whereas the first argument had a technical component, the latter was the equivalent of outright refusal to comply with previously agreed upon principles.

During that period, Washington displayed little willingness to grant Ukraine high-level contacts with the United States. When asked at the end of November 1993 whether the President might stop by in Ukraine during his upcoming trip to Europe, taking place

---

283 Cf. Michael R. Gordon (1993) 'Aspin Meets Russian in Bid to Take Ukraine's A-Arms', *The New York Times*, 6 June.
284 Cf. 'Ukraine Now Says It May Keep Nuclear Weapons', *The New York Times*, 20 October 1993.
285 The White House, Office of the Press Secretary (1993) 'Press Briefing by Dee Dee Myers', Washington D.C., 29 November.

before the START issue was expected to be solved, White House Press Secretary Dee Dee Myers replied that

> [w]e expect the START issue to be resolved, and we're going to continue to press for that, and we don't have any plans at this point; the President has no plans to visit Ukraine.
> [Question from the audience:] by Kravchuk's own word, the issue will not be put to the Parliament before next March, that's obviously after the trip
> [Dee Dee Myers:] Right, but we have no plans to visit Ukraine before March.[286]

But the U.S. resorted to action beyond simply refusing to have the presidents meet. On 29 November 1993 and in response to the *Rada*'s imposing of conditions on START I, President Clinton made a telephone call to President Kravchuk, in order

> to discuss with him our strong hopes for a close U.S.-Ukraine relationship, as well as Ukraine Parliament's recent action on START I ratification [i.e., the Rada's decision to attach conditions to ratification]. The President expressed his concern to President Kravchuk about this incomplete action on START I and the Lisbon Protocol. President Kravchuk then told President Clinton that he planned to resubmit START I and the Lisbon Protocol as a complete package to the new Parliament that will be elected in March, a decision that the President welcomed.[287]

The U.S. strategy thus consisted in, on the one hand, denying high level contacts and urging the Ukrainian president to take action on the matter, while simultaneously working with incentives for Kyiv on the other. In addition to exerting pressure, Washington decided to accommodate Ukrainian concerns and expectations.

The result was the so-called Trilateral Agreement, initiated by the Russian Federation but finalised with U.S. support, signed in Moscow by the presidents of the United States, the Russian Federation and Ukraine on 13 January 1994 and ratified by the Ukrainian

---

[286] The White House, Office of the Press Secretary (1993) 'Press Briefing by Dee Dee Myers', Washington D.C., 29 November.
[287] The White House, Office of the Press Secretary (1993) 'Press Briefing by Dee Dee Myers', Washington D.C., 29 November.

Rada on 3 February that same year.[288] After earlier deploring the "stall mode" of Ukraine's commitment to denuclearisation, officials now praised the Agreement because 'it breaks loose the stall and again lays out a very firm commitment by Ukraine to proceed to eliminate strategic nuclear weapons from its territory in the earliest possible time'.[289] In attaining to Ukraine's ratification of START I and its adherence to the NPT, the Trilateral Agreement was considered to be the solution 'opening the prospect for a very much different kind of ability to conduct relations with Ukraine' by the Clinton administration.[290] In essence, the agreement reached between Russia, Ukraine and the United States reiterates what had been agreed upon previously in the Lisbon Protocol, but added a number of clarifications, being 'essentially yet another package of deals or arrangements that makes [the Lisbon protocol] more concrete and brings it into reality', nonetheless as far as warhead transfers are concerned.[291] Thus, it set forth that further financial means should be provided for Ukraine: the Ukrainian nuclear warheads were to be transported to Russia, processed into nuclear fuel and brought back to Ukraine in order to be used for the generation of electricity. Funding for the processing was to be allocated by the United States, as well as remuneration for the highly enriched uranium that could be gained through the process. For Secretary of State Warren Christopher, the Trilateral Agreement offered valuable incentives to Kyiv:

---

288 For details, see Steven Pifer (2011),'The Trilateral Process: The United States, Ukraine, Russia and Nuclear Weapons', Brookings Arms Control Series, Paper 6, May.

289 The White House, Office of the Press Secretary (1994) 'Background Briefing by Senior Administration Officials', Washington D.C., 14 January.

290 The White House, Office of the Press Secretary (1994) 'Background on Kravchuk Visit', press briefing, Washington D.C., 4 March.

291 The White House, Office of the Press Secretary (1994) 'Background Briefing By Senior Administration Officials', Conrad Hotel, Brussels, 10 January.

> But I say there are very strong incentives for Ukraine to proceed with [denuclearisation]. First, they'll receive security guarantees [sic!]. Second, they'll receive a very substantial amount of Nunn-Lugar funds for the dismantlement of these nuclear weapons. And third, they stand to receive a very substantial amount of compensation for the highly enriched uranium.[292]

Moreover, the agreement provided security assurances for Ukraine, but these would only become valid after Ukraine's fulfilling of all Lisbon Protocol requirements, essentially meaning the country's accession to the NPT.[293] Although these assurances did not go beyond the general assurances[294] by Nuclear Weapons States to Non-Nuclear Weapons States not to use nuclear weapons against them, they did have a certain symbolic value to Ukraine. They nonetheless came to play an important role in the *Rada*'s debates on ratifying the Non-Proliferation Treaty. A senior U.S. administration official, for instance, summarises the U.S. perception of President Kravchuk as follows:

> He said, look, we have to address the concerns of the [Ukrainian] parliament. And he said, I'm willing to do that. Working together with the United States, working together with Russia, we'll deal with — some of their main concerns had to do with compensation, for example. He said, "Then I will be resubmitting the package, the Lisbon Protocol package, which includes START I as well as the NPT part of it, to the Rada. [...] He said he expects to resubmit the package in March or shortly thereafter for another vote. I [senior U.S. official] expect, based on what I have been hearing from some Ukrainian parliamentarians, that they will be satisfied with what they have seen emerge from this deal.[295]

---

292 The White House, Office of the Press Secretary (1994) 'Press Briefing by Secretary Warren Christopher', Conrad Hotel, Brussels, 10 January. The value of the enriched uranium was said to amount to $12 billion, cf. The White House, Office of the Press Secretary (1994) 'Background Briefing By Senior Administration Officials', Conrad Hotel, Brussels, 10 January.
293 The White House, Office of the Press Secretary (1994) 'Background Briefing By Senior Administration Officials', Conrad Hotel, Brussels, 10 January.
294 It is crucial to bear in mind that "security assurances" are not the same as "security guarantees", as also U.S. officials would insist, cf. for instance The White House, Office of the Press Secretary (1994) 'Background on Kravchuk Visit', press briefing, Washington D.C., 4 March.
295 The White House, Office of the Press Secretary (1994) 'Background Briefing by Senior Administration Officials', Conrad Hotel, Brussels, 10 January.

At last, Ukraine unconditionally ratified START I and the Lisbon Protocol on 3 February 1994, following considerable pressure from the United States, especially after the first conditional ratification of November 1993. For President Clinton, Ukraine's becoming a nonnuclear state opened entirely new economic perspectives beyond bilateral U.S.-Ukrainian cooperation:

> [...] Ukraine's decision to become a nonnuclear state opens the possibility of receiving significant economic assistance not just from the United States, but from the International Monetary Fund, the World Bank, the European Bank for Reconstruction and Development, the G-7 nations and other nations who understand the greatness of this nation [Ukraine], its strategic importance and its economic potential. And I believe that in the 21st century, it will be difficult for any nation to be secure unless it is economically strong.[296]

Further discussions on economic assistance would follow. With the Trilateral Agreement settled, it became conceivable for President Clinton to add a stop in Ukraine during his trip to Europe in January 1994 two days before the signing ceremony in Moscow. In granting this favour formerly denied by the U.S. administration, he accepted getting together with President Kravchuk for their first ever meeting at Kyiv's airport, followed by public remarks by both heads of state. In Clinton's words, the meeting began 'a new era' in U.S.-Ukrainian relations, thanks to the 'breakthrough' that the Trilateral Agreement represented.[297] The beginning of that "new era" was, for instance, illustrated by an invitation to join NATO's newly founded Partnership for Peace Programme (*inter alia* meaning Ukraine's military could cooperate with its Western counterparts), as well as to 'expand and enhance the economic ties' between the U.S. and Ukraine. Moreover, Kravchuk received an invitation for an official visit to Washington two months later, in March 1994.[298] During that March 1994 visit, both presidents finalised agreements on an expanded assistance package for Ukraine, focusing on four areas: support for its transition to a market economy, support for

---

296 The White House, Office of the Press Secretary (1994) 'Remarks by President Clinton and President Kravchuk', Kyiv Airport, Kyiv, 12 January.
297 Ibid.
298 Ibid.

Ukraine's capacity to provide social services to its citizens (especially healthcare and food), support for the country's transition to democratic governance as well as support for the transition to a new security regime. The total of this assistance amounted to roughly $ 700 million in 1994.[299] Technically speaking, Kravchuk was nevertheless to be rewarded for fulfilling obligations to which he previously had agreed in the Lisbon Protocol.

In July 1994, Leonid Kuchma succeeded President Kravchuk, allowing for decisive progress on denuclearisation according to views expressed by senior U.S. officials at that time.[300] Several months after unconditionally ratifying START I, Ukraine formally acceded to the Non-Proliferation Treaty (NPT) as a non-nuclear power at a signing ceremony in Budapest during the CSCE summit on 5 December 1994. Nevertheless , the signing ceremony was once more preceded by intensive last minute negotiations due to Ukrainian zigzagging: some days earlier, the Ukrainian parliament had used what Washington considered 'ambiguous wording' in a declaration, which made it sound as if Ukraine considered itself a nuclear power—or at least remained utterly unclear on the question. The issue was solved virtually in the last minute, with Ukraine submitting an accompanying diplomatic note confirming that it did indeed not have any nuclear ambitions.[301] This zigzagging most likely also explains the very late decision by President Clinton to actually attend the ceremony, as well as the unusually short duration of that transatlantic trip which only lasted for seven hours.[302]

As a senior official would explain in hindsight, by the end of 1994, the decision to offer the Ukrainians a 'very intensive economic

---

299 Cf. The White House, Office of the Press Secretary (1994) 'Fact Sheet. Ukraine: U.S. Assistance Package', Washington D.C., 4 March.
300 Cf. The White House, Office of the Press Secretary (1994) 'Background Briefing by Senior Administration Officials on Upcoming Visit of President Kuchma of Ukraine', Washington D.C., 21 November. The senior administration official remains unidentified.
301 Author's interview with a former U.S. official, Washington D.C., 19 October 2007.
302 The White House, Office of the Press Secretary (1994) 'Background Briefing by Senior Administration Officials', Washington D.C., 1 December.

relationship' was 'the key factor that allowed us, then, to go on in January, '93 to sign the trilateral statement in Moscow on nuclear weapons'.[303] President Kravchuk's subsequent visit to Washington in March 1994, unthinkable with at least the contours of a solution on the horizon, was consequently said to represent the 'beginning of a new era in relations toward a kind of normal conduct of business with Ukraine', which could lead to 'a different kind of bilateral engagement with Ukraine, which is really going to be, [according to an unidentified senior official], much broader across the range of things that this government does with sort of full partners and friends in a time when Ukraine is going through some very difficult transition and change.'[304]

IV.2.3 Foreign Policy Tools in solving the nuclear question

As the statements and appraisals made at the numerous background briefings and the like held in connection with Ukraine's denuclearisation indicate, the country clearly qualifies as an undecided state from a U.S. vantage point. During the early years of U.S.-Ukrainian relations, Ukraine hardly displayed a consistent position vis-à-vis the United States. Above all with respect to the nuclear question, Ukrainian policies are most accurately described as zigzagging. This is also the perception that becomes palpable in background briefings by U.S. officials, offering insights on Washington's views on the country and its leadership. Consequently, Ukraine qualifies as an undecided state in its position towards Washington from 1991 to 1994.

The U.S. position on the nuclear question was very clear from the outset: Washington wanted a nuclear-free Ukraine, integrated into the existing international non-proliferation regimes. Ukraine, in turn, was less convinced of the benefits of these objectives. It consequently took Washington some effort to convince Kyiv. In the case of Ukraine's nuclear weapons, the subject on which Ukraine

---

303 The White House, Office of the Press Secretary (1994) 'Background Briefing by Senior Administration Officials on Upcoming Visit of President Kuchma of Ukraine', Washington D.C., 21 November.
304 The White House, Office of the Press Secretary (1994) 'Background on Kravchuk Visit', Washington D.C., 4 March.

and the United States disagreed at the outset was nevertheless very concrete, and it did not in the first instance pertain to more principal matters, steering clear of more complicated issues such as "democracy" or the like. This certainly simplified negotiations, which could be led on the basis of tangible and quantifiable issues and objectives.

The foreign policy tools used in that context cover a wide range, though there is no evidence of negative material power being used:

- Material positive power tools: aid and support under the Nunn-Lugar programme, financial means as agreed upon in the Trilateral Agreement, general aid augmentations, as well as paving the way for assistance from other international organisations such as the IMF, the World Bank or the EBRD
- Positive symbolic power tools: security assurances as agreed upon in the Trilateral Agreement, state visits (Kravchuk in Washington, May 1992 and March 1994), acceptance of high level contacts being directly linked on the United States' part with progress on the non-proliferation agenda
- Negative symbolic power tools: pressure exerted by Washington, for instance translated into the refusal of high level contacts

Quite apparently, friendship with the United States alone was no sufficient motivation for Ukraine to get rid of its nuclear weapons. Kyiv obviously held a powerful tool in its hands in order to demand more (mainly financial) support, with the missiles being an excellent bargaining chip. Ukraine's eventual compliance with U.S. wishes thus certainly paid off in financial terms. Not only was the dismantling of the weapons largely funded by the United States and made possible thanks to American know-how: each time Kravchuk and later Kuchma abandoned earlier commitments, the United States would offer incitements to encourage Ukraine to review its position: the Trilateral Agreement and its accompanying provisions only reiterate commitments already contained in the Lisbon Protocol.

In sum, this first period in post-Cold War U.S. policies towards Ukraine confirms the assumption that both positive and negative power tools of foreign policy are applied towards undecided states.

IV.3 Conventional non-proliferation: Ukraine's accession to the MTCR, Bushehr and the Satellite Deal 1994 to 1998

Following 1994, the nuclear problem was in essence considered solved. When President Clinton visited Kyiv in May 1995, the question was hardly on the agenda. With the nuclear question seen as more or less settled, the United States began to turn its major attention towards conventional non-proliferation. Although the nuclear question was the most urgent one in Washington's view, non-nuclear weapons and assorted risks were not to be neglected either: denuclearisation notwithstanding, the Ukrainian (conventional) missile industry remained a potential risk, nonetheless given the country's desolate economic condition. The temptation to sell weapons for hard foreign currencies was more than theoretical when inflation rates skyrocketed in the early 1990s. Washington thus considered arms proliferation at least equally important as the threat presented by Ukraine's conventional capabilities themselves and was therefore ready to play an important part in solving the matter. Talks about the Ukrainian missile industry started as early as 1992 and 'have been conducted through several political and diplomatic channels' since then.[305] Once the country's ratification of START I and accession to the NPT was secured, conventional non-proliferation consequently moved to the top of the agenda.

---

305 Cf. Gary Bersch and Viktor Zaborksy (1997) 'Bringing Ukraine Into the MTCR: Can U.S: Policy Succeed?', *Arms Control Today*, April.

IV.3.1 Getting Ukraine to join the MTCR

Among the central features of American non-proliferation policies is the Missile Technology Control Regime (MTCR), established in 1987 by the Group of Seven (G7) states.[306] The MTCR is an international mechanism for non-proliferation, which 'rests on common export policy guidelines (the MTCR Guidelines) applied to an integral common list of controlled items (the MTCR Equipment, Software and Technology Annex)'.[307] In short, the MTCR is no organisation strictly speaking, but functions essentially through its members' export control systems, which, in turn, are based on common rules. The regime entirely prohibits the export of one category of weapons, and allows the export of a second category under the condition of very tight control. Contravention is sanctioned by member states, on the basis of national arms export laws.

During President Kravchuk's visit to Washington in March 1994, he and President Clinton

> noted Ukraine's interest in acquiring the status of a full and equal partner in the Missile Technology Control Regime (MTCR). The United States and Ukraine will cooperate closely to help to achieve this goal, which will make an important contribution to international efforts to stem proliferation of ballistic missiles.[308]

Although both the United States and Ukraine agreed on the overall objective of Ukrainian MTCR-membership, consent on details could not be reached at first. Most importantly, Kyiv refused to give up its offensive missile systems whilst Washington insisted on Ukraine abandoning them. At that point, the United States was pushing for new criteria for all states joining the MTCR, among them the requirement not to own offensive missile systems (see below). Ukraine found these new criteria unacceptable. The two countries, however, managed to sign a memorandum of understanding

---

306 The G7 includes Canada, France, West Germany, Italy, Japan, the United Kingdom and the United States. Today, the MTCR has thirty-five members.
307 Cf. the MTCR's homepage at www.mtcr.info.
308 The White House, Office of the Press Secretary (1994) 'Joint Statement on Economic and Commercial Cooperation', Washington D.C., March 4.

in May 1994, with Ukraine agreeing to abide by MTCR rules. Moreover, the U.S. and Ukraine cooperated on the establishment of a Ukrainian export control system, which would be at the core of Kyiv's adherence to the regime and indispensable for Ukraine's effective enforcement of the regime's rules.

In sum, as already was the case in the denuclearisation process, Ukraine first had to be convinced of its interest in joining the MTCR. Nonetheless the question of what Ukraine's rocket industry would become had to be answered, with the economic health of a whole region depending on a viable solution. Ukrainian missiles were therefore not a purely military matter, but had considerable economic implications as well. Ukraine's joining the MTCR thus did not only evolve around the question of the country's offensive missiles. Non-proliferation within the regime and MTCR membership are likewise closely related matters. Arms trade among members of the regime is subject to far fewer rules than the highly regulated transfers to non-members. This, in turn, implies an obvious incentive for states to join the MTCR in order to gain access to technology traded within the regime and to sell weapons without the tight controls required for arms transfers to non-member states. In 1993, these developments had reached a point that made the Clinton administration worry that the MTCR was on its way of becoming a 'missile bazaar'.[309] Imposing stricter rules within the regime was yet a hard way to go, given the principle of unanimity to be applied in the regime's decision-making. The U.S. consequently insisted on a number of criteria new members had to fulfil, being able to do so thanks to the de facto veto right conferred by the principle of unanimity. More specifically, potential members should agree to renounce specific missiles. Among these criteria moreover is good standing with other non-proliferation-regimes, especially the NPT and the Biological and Chemical Weapons Conventions.[310] Ukraine, as noted, was unwilling to give up its short-range ballistic missiles and manufacturing sites and end the production of specific missiles

---

309 Cf. Gary Bersch and Viktor Zaborksy (1997) 'Bringing Ukraine Into the MTCR: Can U.S: Policy Succeed?'.
310 Ibid.

inherited from the Soviet Union. Kyiv's main argument was that the MTCR was about export control and not a disarmament regime, that it needed its missiles for defence purposes and that U.S. demands were discriminatory, since they did not apply to other (member) states.[311].

In order to sweeten the Ukrainian decision to give up the missile programmes, the United States again chose to be generous. The incentives the United States was to offer Kyiv for playing by its rules had to provide Ukraine with a viable perspective for its aerospatial industry in addition to "traditional" economic aid. The reward for Ukraine's acceptance of Washington's MTCR conditions was (and despite protests by U.S. firms active in the sector) access to the highly profitable and growing commercial space launch market.[312]

The situation was thus a classic carrot scenario. Compliance with Washington's wishes would open up lucrative long-term perspectives; yet, the trade-off consisted of abandoning the missile system, and, in a certain way, the sovereignty of autonomous decisions about the nation's military equipment:

> As a result of these dynamics, Ukraine is facing a serious dilemma: comply with the U.S. conditions for full membership in the MTCR — with the resultant prospect for increased space cooperation with other regime members and thereby improving the position of one of the country's most important industries — or continue to be an MTCR "adherent," preserving the right to develop a limited range of military missiles, but thereby restricting cooperative endeavors that could be crucial to the survival of the country's space industry. We believe that the United States can offer Ukraine the "carrots" that will encourage Kyiv to renounce offensive missile programs and join the MTCR in the near future.[313]

In November 1994, Presidents Clinton and Kuchma signed an agreement during Kuchma's first visit to Washington as president,

---

311 Ibid.
312 Interview with former U.S. official, Washington D.C., 19 October 2007.
313 Gary Bersch and Viktor Zaborksy (1997) 'Bringing Ukraine Into the MTCR: Can U.S: Policy Succeed?'.

which allowed for their countries' respective space agencies to cooperate on joint projects without prior political consultations.[314] Signing such an agreement had been on Ukraine's wish list for quite some time. Yet, the U.S. had explicitly established a link with nonproliferation, as for instance stated in November 1994:

> Ukrainians are very interested in expanding into commercial launch markets. And we have taken the view with them that as they get up and over the nonproliferation barrier that we are very willing to talk to them about where they go with commercial launch capabilities. [...] To take into account their interests, bearing in mind that we are very eager to see them first establish themselves as responsible nonproliferation partners with their accession to the NPT [...].[315]

The most important—since most profitable—part of the deal was Ukraine's participation in the Sea Launch Consortium, according to its website an international partnership of American, Russian, Ukrainian and Norwegian businesses under the roof of Boeing; the venture was signed on 3 April 1995.[316] Ukrainian-built rockets were used to launch commercial satellites from a launching platform located in the Pacific ocean, taking advantage of its location on the equator which 'provides the most direct route to geostationary orbit, offering maximum lift capacity for increased payload mass or extended spacecraft life'.[317] The Ukrainian contribution involved providing the first two stages of the Zenith rocket, built in Dnepropretowsk, launch vehicle integration support and mission operations. The project cost more than 500 million U.S. dollars, and the

---

314 Cf. The White House, Office of the Press Secretary (1994) 'Background Briefing by Senior Administration Officials on Upcoming Visit of President Kuchma of Ukraine', Washington D.C., 21 November.
315 Ibid.
316 Information retrieved from http://www.boeing.com/special/sea-launch, accessed 19 October 2007. The partners were: Boeing Commercial Space Company, Seattle / U.S.A. (40 %), Aker ASA, Oslo / Norway (20 %), RSC Energia, Moscow / Russia (25 %) and SDO Yuzhnoye / PO Yuzhmash, Dnepropetrovsk / Ukraine (15 %). Sea Launch stopped operations in 2014 in the wake of the Ukraine crisis, after having re-emerged from bankruptcy a couple of years earlier.
317 http://www.boeing.com/special/sea-launch/information.htm#pag [accessed 5 January 2008, no longer existent in 2017].

World Bank granted Russia and Ukraine 100 million U.S. dollars in loan guarantees each, thanks to U.S. government backing.[318]

In 1996, Ukraine created *Ukrspetsexport*, an arms export agency under government control. Kyiv thus fulfilled one of the major requirements of MTCR-membership, as the regime primarily works through national export control systems. Not all arms sales were however going through *Ukrspetsexport*; several companies were allowed to directly sell abroad. Two years later, in March 1998, the United States and Ukraine reached formal agreement on Ukraine's accession to the MTCR, which became official shortly thereafter at a meeting in Paris. The United States, however, proved to be unable to insist on new rules for membership stipulating that all states (with the exception of the five permanent members of the United Nations' Security Council) had to abandon all their offensive missile programmes. The compromise brokered with Kyiv implies that 'Ukraine will keep its hundreds of Scud missiles – the type of rocket MTCR was specifically designed to counter – through the end of their service lives, and will not forswear future production of short-range missiles should Kyiv find it necessary'.[319] When asked about explanations for this radical change of policy, U.S. officials declared: 'We've discussed their plans, and we're content their plans are compatible with MTCR membership'.[320]

IV.3.2 The Policy of issue linkage: non-proliferation, nuclear power plants and satellites

This reassessment by Washington was almost certainly linked to parallel developments involving the Bushehr nuclear reactor in Iran, lowering the MTCR accession requirements in return for Ukraine's withdrawal from contributing to that project. The Ukrainian company *Turboatom* of Kharkiv was involved in the construction of the Bushehr nuclear power plant in Iran alongside a

---

318 William J. Board (1998) 'Offering a Cheaper Ride to the Orbit from the Middle of the Ocean', *The New York Times*, 16 June.
319 Howard Diamond (1998) 'U.S., Ukraine Sign Nuclear Accord, Agree On MTCR Accession', *Arms Control Today*, March.
320 Ibid.

Russian state company, *Atomstroyexport*, contributing especially designed and manufactured turbines. The power plant had initially been designed and built by the German Siemens Corporation, which however abandoned it after the 1979 Iranian revolution. Years later, Russians revived it. Needless to say, the project was strongly opposed by the United States.

Washington eventually succeeded in getting Kyiv to force *Turboatom* out of the project, although this equalled *Turboatom*'s losing a contract worth several millions of dollars. The decision was announced after Madeleine Albright's visit to Kyiv in March 1998.[321] In the White House's press services' own words, Washington had thus managed to 'obtain Ukraine's commitment to cease collaboration with the Government of Iran on the Bushehr nuclear power project'.[322] The Ukrainian withdrawal at least led to delays in the construction, though the power plant continued to be built with turbines provided by a Saint Petersburg firm. Before Albright's trip, 'Ukraine's ambassador to Washington at the time, Yuri Shcherbak, was told that the administration would prevent Ukraine from purchasing fuel for its aging nuclear reactors from American companies unless Turboatom gave up the Iran project. There were carrots as well sticks, the Kharkiv Initiative among the carrots, along with promises of Ukrainian participation in space exploration.'[323] Participation in space exploration, however, was only indirectly linked to the Bushehr issue through the linkage with Ukraine's accession to MTCR. Whilst access to the space launch market was the reward for joining the regime, compliance with U.S. wishes in the Bushehr question probably led to Ukraine's being allowed to keep its offensive missiles.

---

[321] Cf. Michael R. Gordon (1998) 'Russia Plans To Sell Reactors to Iran Despite U.S. Protests', *The New York Times*, 7 March.

[322] Cf. The White House, Office of the Press Secretary (1998) 'Promoting Democracy and Sovereignty in the Newly Independent States', Washington D.C., 21 May.

[323] Patrick E. Tyler (2000) 'Deprived Ukraine City Finds U.S. Help No Help', *The New York Times*, 6 June.

Besides joining the MTCR with its offensive missiles, the pay-off for Ukraine's withdrawal from the Bushehr project involved the signature of an agreement on civil nuclear cooperation.[324] The agreement included the option for Ukraine to buy nuclear fuel from Westinghouse. Seen from a strategic perspective, the deal was intended to promote Ukraine's *marge de manœuvre* vis-à-vis Russia, securing partial independence in terms of energy. The actual value of the deal in terms of increased independence was rather limited, however.

In addition to the nuclear fuel duel, the so-called Kharkiv Initiative was negotiated within the framework of the Gore-Kuchma commission (see below) and described in a U.S. embassy press release as a 'multi-faceted partnership involving the Kharkiv Oblast Administration, local governments within the Kharkiv Oblast, the U.S. government, and the Government of Ukraine'.[325] The objective of the Initiative consisted of compensating the Kharkov region, where Turboatom is one of the largest companies and the consequences of withdrawing from the Bushehr project were widely felt. In the words of its director, '[t]his was one of our biggest contracts, and losing it has been a very serious blow to the economy of our region'.[326] Through aid given directly to the regions, the loss of the contract should at least be eased. Overall, the Ukrainian side seemed rather dissatisfied with its outcome.[327]

IV.3.3 Foreign Policy Tools in making Ukraine join the MTCR

The United States' disappointment over Ukraine's involvement in Iran stands in sharp contrast to the exclusively positive aspects of U.S.-Ukrainian relations mentioned in State Department Background Notes from the years 1994 to 1998. At the same time, none

---

324 Cf. U.S. Embassy to Ukraine (1998) 'United States and Ukraine Sign Agreement to Develop Peaceful Nuclear Energy', press release, Kyiv, 6 May.
325 U.S. Embassy to Ukraine (1999) 'Kharkiv Oblast Hospitals To Receive $ 16.5 Million In Medical Humanitarian Assistance From United States', press release, Kyiv, 25 August.
326 Patrick E. Tyler (2000) 'Deprived Ukraine City Finds U.S. Help No Help'.
327 Ibid.

of these Notes tellingly contains qualifications of the bilateral relationship's qualitative nature—as is usually the case in Background Notes on Washington's friends.[328] Taken together with statements made during the overlapping period to be analysed in section IV.4. below, considering Ukraine an undecided state from a Washington perspective seems to be more than fair. Kyiv moved back and forth between complying with U.S. requests and opposing them, and these moves determined Washington's view in the country as reflected in background briefings and expert interviews—and induced the U.S. to apply a policy of carrots and sticks.

With respect to conventional non-proliferation, the United States clearly articulated its expectations and demands that Ukraine should adhere to the existing non-proliferation regime, i.e., the MTCR. The conflict of interest is obvious: whilst the U.S. wanted Ukraine to join the MTCR, without its offensive missile systems, Kyiv did not unequivocally share this position. Just like in the case of Ukraine's nuclear weapons, the conflict of interest was mainly kept at the level of concrete matters, hence avoiding that the MTCR question degenerated into a more categorical conflict over basic principles. Although the latter was constantly lingering in the background, it never came to the fore at this stage in U.S.-Ukrainian relations. Regarding the MTCR, the United States decided to operate with incentives and threats. Yet, foreign policy tools applied mainly fell into the realm of positive power.

- Positive material power tools: access to the U.S. satellite market, the so-called Kharkiv initiative, agreement on civil nuclear cooperation

The negative power tools which appear in the sources remain at the level of threats, and are thus somewhat hard to classify in terms of symbolic / material categories (but classified here as material, as they would definitely be material had they been implemented):

---

328 For a comparison, cf. the above chapter on U.S. approaches to Poland. Cf. also respective Notes on e.g. NATO allies.

- Negative material power tools: denying Ukraine the right to buy nuclear fuel

The fact that Ukraine—with respect to the Bushehr issue—was in possession of a most relevant bargaining chip restricted American policies. The Iranian question led to a more balanced relationship between Washington and Kyiv, reducing asymmetries in favour of the latter: with Iran involved, the matter became immediately relevant to U.S. interests and national security, hence reducing Washington's leeway. Ukraine's withdrawal from building the reactor became incorporated into the MTCR deal, despite originally being situated in another context. Because it happened to coincide in purely chronological terms, the MTCR and Bushehr issues became a conglomerate to be negotiated in connection. This almost certainly weakened the American position and narrowed Washington's range of manoeuvre. Although counterfactuals are impossible to prove accurate, it does not seem unlikely that the U.S. would have been more determined on the MTCR-issue if Iran had not entered the picture.

In sum, developments covered above indicate that tools based on both positive and negative power come to use towards Ukraine as an undecided state.

IV.4 Euro-Atlantic integration: Ukraine in its wider context 1994 to 2004

IV.4.1 The U.S.-Ukrainian honeymoon: broadening relations

Nineteen ninety-four not only marks the end of the nuclear question, but also the beginning of U.S. efforts to think about the future role of Ukraine in Europe. The significance of solving the nuclear question for U.S.-Ukrainian relations at that point in time can hardly be overstated. The Clinton administration assumed that although its relationship with Ukraine was 'a relationship that was focused primarily on nuclear issues' it also was 'a relationship that President Clinton felt from the very beginning was one of the key foreign policy relationships that he had to develop as President'.[329] In other words, Washington ceased seeing Ukraine through the narrow non-proliferation prism and began to look for perspectives in a wider context. Thus, at a press conference with his Ukrainian counterpart, President Clinton for instance declared in March 1994:

> The United States recognizes that it is very important to be supportive as Ukraine tries to reform and get through this period of economic transition. One of the things that we've been able to do in the last year or so is to take a broad view of the need for defense conversion measures as the denuclearization occurs.[330]

Ukraine's ratification of START and accession to the NPT and the beginning agreement on the MTCR opened the door to broadening the relationship. The year 1994 therefore marks a watershed in Washington's approach to Ukraine, with attempts at engaging Kyiv beyond non-proliferation and military matters. Especially in the aftermath of Leonid Kuchma's accession to power, the view on Ukraine—as well as on Eastern Europe in general—gradually changed towards becoming broader and less centred on Russia. The official rhetoric of the time was characterised by optimism. The White House Press Secretary consequently declared that '[w]ith Ukraine's accession to the NPT, the United States and Ukraine are entering a new era of expanded cooperation'.[331]

When President Kravchuk visited Washington in March 1994 following the breakthrough of the Trilateral Agreement, economic cooperation was high on the agenda. It was President Clinton's view that

---

329 The White House, Office of the Press Secretary (1994) 'Background Briefing by Senior Administration Officials on Upcoming Visit of President Kuchma of Ukraine', Washington D.C., 21 November.
330 The White House, Office of the Press Secretary (1994) 'Press Conference by President Clinton and President Kravchuk of Ukraine', Washington D.C., 4 March.
331 The White House, Office of the Press Secretary (1994) 'Ukraine's Vote To Accede To The Non-Proliferation Treaty', statement by the Press Secretary, Washington D.C., 17 November.

> [w]hile Ukraine is going through a difficult period of transition, it remains a nation with enormous economic potential, endowed with abundant natural resources and human talent. To develop the full measure of these resources, Ukraine's most promising future clearly lies with market reform.[332]

Supporting economic reform was therefore a declared priority, and Washington was ready to let deeds follow words, as Clinton explained at the same occasion:

> As Ukraine proceeds with reform, the United States is prepared to mobilize support from the G-7 nations and from international financial institutions. We're also prepared to increase our bilateral economic assistance [...]. Total U.S. assistance available to Ukraine this year will, therefore, be $700 million. This represents a major increased commitment to an important friend in the region.[333]

Some months later, for President Kuchma's first visit to the United States in November 1994, the U.S. administration had identified two central policy issues, namely 'the nuclear future between [the U.S. and Ukraine] and the economic future of Ukraine and what the United States can do to support that future'.[334] It is fair to say that the first Kuchma years represent something like a honeymoon period in U.S.-Ukrainian relations, a time when U.S. officials could, in a background briefing, declare that 'we find ourselves with Ukraine probably at the strongest point that we have ever been in our relations with that country.'[335]

As far as the economic realm was concerned, Washington decided to provide substantial support for President Kuchma's reform policies, increasing aid and assistance with the result that Ukraine became the fourth largest recipient of the United States anywhere

---

332 The White House, Office of the Press Secretary (1994) 'Press Conference by President Clinton and President Kravchuk of Ukraine', Washington D.C., 4 March.
333 The White House, Office of the Press Secretary (1994) 'Press Conference by President Clinton and President Kravchuk of Ukraine', Washington D.C., 4 March.
334 The White House, Office of the Press Secretary (1994) 'Background Briefing by Senior Administration Officials on Upcoming Visit of President Kuchma of Ukraine', Washington D.C., 21 November.
335 Ibid..

in the world, and the largest in the post-Soviet sphere.[336] Economic cooperation and assistance, however, was contingent on economic reform in Ukraine, which Washington deemed to be insufficient in 1994. Still under Kravchuk, and in the final negotiation phase of the Trilateral Agreement, the U.S. announced its willingness to commit $155 million in economic aid to Ukraine, to be increased if need be as a senior administration official made clear:

> I can tell you the $155 million is a floor, and we're willing to go above that. They [Ukraine] have to show us some evidence that they are ready to move energetically on reform. We are willing to work with them on that.[337]

In other words, there were rewards to be distributed by Washington provided Ukraine took to measures desired and expected by the U.S. administration. Also after the Kravchuk years, economic support clearly was (at least partly) linked to progress made possible by Kuchma's accession to power, as Presidents Clinton and Kuchma noted in their joint summit statement on the occasion of the Ukrainian head of state's visit to Washington in November 1994: 'This United States economic support is in recognition of Ukraine's major initiative to launch a comprehensive economic reform program'.[338] American economic support for Ukraine included direct aid, advocacy of Ukraine's interests at the G7, the IMF and with respect to GATT agreements. Moreover, Washington chose to take the unusual step of providing Kyiv assistance for its balance of payments problems, a first in U.S. history: 'we're making an exception in this case because of the unique situation in which Ukraine finds itself, and also I [unidentified Senior Administration Official] think

---

336 Cf. The White House, Office of the Press Secretary (1994) 'Fact Sheet: State Visit of Ukrainian President Kuchma. U.S. Bilateral Assistance to Ukraine', Washington D.C., 22 November.
337 The White House, Office of the Press Secretary (1994) 'Background Briefing By Senior Administration Officials', Conrad Hotel, Brussels, 10 January.
338 The White House, Office of the Press Secretary (1994) 'Joint Summit Statement By President Clinton and President of Ukraine Leonid D. Kuchma', Washington D.C., 22 November.

because of the unique importance of Ukraine to the United States'.[339]

The search for ideas about Ukraine's future fell in a period of general reorientation of Washington's policies towards Europe's Eastern parts, to a large extent triggered by concerns about developments in Russia and the coming of a new U.S. administration in 1993. As a consequence, greater importance was attached to Ukraine, going beyond proliferation and denuclearisation issues. More and more observers were arguing for a genuine European policy and a consequent end of the Russocentrism in U.S. views on the region. Within Central and Eastern Europe, Ukraine was identified as a key state. As Zbigniew Brzezinski argued, '[t]he problem of Ukraine cannot be deferred. Ukraine is just too big, too important, and its existence too sensitive a matter to both Russia and the West'.[340] A parallel development in Washington was the new focus on Democratisation by the Clinton administration, with Ukraine being one of the countries identified as a key target of respective policies.

In short, the U.S. view on Ukraine became more centred on Ukraine itself, moving away from solely seeing the country as a non-proliferation problem and recipient of economic aid. On the official side, Deputy Secretary of State Strobe Talbott, in a Statement before the Subcommittee on European Affairs of the Senate Foreign Relations Committee, stated in June 1993 that

> [a]s a large and resource-rich country in the center of Europe, Ukraine has a crucial role to play in the security of Central and Eastern Europe. Ukrainian independence and sovereignty are important to the national interest of the United States; we want to see the young Ukrainian state prosper. Our relationship with Ukraine is independent of our relationship with Russia; strong

---

339 The White House, Office of the Press Secretary (1994) 'Background Briefing by Senior Administration Officials on Upcoming Visit of President Kuchma of Ukraine', Washington D.C., 21 November.
340 Cf. for example Zbigniew Brzezinski (1995) 'A Plan for Europe', p. 37.

relationships with both countries are in our national interest, as are good relations between Russia and Ukraine.[341]

At a more symbolic level, a U.S.-Ukraine Charter was signed during the above mentioned first visit of President Kuchma in Washington, containing general statements on security, political and economic cooperation. Furthermore, 1994 was proclaimed "year of Ukraine" by Vice President Al Gore. Concrete steps followed. Vice President Al Gore met President Kuchma; their meeting led to the establishment of the U.S.-Ukrainian Binational Commission (also known as the Gore-Kuchma Commission) in 1996. It held its first plenary session in May 1997, offering a forum for regular high-level consultations on a broad range of issues.[342] The Commission had four committees, focusing on trade, energy and the environment, defence and economic cooperation, respectively. It met about once a year at the highest level, President / Vice President.[343] Also in 1996, the relationship became a "strategic partnership" and was formally declared so. Although the label does not confer any specific advantages and tends to be more valued by the respective "strategic partners" than by the United States itself, its symbolic value must not be underestimated.

IV.4.2 Setbacks and frustration

Engaging with Ukraine in broader terms proved to be difficult, as the Kuchma-regime did not always qualify as a reliable partner as seen from the U.S. A number of affairs put their mark on bilateral relations from the mid-nineties onwards. In 1997, non-proliferation again became a big issue between Ukraine and the United States

---

341 Strobe Talbott, Ambassador-at-Large and Special Adviser to the Secretary on the New Independent States (1993) 'The United States and Ukraine: Broadening the Relationship', Statement before the Subcommittee on European Affairs of the Senate Foreign Relations Committee, Washington, D.C., 24 June. Cf. U.S. *Department of State Dispatch* 4(27), 5 July 1993.

342 Cf. The White House, Office of the Vice President (1997) 'Opening Statement by Vice President Al Gore, First Plenary Session, U.S.-Ukraine Binational Commission', Washington D.C., 16 May.

343 The incoming Bush-administration chose to abolish the Commission, but two of its four committees continued their work (defence and economic cooperation).

with the Bushehr project (see above). And the relationship would deteriorate further. Towards the end of the decade, Washington's faith in Ukraine's commitment to economic reform was low, not to mention very legitimate concerns about democratic development and—again—the proliferation of weapons and military materiel:

> Beginning in 1998, I think, we began to run into a period where some of the difficulties began to accumulate. There were a number of factors for this: one, the economic reform in Ukraine slowed down. [...] There was on both sides an increasing frustration. In part, on the U.S. side, that frustration reflected exaggerated expectations about how fast Ukraine could change. Sometimes we failed to recall what Ukraine was doing, that beginning in 1991, there was not one or two but three different revolutions: one, moving from a communist to a democratic political system; two, moving from a command economy to a market economy; and three, going from one part of this thing called the Soviet Union to an independent state with an independent foreign policy. [...] There was also some frustration generated by a tendency that we would see in Kyiv to say "yes" to issues, "yes" to solutions, without, perhaps, fully thinking through what was the follow-up necessary, in fact, to implement the agreement. So, frustrations would grow sometimes, because we thought we had something agreed and in the box, but then later on, five, six, eight months down the road, it still was an open issue, we had not found the right path to implement the agreement.[344]

In addition to general dissatisfaction with Kyiv's performance, concrete concerns about elections were added in 1999 when Ukrainians were to vote for a new president. The U.S. embassy held strong suspicions that the run-up to the election did not match democratic criteria, indeed observing a strange coincidence between business contributions to Kuchma's rivals and a sudden interest of the tax authorities in the respective contributing businesses. The press reported one-sidedly—with the only TV station reporting in a balanced way being subject to tax investigations. The embassy communicated its concerns to the Ukrainian Ministry of Foreign Affairs. Upon not getting any response, the decision was finally taken to go

---

344 Steven Pifer, Deputy Assistant Secretary for European and Eurasian Affairs (2003) 'The U.S.-Ukrainian Relationship: Looking to Move Forward'. Remarks to Russia and Eurasia Program Policy Leaders Forum, Center for Strategic and International Studies, Washington D.C., 13 February.

public in late October 1998.[345] However, even publicly raised concern did not have much effect, except that it allowed the United States to prove its commitment to democracy and fair elections.

The release of (at least parts of) the so-called Melnychenko tapes in November 2000, in connection with the Gongadze affair, was at the heart of an even deeper crisis. The tapes are a recording of conversations that took place in President Kuchma's office, covering a period of three years between 1998 and 2000. Excerpts of the recordings were published in 2000 in the aftermath of Georgyi Gongadze's disappearance, a journalist and editor-in-chief of the critical on-line newspaper *Ukrayinska Pravda*. His headless body had been found in a forest two months after he was kidnapped. The recordings contain discussions between President Kuchma, former President Kravchuk and an unidentified third person, linking President Kuchma to the abduction (though not killing) of the journalist.[346] Kuchma always claimed that the recordings were forged. Despite valid objections being raised against the mere technical feasibility of such an undertaking as taping conversations in a presidential office without detection, the recordings were tested and found authentic by analysts in the United States. Washington at first considered the matter a domestic question, but later on requested Ukraine to set in motion a process of investigations.[347]

However, the biggest blow for Washington was yet to come. Whereas the Gongadze affair certainly did not do any good for Ukraine's credentials as a democracy functioning under the rule of law, it had not directly touched U.S. interests. Ukrainian violations of non-proliferation rules, in turn, did — and were not limited to one occasion: not only did Kyiv export weapons to Macedonia (where NATO's peace-keeping mission Allied Harmony was ongoing), President Kuchma moreover authorised the transfer of a new, state-

---

345 Interview with former U.S. official, Washington D.C., 19 October 2007.
346 For translated excerpts of the transcription, see: Radio Free Europe / Radio Liberty (2005) 'Transcript: "What Do Melnychenko's Tapes Say About Gongadze Case?"', 3 March.
347 Author's interview with a former U.S. official, Washington D.C., 19 October 2007.

of-the-art Kolchuga passive radar system to Iraq, potentially endangering U.S. (and other) aircraft.[348] The arms sale to Iraq moreover was tantamount to a clear violation of a U.N. embargo against Saddam Hussein's regime. In short, U.S.-Ukrainian relations had thus reached a new low point, with very little confidence for Kyiv left in Washington:

> In the [years 2001-2003] we have had a period where problems have grown. [...] The question of arms transfers to Macedonia, which was an issue not just between the United States and Ukraine, but between NATO and Ukraine, where, at several points, we thought we had an agreement, and then that agreement appeared to come undone. There have been some democracy questions. [...] Election problems that we saw even last March [2002] in terms of an election process that was not at all that bad by the terms of the region, but was still less than we had hoped for or would have expected [...]. All of this in September [2002] led to a decision by the government to take a look at the relationship between the United States and Ukraine. That review ran a bit longer than we expected, in part because we wanted to have the visit of the U.S. experts team on Kolchuga to Ukraine, once they had the invitation from the Ukrainian Government. Then it took a while to digest that.[349]

On the Kolchuga issue, there was a certain willingness in Washington to accept Kuchma declaring that he actually 'had not meant it', i.e., that he simply had acquiesced in order to get 'people out of his office' and would later on revoke his approval (as he supposedly had done on many occasions earlier).[350] Yet, the Ukrainian side strictly denied the authorisation ever taking place, contrary to — as the U.S. believed — evidence provided by the Melnychenko recordings.[351] In reaction to Washington's anger, Kyiv invited American and British investigators to Ukraine in order to verify that a transfer

---

348 The system is "passive" because it does not emit signals itself, which in turn means it cannot be detected or localised. It hence allows for the tracking of aircraft without being noticed.
349 Steven Pifer, Deputy Assistant Secretary for European and Eurasian Affairs (2003) 'The U.S.-Ukrainian Relationship: Looking to Move Forward'.
350 Author's interview with a former U.S. official, Washington D.C., 19 October 2007.
351 U.S. Department of State, Richard Boucher, Spokesman (2002) 'Daily Press Briefing', Washington D.C., 6 November.

of the radar system had not taken place.[352] The team came back with more questions than answers and the impression that 'something was hidden there'.[353] Washington was clearly dissatisfied with the investigations' outcome, as Ukrainian authorities were said to have

> failed to provide our teams, our US / UK team, with satisfactory evidence that the transfer to Iraq did or could not have taken place. So the question is still open. If they had wanted to answer it they could have answered while our team was there. We've asked them follow-up questions now, which they have not responded to.[354]

On the democracy side, the United States informed Kyiv early in 2002, that if the elections to be held later that same year would be acceptable, then Washington was willing to turn the page on previous irritations and finally fulfil Kuchma's wish to meet with President Bush in Washington. Again, Kyiv chose to not respond, despite constant claims that it wanted better relations.[355]

All these events eventually led Washington to reassess its relations with Ukraine.[356] Despite all the setbacks described above, the United States could not afford to abandon Ukraine, however. Although the relations were difficult, they were at least continued. Washington offering indulgence (yet ignored by Kyiv) illustrates the existing interest in better relations with Ukraine, although the perspectives were less than promising in the years 2002 / 2003. Financial aid from the U.S. to Ukraine was frozen as a consequence. Conclusions reached during the review process were that

---

352 U.S. Department of State, Philip T. Reeker, Deputy Spokesman (2002) 'Daily Press Briefing', Washington D.C., 2 October.
353 Author's interview with a former U.S. official, Washington D.C., 19 October 2007.
354 U.S. Department of State, Richard Boucher, Spokesman (2002) 'Daily Press Briefing', Washington D.C., 6 November.
355 Author's interview with a former U.S. official, Washington D.C., 19 October 2007.
356 Cf. 'US punishes Ukraine over Iraq claim', BBC News Online, 1 February 2003.

Ukraine still matters to the United States. It is important to us that Ukraine succeed, and our definition of success is that Ukraine develop as a stable, independent, democratic state with a strong market economy that is increasingly linked to Europe and European and transatlantic institutions.

Pifer continued by stressing that

while we have had some problems in the last couple of years, it remains in our interest to seek to engage Ukraine in a broad manner and a robust manner to try to address the problems that we have on the bilateral agenda.[357]

For that reason, the policy of the United States towards Ukraine was designed to continue to be a policy of engagement, in economic, foreign policy, defence, and democracy issues. Despite continued engagement, then U.S. Ambassador to Ukraine Carlos Pascual however stated that 'Ukraine right now [January 2003] represents one of, if not the biggest, unsolved security challenges in Europe'[358], adding that '[he] would characterize the relationship between the United States and Ukraine as perhaps the most difficult since independence', adding that 'trust has been eroded'.[359]

IV.4.3 Multilateralising Ukraine's transformation: Ukraine and NATO

Given that Washington's ideas about the future of Central and Eastern Europe's security landscape mainly consisted of integration into Euro-Atlantic structures, the question of Ukraine's relations with NATO was central. With Ukraine's accession to the WTO settled[360], NATO membership remained the last major question to be solved. Yet, Ukraine's relations with the Alliance followed a pattern similar to that of its relations with the United States, i.e., characterised by progress followed by setbacks and a general dissatisfaction

---

357 Steven Pifer, Deputy Assistant Secretary for European and Eurasian Affairs (2003) 'The U.S.-Ukrainian Relationship: Looking to Move Forward'.
358 Carlos Pascual, U.S. Ambassador to Ukraine (2003) 'U.S.-Ukraine Relations', remarks at the Russia and Eurasia Program Policy Leaders Forum, Washington D.C.: Center for Strategic and International Studies, 9 January.
359 Ibid.
360 Ukraine joined the WTO in 2008, cf. WTO (2008) 'WTO welcomes Ukraine as a New Member', WTO press release 2008/511, Geneva, 5 February.

with Kyiv's achievements and commitments in Brussels and various other capitals.

When starting to think about the future role of Ukraine in Europe, Washington realised that it needed a Ukrainian parallel of the NATO dual track processes with Russia, given the country's importance.[361] Since membership was unthinkable then (and continues to be unlikely for the foreseeable future), the solution eventually sought was a "distinctive partnership" between Ukraine and the Alliance, going beyond the mechanisms and consultation framework the Partnership for Peace programme had to offer. After having been a Partner Country within the Alliance's Partnership for Peace framework since 1994, Ukraine obtained closer links with the Alliance with the signature of the "Charter on a Distinctive Partnership between the North Atlantic Treaty Organisation and Ukraine" at NATO's 1997 Madrid summit.[362] In the words of then Deputy Secretary of State Strobe Talbott,

> [...] a lot of work went into the selection of that word "distinctive". Some of us literally thumbed through the thesaurus to make sure we ended up with exactly the right adjective. Part of the task—strategic as well as semantic—was to ensure that the NATO-Ukraine relationship had independent, indeed, distinctive significance, while taking into account the importance—to the US, to Ukraine, to NATO—of Russia's own evolving relationship with the alliance.[363]

On the institutional side, the Charter established the NATO-Ukraine Commission (NUC) with the task 'to ensure proper implementation of the Charter's provisions, broadly assess the development of the NATO-Ukraine relationship, survey planning for future activities and suggest ways to improve or further develop co-operation'.[364] The first meeting of the NATO-Ukraine Council to take place on a leadership level was held during the 1997 Madrid

---

361 Interview with former U.S. official, Washington D.C., 19 October 2007.
362 Available at NATO's homepage, www.nato.int.
363 Strobe Talbott, Deputy Secretary of State (1998) 'The New Ukraine in the New Europe', Address at the Workshop on Ukraine-NATO Relations sponsored by the Harvard University Project on Ukrainian Security and the Stanford-Harvard Preventive Defense Project, Washington D.C.: Brookings Institution, 8 April. Cf. U.S. *Department of State Dispatch*, May 1998, pp. 14 ff.
364 Cf. NATO's homepage at www.nato.int.

summit. The desired scenario was to gradually build a closer relationship between the Alliance and Ukraine.

Yet, Ukraine itself torpedoed its chance to engage in an even closer relationship with NATO. The Kolchuga affair occurred only shortly before the November 2002 NATO summit in Prague, at which, according to initial plans, Ukraine should obtain closer links with the Alliance. Although the summit's main event was the invitation to join the Alliance for seven Central European countries, the NATO-Ukraine Action Plan was designed to constitute an important step forward for Kyiv. Yet, the North Atlantic Council decided ahead of the summit that the NATO-Ukraine Commission meeting to be held there should take place at ministerial level only, thus effectively withdrawing the invitation for Leonid Kuchma.[365] The Kolchuga issue hung like a cloud over Ukraine during the summit — especially when Kuchma eventually turned up on its second day. In a last minute action which figures among the more creative moments of diplomatic history, Secretary General George Robertson allegedly decided to base the alphabetically determined seating order for the final meeting of heads of state and government on French country names instead of using the usual English. By switching to NATO's second official language, it could at least be avoided that the Ukrainian president would be sitting in between the prime minister of the United Kingdom (*Royaume Uni*) and the president of the United States (*États-Unis*), instead ending up seven seats away from the former and thirty from the latter.[366] At the same time, the fact that the Secretary General had to resort to that kind of means illustrates the degree to which NATO-Ukrainian relations had been damaged.

---

365 Cf. The U.S. Department of State, Richard Boucher, Spokesman (2002) 'Daily Press Briefing', Washington D.C., 31 October.
366 For an account, see for instance Stephen Castle (2002) 'Diplomacy in French saves embarrassment for Nato', *The Independent*, London, 23 November.

Ukraine nevertheless took part in a number of NATO exercises and peacekeeping missions, among them operations in Bosnia-Herzegovina and Kosovo.[367] When adopting a new military doctrine in 2004, 'Euro-Atlantic integration' was declared a foreign policy priority, although there was no explicit mention of the Alliance.[368] After the Orange Revolution at the end of 2004, things evolved more drastically. The newly elected president, Victor Yushchenko, 'pushed for acquiring a NATO-MAP'.[369] A MAP—or Membership Action Plan—firmly sets a country on the road towards membership by gradually implementing NATO standards in all relevant fields. Consequently, obtaining a MAP would have been a very significant step for Ukraine. Yet, Kyiv itself once more prevented closer ties with the Alliance, as 'the prospects of Ukraine receiving a MAP program at NATO's Riga summit in November 2006 rapidly evaporated after the election of the Yanukovych government in the summer of 2006.'[370] The comeback of Victor Yanukovych as Prime Minister marked the return of the pro-Russian forces in Ukrainian politics, hence also establishing NATO critics among the leading figures of government. An incident led to the cancellation of an annually held routine exercise, when the Crimean peninsula was declared a "NATO-free zone" in May 2006. In September that year, Yanukovych, referring to insufficient popular support, declared that because of the political situation in Ukraine, 'we will have to take a pause' in Ukraine's efforts to join the Alliance.[371]

---

[367] Cf. the Ukrainian Mission to NATO's homepage for details: www.ukraine.be, then "Ukraine-NATO" (accessed 8 March 2008).

[368] Janusz Bugajski (2007) *The Eastern Dimension of America's New European Allies*, p. 33.

[369] Janusz Bugajski (2007) *The Eastern Dimension of America's New European Allies*, p. 33.

[370] Janusz Bugajski (2007) *The Eastern Dimension of America's New European Allies*, p. 34.

[371] NATO, NATO Press Services (2006) 'Press Point with NATO Secretary General, Jaap de Hoop Scheffer and the Prime Minister of Ukraine, Viktor Yanukovych after the meeting of the NATO-Ukraine Commission at ambassadorial level', NATO Headquarters, Brussels, 14 September.

The Bush administration's objective of making Ukraine enter NATO took another blow in 2008, although elections had brought "Orange" forces back to power. At the Alliance's April 2008 Bucharest summit, the U.S. and Poland suffered a setback in promoting the country's accession to the Alliance, running into the open opposition of major Western European allies. In the end, the concrete decision on whether Ukraine should or should not be granted a Membership Action Plan (MAP) was postponed until at least the Foreign Ministers' meeting in December 2008, although NATO members agreed in principle that Ukraine should become a member of the Alliance — without, however, any concrete decisions on a timeframe.[372] At December's Foreign Minister's meeting at the Alliances Headquarters in Brussels, enlargement was then *de facto* postponed indefinitely. Yet again, resistance by some of the European allies — most prominently France and Germany — left no choice for the U.S. but to agree that Georgia and Ukraine 'are not ready for membership and still have many, many standards that they would have to meet'.[373] NATO nevertheless decided to enhance cooperation with Ukraine within the framework of its existing partnership.[374] As of 2017, Ukraine's accession to the Alliance seems more distant than ever.

IV.4.4 Foreign Policy Tools in promoting Ukraine's Euro-Atlantic integration

U.S.-Ukrainian relations as described in the above section clearly allow for classifying Kyiv as undecided from a Washington vantage point. With respect to the question of Ukraine's integration into

---

372 Cf. 'Joint Statement', Meeting of the NATO-Ukraine Commission at the level of Heads of State and Government, Bucharest, 4 April 2008 (NATO Press Release (2008)051).
373 U.S. Department of State, Office of the Spokesman (2008) 'Remarks on the NATO Foreign Ministers Meeting', remarks by Secretary Condoleezza Rice, Washington D.C., 26 November.
374 Cf. NATO Press Services (2008) 'Introductory Remarks by Secretary General Jaap de Hoop Scheffer at the meeting of the NATO-Ukraine Commission with Invitees at the Level of Foreign Ministers', Brussels, 3 December.

transatlantic frameworks, the country once more qualified as an undecided state as seen from Washington. This is also underlined by the 2008 assessment that

> The previous Ukraine Government [i.e. the Kuchma government prior to the Orange Revolution] balanced Ukraine's relationship with Europe and the United States with strong ties with Russia, including pursuing the Single Economic Space project with Russia, Belarus, and Kazakhstan.[375]

Back in 1994, hopes for improved relations were not only expressed at the occasion of state visits, but truly characterised U.S. thinking on Ukraine. Reality, however, soon brought deception. The Kolchuga affair is thus explicitly mentioned as the cause for a 'setback' in bilateral relations in the above quoted version of the Background Note:

> Bilateral relations suffered a setback in September 2002 when the U.S. Government announced it had authenticated a recording of President Kuchma's July 2000 decision to transfer a Kolchuga early warning system to Iraq.

In sum, a lack of continuity characterised U.S. views on Ukraine's status, therefore justifying Kyiv's categorisation as an unfriendly state.

Unlike the previous matters (denuclearisation and Ukraine's accession to the MTCR), the question of Ukraine's Euro-Atlantic future is not a matter to be negotiated with a concrete result to be obtained. In other words, in addressing the question of Ukraine's future within the wider Euro-Atlantic framework, Washington entered the realm of principles and abstract issues. Expectations expressed by the United States thus mainly concerned the respect of specific codes of conduct, both domestic and international. At first, as long as Washington was satisfied with the path taken by Kyiv, positive power was the dominating approach.

---

375 U.S. Department of State (2008) 'Background Note: Ukraine', Washington D.C., May.

- Positive material power tools: considerable financial support, at least partly contingent on progress on specific issues (i.e., ratification of START I and joining the Non-Proliferation Treaty)
- Positive symbolic power tools: allowing Ukraine to enter the international political stage (Gore-Kuchma Commission since 1996 etc.), providing a forum for Ukraine through superpower backing and demonstrative high-level contacts, engaging Ukraine in NATO (NATO-Ukraine Charter of 1997), seven visits to the United States by President Kuchma between 1996 and 1999

By about 1998-99, when bilateral difficulties became increasingly apparent, the use of positive power diminished at the expense of more and more negative power. High-level contacts became increasingly rare, President Kuchma was denied contact with President Clinton, and the country was the object of public criticism on more than one occasion.

- Negative symbolic power tools: denied high-level contacts, voicing public concern over Ukrainian developments (democracy), denying displayed good relations (change of the seating order at NATO's 2002 Prague summit), no more presidential visits to Washington (until 2005, i.e. after the Orange Revolution), public announcement of intentions to review relations with Ukraine
- Negative material power tools: freezing financial aid

Previously granted advantages and aid were thus withdrawn, which even increases the measures' character of punishment.

The apparent tendency when it comes to U.S. attempts at promoting Ukraine's Euro-Atlantic integration as well as the country's general behaviour in international politics is thus that the use of positive and negative power tools is linked to the target country's attitude. The friendlier Ukraine positions itself vis-à-vis Washington, the more foreign policy tools applied by Washington are based on positive power. *Vice versa*, the more unfriendly Kyiv appears from an American vantage point, the more Washington is inclined to resort to negative power tools.

IV.5 After the Orange Revolution: diminished U.S. interest 2004 to 2008

IV.5.1 Few illusions left: the Orange Revolution and its aftermath

Ukraine's presidential elections in October and November 2004 resulted in a several weeks' long tug-of-war between the proclaimed winner, Victor Yanukovych, and the opposition leader and pro-Western candidate, Victor Yushchenko. Not only did Yushchenko supporters quickly raise accusations of election fraud. The subsequent struggle between the two camps became known as the Orange Revolution. The standoff eventually resulted in a victory of the opposition after a new round of elections which was agreed upon in November 2004 and held in December that same year. In January 2005, Victor Yushchenko officially became Leonid Kuchma's successor as president of Ukraine. One month later, the *Rada* confirmed Yulia Timoshenko as head of government. While the events were unfolding, the United States acted with restraint, although Washington was not entirely passive. In a statement on 24 November, Secretary of State Colin Powell hence declared that

> [i]ndeed, this is a critical moment. It is time for Ukrainian leaders to decide whether they are on the side of democracy or not, whether they respect the will of the people or not. If the Ukrainian Government does not act immediately and responsibly, there will be consequences for our relationship, for Ukraine's hopes for Euro-Atlantic integration and for individuals responsible for perpetrating fraud.[376]

Yet, the "consequences" to which Powell referred were never specified. Later on, Senators McCain and Lugar were Bush's special envoys to Ukraine under the second round of elections in 2004. Among the most credible allegations on American non-official support for the democratic forces is, for example, German Marshall

---

376 U.S. Department of State, Secretary Colin L. Powell (2004) 'Briefing by Secretary of State Colin L. Powell', Washington D.C., 24 November.

Fund support for youth organisations. Overall, however, Washington chose to avoid large-scale intervention for several reasons; most importantly, Washington had confidence in the Europeans', especially Polish president Kwaśniewski's, ability to assist in solving the crisis.[377] During press briefings, it thus sounded as if the United States was keeping a low profile, as the State Department spokesman for instance explained after a telephone conversation between Secretary Powell and Leonid Kuchma, pertaining to the ongoing debate on whether new elections should be held:

> QUESTION: But you are confident that the new election idea did not come up in the Secretary's conversation with the President? Because, I mean, the reason why we're asking is because this has got some similarities -- not a lot, but it has some -- to what happened in Georgia, where after the Secretary's intervention with President Shevardnadze in a different situation -- he wasn't stepping down, he wanted to stay in power -- but, you know, things happened as a result of intervention by the US, by the Russians, by others. So that's why --
> MR. BOUCHER [State Department Spokesman]: And we certainly would hope that things would happen as a result of the Secretary's phone calls and the intervention, what the U.S. Embassy is doing and what other nations are doing. The OSCE is very involved. European nations are very involved in making their position known. And we would certainly hope, first of all, that the international community would pursue this, as we seem to be doing perhaps a little more now, by all pointing in the same direction, by all pointing in the direction of using these legal and political processes in Ukraine to resolve it. Second of all, we hope the Ukrainians will take that seriously and that all the parties in Ukraine will maintain a peaceful approach to this matter and try to look for ways to help solve these matters. So certainly we believe that our intervention is designed to try to move things forward and help them work it out, but precisely which outcome they arrive at is not the most important thing to us. The most important thing to us is that it's an outcome that respects the Ukraine, respects the will of the people of Ukraine, and respects the legal institutions and processes and the political process that they have within the country.[378]

---

377 Cf. U.S. Department of State, Spokesman Richard Boucher (2004) 'Daily Briefing', Washington D.C., 29 November, see also Steven Pifer (2007) 'European Mediators and Ukraine's Orange Revolution', *Problems of Post-Communism* 54(6), pp. 5-53.

378 U.S. Department of State, Office of the Spokesman (2004) 'Daily Briefing', briefing by Spokesman Richard Boucher, Washington D.C., 29 November.

In the aftermath of the revolution, the newly elected President Yushchenko was warmly welcomed by the U.S. administration. President Bush called him on the telephone, and Secretary Powell attended his inauguration in Kyiv in January 2005, looking forward to improved relations with Ukraine and progress on specific issues:

> We will make clear to them the kinds of things that we're expecting and hoping to see happen with respect to intellectual property rights and other structural issues that they have to deal with. They know what these issues are, and now they have a new president who will have to take on these issues and resolve them. But we shouldn't let the challenges that are ahead in any way diminish the historic nature of tomorrow's inauguration. He's taking over with a great deal of energy, and with the best wishes of the Ukrainian people and the international community, and I think he fully understands the challenges that are ahead and that he has to deal with. The United States will help him.[379]

Revolutions tend to be seen as watersheds in history. Yet, although the revolution was successful, it could not resist eating its own children shortly thereafter. In September 2005, President Yushchenko discharged Yulia Timoshenko from the post of prime minister, where she was eventually replaced by Yushchenko's former opponent, Victor Yanukovych. As a consequence, Ukraine's unified pro-Western leadership was a matter of the past, as soon became obvious. The ensuing chaos around the formation of a new government eventually led the United States to cancel a planned state visit by George W. Bush to Kyiv in June 2006.[380] Most notably however, in early June 2006, the Crimean regional parliament declared the peninsula a "NATO-free zone", thereby preventing the US / NATO "Sea Breeze 2006" exercise.[381] When asked on the day of the announcement of Bush's trip to Hungary—the replacement for Ukraine—why the President wasn't going to Kyiv, White House spokesman Tony Snow replied

---

379 U.S. Department of State, Office of the Spokesman (2005) 'Remarks En Route To Kiev', remarks by Secretary Colin L. Powell, Kyiv, 22 January.
380 Cf. The White House, Office of the Press Secretary (2006) 'Press Briefing by Tony Snow', Washington D.C., 8 June.
381 Cf. for instance Deutsche Welle (2006) 'Regionalparlament der Krim protestiert gegen NATO-Manöver', 8 June.

> [t]he President will be going to Kiev. We've just postponed the trip. There will be a trip, but we're going to go to Budapest. This wasn't a good time, and we're going to find a better time.[382]

Domestically in Ukraine, tensions between the Yanukovych and Yushchenko camps were unavoidable and in April 2007, Yushchenko resorted to dissolving the parliament. The September 2007 elections resulted in victory for the (again allied) coalition between the respective parties of President Yushchenko and former Prime Minister Yulia Timoshenko. Although the coalition lost its majority in 2008, the Timoshenko government continued to work in minority through a number of crises.

After a short renewed bloom, relations between Washington and Kyiv were back to their pre-revolution moroseness. In U.S.-Ukrainian relations, the Orange Revolution thus had little major long-term effect. For some time, the events on the *Maidan* and Yushchenko's subsequent victory helped to overcome the lingering Ukraine-fatigue in Washington. As Ukrainian politics returned to pre-revolutionary patterns, however, the Revolution's effects quickly faded. With, moreover, Ukraine's WTO accession now settled and its NATO membership highly unlikely in the foreseeable future, there were rather few concrete issues left to be resolved. The Bush II Administration's focus on other regions in the world and September 11 and its aftermath did not contribute to keeping Ukraine on top of the agenda either. A certain U.S. disengagement from Ukrainian affairs consequently followed.

In light of relative U.S. disengagement, and borrowing the term of non-policy from Geir Lundestad, it is thus worth looking at what was actually *lacking* in U.S.-Ukrainian relations. Despite considerable activity in the security field throughout the 1990s and until today, as well as continuous calls for democracy and free market economy, U.S.-Ukrainian relations were in fact characterised by the absence of policy elements usually present in friendly relations.

---

382 The White House, Office of the Press Secretary (2006) 'Press Briefing by Tony Snow', Washington D.C., 8 June.

U.S. approaches to Ukraine continued to be mainly focused on security issues. As a consequence, other fields such as trade and cultural exchange were neglected.

At a general level, high-level contacts notably diminished in frequency since the 1990s. The Gore-Kuchma Commission was abolished, and the United States withdrew from the Polish-American-Ukrainian Cooperation Initiative. Ukrainian citizens continued to have to go through a long application process in order to obtain a visa for the US, including tourist visits. Even before Ukraine's accession to the World Trade Organisation (WTO), specific steps could have been taken to facilitate trade between the United States and Ukraine—but were not taken. Visa regulations in force did not facilitate trade. Ukraine's "graduation" from the Jackson-Vanik Amendment (restricting trade) took place on 8 March 2006, but the United States did not seem to be particularly interested in bilateral investment agreements. Soon afterwards, the U.S. and Ukraine signed a new Trade and Investment Cooperation Agreement, establishing a forum for discussion of bilateral trade and investment relations.[383] Yet, such an Agreement is less important than a free-trade agreement—which was never on the agenda in Washington. In economic and trade terms, Washington was thus rather standing by whereas the European Union took active steps towards Ukraine's integration in the European economy.[384] Particularly, U.S.-Ukrainian trade relations continued to be characterised by problems. During the late 1990s, business disputes poisoned the investment climate, with Ukraine being either unwilling or unable—or perhaps both—to solve the problems. Among the core issues were questions related to copyright and intellectual property, as Ukraine was considered Eastern Europe's main producer of pirated

---

[383] Office of the United States Trade Representative (2008) *Trade and Investment Co-operation Agreement Between the Government of Ukraine and the Government of the United States of America*, Washington 28 March and Kyiv 1 April.

[384] EU-Ukrainian trade relations were at that point based on a Partnership and Co-Operation Agreement (PCA). Negotiations on the Association Agreement began in 2012.

goods (especially music, videos and computer software), with intellectual property rights being traditionally dear to Washington.

As far as security is concerned, Washington and Kyiv signed the "United States-Ukraine Charter on Strategic Partnership" in December 2008.[385] The Charter foresaw intended cooperation in the fields of defence, security, economics and trade, energy security as well as cultural exchange. More importantly, it also reiterated the United States' commitment to Ukraine's accession to NATO. Yet, little concrete action followed — very likely due to the fact that the Charter was signed in the last weeks of the Bush II administration, thus perhaps representing some sort of legacy to Obama rather than a forceful act of foreign policy. At the same time, the Charter may well be viewed as Washington's plan B after it failed to obtain an invitation for Kyiv to join NATO at the Bucharest summit earlier that year. In that sense, its concrete implications are less important than its symbolic value.

All these measures notwithstanding, declined interest is obvious as well as a tendency to "outsource" its Ukrainian policies to Warsaw in the late years of George W. Bush's administration. What perhaps most evidently became apparent during the Orange Revolution, when Washington trusted Kwaśniewski's ability to solve the crisis, had in fact been developing for a number of years. With regard to Ukraine, Poland and the United States largely share the same strategic vision of a Ukraine (institutionally) anchored in the West. From early on, Poland has seen itself in the role of an advocate for Ukraine, and has likewise been willing to be a Western 'ambassador' in Kyiv. Anchoring the neighbour in the West was thus a declared ambition of Polish foreign policy, reiterated in many foreign policy declarations such as the following:

---

[385] Cf. U.S. Department of State, Bureau of European and Eurasian Affairs (2008) *United States-Ukraine Charter on Strategic Partnership*, Washington D.C., 19 December.

we are proponents of integration of the European Union, of further enlargement of the European Union, primarily through the accession of such countries as Ukraine and Moldova, of further expansion of the European Union eastwards.[386]

In order to realise these objectives, Warsaw actively sought support in Washington, which eventually led to a number of trilateral instruments. The founding of the Polish-American-Ukrainian Partnership Initiative (PAUCI) in 1999 illustrated Poland's reinvigorated ambitions as well as the American desire to engage Ukraine. The main purpose of the Initiative was to provide technical assistance, based on an idea that it indeed seems sensible: instead of learning from the Americans, Ukrainians should benefit from the Polish experience with economic transformation. At a more abstract level, it moreover intended to 'strengthen the emerging cooperative relationship between Ukraine and Poland'.[387] The Initiative had a rocky start with problems on all three sides, but eventually turned out to be a workable channel. Several million dollars were invested by Washington via the United States Agency for International Development (USAID), which were administered by Freedom House. Throughout the years of its existence, 'PAUCI funded 185 partnership grants to 424 organizations throughout Ukraine and Poland totalling 4,332,628 million U.S. dollars'.[388] Three years after PAUCI was founded, Ukraine suggested adding a political dimension in 2002. This suggestion was received positively and resulted in the creation of a channel at the level of deputy assistant secretaries, who met approximately once every six months. The first session took place in Washington D.C. in 2002. Initial concerns that the Polish, seen as advocates for Ukraine, would be unable to deliver tough messages to the Ukrainians proved wrong. Matters of interest encompassed the improvement of Ukraine's relations with the EU and NATO as well as questions of energy security. The PAUCI-channel was generally considered valuable in Washington.[389]

---

386 Cf. Anna Fotyga (2007) 'Annual Address to the Sejm', Warsaw, 11 May.
387 Cf. www.pauci.org, accessed 13 November 2007.
388 Cf. www.pauci.org. accessed 13 November 2007.
389 Author's interview with a former U.S. official, 19 October 2007.

Nevertheless, after years of comparably high activity in Eastern European affairs, a decline in U.S. involvement is observable since the end of the Clinton Administration. The United States withdrew from a number of trilateral initiatives pursued throughout the 1990s. Particularly, the U.S. has considerably reduced its engagement since George W. Bush came to power in 2001. For instance, the Polish-American-Ukrainian Cooperation Initiative has been renamed and remodelled in 2005, and, along the process, became a bilateral Polish-Ukrainian instrument. Yet, PAUCI's 'key focus areas' are still defined as 'advocacy for closer integration with Euro-Atlantic structures, administrative and local government reform, international and EU business standards, ethical standards in public life and youth empowerment'.[390]

Washington's decreasing presence coincided with a more assertive Polish foreign policy, with Warsaw expressing the ambition to provide regional leadership. As long as this regional leadership did not interfere with U.S. global ambitions, Washington's look upon Polish efforts was favourable. The United States indeed welcomed Poland's more prominent role in Ukraine, qualifying the country as 'Ukraine's gateway to the West'.[391]

IV.5.2 Foreign policy tools 2004 to 2008

As regards Ukraine's status, the pattern of earlier years is again observable: after a brief intermezzo commonly referred to as the Orange Revolution, Ukraine went back to holding an undecided position vis-à-vis the United States. According to the May 2008 Background Note,

---

[390] Cf. the PAUCI-homepage at http://pauci.org/en/about/, accessed 13 November 2007
[391] U.S. Department of State, Office of the Spokesman (2007) 'Poland as Ukraine's Gateway to the West', remarks by Paula J. Dobriansky, United States Under Secretary for Democracy and Global Affairs at the Heritage Foundation, Washington, D.C., 18 January.

> Ukraine's democratic "Orange Revolution" has led to closer cooperation and more open dialogue between Ukraine and the United States. U.S. policy remains centered on realizing and strengthening a democratic, prosperous, and secure Ukraine more closely integrated into European and Euro-Atlantic structures.[392]

The relationship however continued to be characterised by occasional disagreement over issues considered central by Washington, thus leading U.S. officials to view Kyiv overall as undecided even after the Orange Revolution.

American expectations with regard to Ukraine from 2004 to 2008 were a continuation of the U.S. approach prior to the Orange Revolution. Thus, Washington again mainly asked for the respect of key principles and Kyiv's promise to behave like a reliable member of the international system. At the same time, it is also apparent that U.S. policies towards Ukraine had lost momentum. A decreased level of engagement on the United States' part is observable. The major questions pertaining to nuclear weapons and nonproliferation were solved; remaining issues like a Ukrainian NATO membership did, in turn, seem unsolvable. In other words, what could be done had been done. Matters were getting more and more abstract, being related to principles of good governance, democracy and economic reform rather than concrete issues to be tackled by hands-on measures.

- Negative symbolic power tools: threatening with (unspecified) consequences for bilateral relations in case of electoral fraud, threatening with personal consequences for those engaged in fraud, cancelling the June 2006 state visit
- Positive symbolic power tools: promoting Ukraine's NATO membership, promoting Ukraine's WTO membership, state visits (Yushchenko in Washington, April 2005; Bush in Kyiv, April 2008), signature of the United States-Ukraine Charter on Strategic Partnership

---

392 U.S. Department of State (2008) 'Background Note: Ukraine', Washington D.C., May.

Washington's continued promotion of Ukraine's membership in the World Trade Organisation (successfully) and NATO (unsuccessfully) cannot belie the fact that U.S. policies towards Ukraine declined in intensity. In sum, post-Orange Revolution American towards Ukraine illustrate that undecided states are met with both positive and negative power tools.

IV.6 Conclusions on U.S. foreign policies towards Ukraine

As became clear in the above account of U.S.-Ukrainian relations from 1991 to 2008, Ukraine indeed qualified as an undecided state, moving back and forth between friendship with the United States and relations characterised by a high degree of tension and dissatisfaction.

The described ambivalence on Kyiv's part led to the necessity, for Washington, to deal with Ukraine wearing velvet gloves, lest provoking a shift in attitude towards permanent unfriendliness. The foreign policy tools observable in U.S. policies towards Ukraine in the years 1991 to 2008 therefore belong to both positive and negative categories of power. The Ukrainian case hence confirms the assumption that both positive and negative power tools are used in addressing undecided states.

At the core of U.S. approaches towards Ukraine were two very different issues: Washington, on the one hand, wanted Kyiv to get rid of something it owned (nuclear weapons) and to adopt something it lacked (free market economy and democracy). These two core elements were essentially different in nature, with respect to the foreign policy tools applicable. Compliance with U.S. demands was not necessarily in Ukraine's interest. Whilst possessing nuclear weapons could in general be seen as an asset rather than a liability, the ruling elites in Ukraine probably benefited more from opaque economic governance intrinsically intertwined with politics than from democracy and Western-style free market economy. In other words, "shared values" were no incentive in its own right from Kyiv's perspective, which meant that additional incentives had to come into play.

Throughout the 1990s, relations with Ukraine were of a kind that did not allow for the trust usually characterising friendship among states. Ukrainian compliance with U.S. wishes each time came at a considerable cost for Washington: for every concession Ukraine was to make, the United States had to provide generous compensation. Given that the U.S. administration considered the issues at hand crucial to its own interest (most importantly, denuclearisation and making Ukraine join the MTCR), Washington at last essentially resorted to paying for what it wanted from Kyiv. Compensation could be financial (or lead to financial gains such as the space launch market deal) or symbolic (security "assurances"). This, however, is not the way friends deal with each other, as U.S. officials were quick to point out. In sum, if U.S. Ukrainian relations were to be characterised in one single term, "expensive" would be the word.

U.S.-Ukrainian relations 1991–2008 were hence more a matter of carrots than a matter of sticks. Lacking leverage over Ukraine, the United States did not have many negative power tools with which to exert power over Ukraine—at least no such tools which could be used at reasonable costs and in a way effective over the longer term. Washington thus used positive power, offering direct or indirect financial incentives each time it really wanted a specific outcome. The limits of that approach first became obvious in the context of Ukraine's accession to the MTCR, when Washington's capability to exert power was not sufficient so as to allow the U.S. to assert itself on the offensive missile issue. It later on became even more obvious when the more abstract issues of democratisation and economic reform were on the agenda.

Compared to security matters (first and foremost: denuclearisation), Washington has been less successful when it comes to democracy in Ukraine. Yet, democratisation never was the primary U.S. objective in the country either, although it certainly did qualify as a desirable outcome from Washington's perspective. In the long run, if the vision of a Ukraine anchored in the West were to become reality, it even is indispensable. For Euro-Atlantic integration to be the solution to the Ukrainian question, it is unavoidable for Ukraine to have a clean democratic record, to implement economic reforms and to show true and believable commitment to non-proliferation. By 2008, however, U.S. efforts in this respect were rather limited. That specific steps in order to facilitate trade were not taken was of course largely due to the lack of necessary reforms, which would have needed to be initiated by Ukraine. Yet, the U.S. would certainly have held powerful tools of conditionality in its hands if it had been pushing for these reforms. That Washington chose not to do so hence illustrates the "non-policy" towards Ukraine, naturally amplified by major Western European states' refusal to let the country join NATO within the foreseeable future. With denuclearisation achieved, the Ukrainian question had lost in urgency. Establishing sustainable trade relations seemed to be more important from Kyiv's perspective than from Washington's. Accordingly, the United States' policy mainly consisted of protecting its own businesses from product piracy and violation of intellectual property. This, however, was not specific for Ukraine but rather the general U.S. approach to international trade.

Ukraine's relative failure on the democratisation side moreover illustrates the absence of strong "soft power" on the United States' part in the Ukrainian context. The American Way of Life and American values obviously were not appealing enough to trigger Ukrainian desires to emulate the American model. Gift-wrapped rhetoric such as the declaring of a "strategic partnership" deflagrated to no effect. The U.S.-Ukrainian relationship remained narrow in nature, with a strong focus on security. Although U.S. support for the country's accession to NATO by no means was a minor occurrence, the question is to what extent this primarily was related to U.S. efforts at maintaining a specific relationship with Ukraine. Rather, it seems fair to consider the matter as part of the Bush II administration's overall master plan for the post-Cold War redefinition of the European security landscape—thus, in essence, a policy that stems from the U.S. approach to (a reinvigorated) Russia and hence a return to the patterns of the early 1990s. The fact that the incoming Obama administration toned down the matter further indicates that Ukraine *per se* was no priority (anymore) for U.S. foreign affairs.

As Taras Kuzio wrote in 2003, the pattern of Ukraine's relations with the West followed the opposite of the West's relation with Russia: When relations with Ukraine have improved, this has tended to occur simultaneously with a decline in relations between the West and Russia, and vice-versa.'[393] He distinguished different periods in Western-Ukrainian relations prior to the Orange Revolution:

> The first period is disinterest during 1992–94 when the West prioritised relations with a reformist Russia. The second period was 1995–99 when Ukraine and the West developed a strategic partnership. From 2000, Ukraine's relations with the West are best described as disillusionment due to the growing gap between official rhetoric of integration into Euro-Atlantic structures and Eurasian domestic policies.[394]

Whether the end of the line really has been reached in U.S. attempts at making Ukraine become a "Western" state remains to be seen.

---

393 Taras Kuzio (2003) 'Ukraine's Relations With the West: Disinterest, Partnership, Disillusionment', *European Security* 12(2), p. 21.
394 Ibid.

V U.S. Foreign Policies Towards Belarus

Located in Central Europe, Belarus shares its borders with Poland, Ukraine, Russia, Latvia and Lithuania. Historically part of the Russian empire, the country was occupied by Germany during World War I and declared independence in March 1918, only to become the Byelorussian Soviet Socialist Republic (BSSR) shortly thereafter in 1919. Three years later, Belarus became a founding member of the Union of Soviet Socialist Republics. On 25 August 1991, the Republic of Belarus declared itself independent from the USSR. The Belarusian nation is a recent and still disputed construct.[395] Belarusian as a language is less widely spoken than Russian, and throughout the late 1990s and the early 2000s, the idea of a Russian-Belarusian union state was on the agenda between Moscow and Minsk. Aleksandr Lukashenka's accession to power in 1994 was the tone-setting event for the country's relations with the West.

Belarus was and continues to be referred to as the last dictatorship in Europe. The United States government does not have any high level contacts with Belarusian representatives, the U.S. ambassador was forced out of the country in 2008. In short, relations with Belarus are among the worst the United States maintains with other countries.

In five sections, this chapter sets out to provide a chronological overview of U.S.-Belarusian relations in order to determine Belarus' friend / non-friend / undecided status vis-à-vis the United States and to analyse the foreign policy tools employed by the United States. Section V.1 introduces the general context of Belarus' relations with the West. This introductory section is then followed by three more detailed sections, each concluded by an analysis of foreign policy tools employed by Washington. Section V.2 deals with the early years of U.S.-Belarusian relations. The policy of Selective

---

395 Cf. Alexandra Goujon (2005) 'Nationalisme et identité en Biélorussie', in: Dov Lynch (ed.), *Changing Belarus*, Paris: EUISS Chaillot Paper no. 85.

Engagement and the Belarus Democracy Act are discussed in section V.3. Belarus and the wider international context is the topic of section V.4. Finally, the chapter ends with concluding remarks in section V.5.

V.1 Introduction: At odds with the West

After independence, Belarus' relations with the West seemed promising at first. The country quickly established diplomatic relations with the United States, Germany and other leading Western nations during the early 1990s. Under its first formal head of state, President Shushkevich, Belarus engaged in economic reform and a process of democratisation. Perhaps more importantly, Shushkevich agreed to dispose of all nuclear weapons, thus avoiding a Belarusian parallel to the Ukrainian nuclear question. These positive developments lasted, however, only until President Lukashenka took office in 1994. Since Lukashenka's accession to power, Belarus has become a *de facto* dictatorship. The 1996 referendum, deemed undemocratic by all Western observers and governments, confirmed most apprehensions. Belarus' relations with the European Union and the United States deteriorated further. In September 1997, the General Affairs Council of the EU took the decision to limit political relations until the Belarusian regime shows commitment to democracy and the rule of law and took additional steps such as withdrawing its support for Belarus's membership in the Council of Europe. Among other things, the EU declared to be 'especially concerned by the political and constitutional situation and by the recurrent violations of human rights and fundamental freedoms, in particular the freedom of the media' and 'regrets the Belarusian authorities' non-constructive, indeed obstructive, attitude to its relations with the European Union'.[396] Relations with the West hence gradually deteriorated, culminating in the so-called Drosdy affair of 1998[397]: In

---

396 Cf. the 2027th General Affairs and External Relations Council's press release 269 no. 10368/97 of 15 September 1997.
397 The United States and the EU countries eventually decided to withdraw their respective ambassadors on 22 June 1998, who did not return for more than a

clear violation of international law, the Belarusian authorities tried to force Western diplomatic missions to move their respective ambassadorial residences from Drosdy, a district of the capital city of Minsk. Coercive measures included intrusion on exterritorial grounds, preventing access by car to the U.S. residence as well as the issuing of various categorical deadlines.

The U.S. consequently failed to build a constructive rapport with Minsk. In 2005, for instance, relations with Poland reached a new low after members of the Polish minority were attacked and Polish diplomats forced to leave the country. Lukashenka took to 'actions straight out of Soviet Political Methodology 101', undermining the association of ethnic Poles' leadership with its security agents.[398] The inability of the EU to—unlike during the Drosdy affair—come up with a common position did not contribute to solving the crisis.[399] Once more, relations with Russia were deemed more important than taking a tougher stance on Belarus, as '[t]he EU, not wanting to harm relations with Belarus's historic big brother, Russia, has tried appeasing Minsk for the better part of a decade.'[400] In short, Belarus never became a Western oriented state. It has not undergone a successful transition towards becoming a democratic state under the rule of law, with a free market economy and citizens able to express themselves freely. Compared to its neighbours in the region, the country was even characterised as an 'anti-model' in terms of domestic politics.[401]

---

year. The European Union reacted by adopting travel restrictions for a list of senior Belarusian officials, shortly thereafter joined by the U.S. with a similar a list and suspending parts of its bilateral military cooperation programs.

398 Mark Lenzi (2005) 'Poles deserve the West's support', *The International Herald Tribune*, 30 July.
399 Cf. Rainer Lindner (2005) *Selbstisolierung von Belarus. Konflikte mit Polen und anderen Nachbarstaaten als Sicherheitsproblem der EU*, Berlin: SWP-Aktuell no. 43.
400 Mark Lenzi (2005) 'Poles deserve the West's support'.
401 Heinz Timmermann (2002) *Die widersprüchlichen Beziehungen Rußland-Belarus im europäischen Kontext*, Berlin: SWP-Studie no. 37, p. 7.

V.2 Belarus and the US: the early years

V.2.1 Belarus: The unproblematic answer to the nuclear question

During the early years of independence, Belarus as such was no major preoccupation in Washington, with one notable exception: Nuclear weapons. The dismantling of the Soviet nuclear arsenal and non-proliferation was the lens through which the ex-Soviet, now independent states, were perceived. Belarus thus was included in the Cooperative Threat Reduction Program (CTR), commonly referred to as the Nunn-Lugar Programme, created on the basis of legislation sponsored by senators Sam Nunn (D, Georgia) and Richard Lugar (R, Indiana). Together with Ukraine and Kazakhstan, Belarus signed the Lisbon Protocol of START I in May 1992, thereby committing itself to getting rid of all its nuclear weapons. Belarus joined the NPT as a nuclear-free state in July 1993, after having ratified START I in February the same year. All nuclear weapons stationed on its territory were accordingly transferred to Russia. Today, Belarus has no weapons of mass destruction in its possession.[402]

Over the relatively smooth denuclearisation, domestic developments in Belarus were perhaps neglected. Before Aleksandr Lukashenka came to power in 1994, Belarus was taking hesitant steps towards transition. For some, the negative developments in Belarus were a consequence of missed opportunities in supporting the country's democratic transition. In the view of David H. Swartz, the first U.S. ambassador in Minsk in office from 1991 to 1994, the 'mess in Belarus' is at least to some extent the State Department's fault, *inter alia* due to the Russocentrism of American policies towards Central Europe:

---

402 Cf. Nuclear Threat Initiative (2007) *Belarus Profile*, available at www.nti.org (accessed 25 October 2007).

Specifically, the following U.S. actions contributed to the rise of the seemingly populist but in fact repressive Lukashenko regime in Belarus: the Clinton administration's Russia uber alles policy; the near total absence of effective technical assistance to Belarus when it could have counted; the provision of over $200 million in agricultural commodities whose only "benefit" was to allow the Soviet-style agricultural system—and its super-conservative managers (the heart of Mr. Lukashenko's political support)—to survive post-Soviet market realities; the Clinton team's naive belief that Stalin-bashing via the president's visit to the Kuropaty killing field near Minsk would promote reform in Belarus; and—related to this—the administration's nearly complete lack of understanding of the political constellation of forces there.[403]

Russocentrism as an accusation is hardly surprising in the context. In the Belarusian case, once Lukashenka had become president and established his regime, it was in any case too late for the successful promotion of democracy. Swartz is not alone in his assessment that the West simply neglected Belarus. As Kaare Dahl Martinsen notes, '[o]fficial statements, politely encouraging strengthening reforms that were never implemented were issued from time to time by Western organisations'[404], the amount of aid for Belarus not being anywhere near the sums offered to other countries in the area.

Ironically, disposing of its nuclear arsenal without greater reluctance or attempts at capitalising on the weapons somehow turned out to be Belarus' greatest diplomatic error. Behaving in such an unproblematic way, compared with for instance Ukraine, diverted Washington's attention from Belarus, at a time when, in Ambassador Swartz's and many others' opinion, American support and aid could have made a difference. As the then Director for Russian and Eurasian Affairs at the National Security Council, Steven Pifer, explained in hindsight in 1996, the U.S. never felt the need to intervene in Belarus's denuclearisation process.[405] Thanks to its zigzag course, Ukraine managed to get out a lot more of its consent to

---

403 David H. Swartz (1997) 'The mess of Belarus, care of the State Department', *The Washington Times*, 5 June, p. A21.
404 Kaare Dahl Martinsen (2002) *The Russian-Belarusian Union and the Near Abroad*, Oslo: Institutt for Forsvarsstudier, p. 29.
405 U.S. Department of State, Office of the Spokesman (1996) 'Press Briefing by Mike McCurry; Bob Bell, Senior Director for Defense and Arms Control Policy at NSC; and Steven Pifer, Director for Russian and Eurasian Affairs at NSC', Washington D.C., 3 June.

denuclearisation (see above), whereas Belarus in effect never was rewarded for its cooperative approach. The 1990s, sometimes called the "lost decade" in U.S. foreign policy, are thus at least characterised by missed opportunities in Belarus.

V.2.2 Foreign policy tools in early U.S.-Belarusian relations

During the period covered in the above section, it seems hardly appropriate to speak of U.S.-Belarusian relations at all. For Washington, Minsk was far from being an issue on the agenda. For the years 1991 to 1994, little proof of U.S. expectations regarding Belarus (beyond denuclearisation, in which the United States was, however, not involved) could be found. Whether the United States should have provided more support for Belarus is ultimately a normative question and hence not — strictly speaking — relevant in the present context. Yet, what is clear is that the very low level of involvement left Washington bereft of vehicles for the U.S. to exert power over Belarus. In sum, the United States failed to lay the foundations for a relationship within the framework of which the basis for U.S. influence could emerge.

The list of foreign policy tools applied is therefore short to the extent of being inexistent: Belarus did not receive aid or attention beyond measures taken with respect to all post-Soviet countries. Funding provided by the Nunn-Lugar programme and similar measures hardly qualify as specifically "Belarusian" foreign policy tools. With some reservations, it could therefore be argued that Washington resorted to positive material power tools during Belarus's first years of independence — although these tools were not exclusively focused on Minsk but rather treated Belarus as just one representative of the much larger and disparate group of former Soviet countries.

With respect to the interrelationship between friend / nonfriend / undecided status and foreign policy tools, it may thus be concluded that unawareness of a specific state also implies the absence of a foreign policy towards that country.

V.3 Lukashenka and "Selective Engagement" with Minsk

V.3.1 Rigged elections and referenda: Deteriorating relations

Aleksandr Lukashenka won the 1994 presidential elections by a large margin, campaigning on the classic post-Communist topic of corruption. Soon after Lukashenka's election, bilateral U.S.-Belarusian relations 'cooled'[406] (In 2017, they are still characterised as 'anything but a smooth relationship with Belarusian authorities' on the homepage of the U.S. embassy to Belarus.[407]) Internal developments in Belarus were the major concern since Lukashenka's accession to power, i.e., the regime's democracy record (or rather, lack thereof), violations of human rights and the country's self-isolation. Lukashenka dissolved the parliament, removed judges and other critics and stopped all market economy reforms, instead emphasising the Soviet Union's great achievements. Especially the 1996 referendum, which "confirmed" him as president, was seen as a major violation of democratic principles, as were all subsequent "elections". Bilateral relations deteriorated quickly, leading the U.S. State Department to issue a new policy towards Belarus in 1997, motivated by the fact that 'the United States, other OSCE member states and the European Union have viewed with concern the developments in Belarus over recent months'.[408] In the wake of the 1996 referendum, the U.S. thus decided to implement a policy of 'selective engagement' with the Government of Belarus from 1997 onwards. Washington consequently

---

[406] Cf. for instance U.S. Department of State (2001) 'Background Note: Belarus', Washington D.C., January. The same formulation is contained in all other Background Notes subsequently issued.
[407] Cf. U.S. Embassy to Belarus, https://by.usembassy.gov/our-relationship/policy-history/ (accessed 1 May 2017).
[408] Cf. U.S. Department of State, Office of the Spokesman (1997) 'New U.S: Policy Toward Belarus', Washington D.C., 28 February.

notified the government of the Republic of Belarus that our bilateral diplomatic contacts will be conducted at a level commensurate with U.S. objectives. Policy-level contacts will be infrequent. We will enhance contact with, and we will encourage, democratic elements in Belarus, the independent media and non-governmental organizations.[409]

Contacts with the Belarusian parliament and the Constitutional court were to be limited to 'essential business'.[410] Government-to-government contacts were downgraded to the level of Assistant Secretary and below. The U.S. would no longer provide assistance to Belarusian authorities, thenceforward rechanneling USAID programmes and the like towards the promotion of democracy through non-governmental organisations. The only permitted purposes were humanitarian assistance, educational exchanges, limited non-proliferation assistance, and 'other contacts that advance clearly-defined U.S. security and law enforcement interests'.[411] Humanitarian aid for the victims of radiation yet continued (and continues to this day), an important aspect given that Belarus still suffers from the consequences of the 1986 nuclear disaster in Chernobyl.

In the wake of the 1998 Drosdy affair, the U.S. ambassador to Belarus was recalled to Washington for 'consultations', while Belarus was informed that it would be 'inappropriate for the Belarusian ambassador to the United States to return to Washington until further notice'.[412] The ambassadors of several other countries, including EU member states, left Belarus, reflecting 'the view of the international community that the Belarusian government's actions are

---

409 Cf. U.S. Department of State, Office of the Spokesman (1997) 'New U.S: Policy Toward Belarus', Washington D.C., 28 February.
410 Cf. U.S. Department of State, Office of the Spokesman (1997) 'New U.S: Policy Toward Belarus', Washington D.C., 28 February.
411 Cf. U.S. Department of State, Bureau of European and Eurasian Affairs (2006) 'Report on Belarus, the Last Dictatorship in Europe, including Arms Sales and Leadership Assets', Washington D.C., 16 March.
412 U.S. Department of State, Office of the Spokesman (1998) 'Recall of Ambassador Speckhard', press release, 22 June.

totally unacceptable'.[413] What followed was an exchange of statements between President Lukashenka and the United States, with the U.S. embassy officially refuting his remarks and declaring that withdrawing the ambassador did not equal ending diplomatic relations and that the U.S. would continue its commitment to medical treatment for children victim to the Chernobyl accident.[414] Ambassador Speckhard returned to Minsk in September 1999, at a crucial moment when the OSCE was 'attempting to initiate a dialogue between the Belarusian government and opposition on the conduct of free and fair elections and the strengthening of democratic institutions in Belarus' in 2000.[415] Yet, the conclusion the OSCE mission would reach in its final report was that

> [t]he 15 and 29 October parliamentary elections in Belarus failed to meet international standards for democratic elections, including those formulated in the 1990 Copenhagen Document of the OSCE. In particular, the elections fell short of meeting the minimum commitments for free, fair, equal, accountable, and transparent elections.[416]

The report condemned almost any aspect of the elections, from the treatment of the opposition during the campaign to intimidating voters on Election Day. The OSCE mission observed more than eighty ways to manipulate the counting of votes. In the elections' aftermath, the U.S. Congress passed a Resolution on Parliamentary Elections in Belarus, denouncing the Lukashenka regime on the grounds of all events related in the OSCE report.[417]

Unsurprisingly, the 2001 presidential "elections" did not match any international standards either, as the OSCE once more

---

413 U.S. Department of State, Office of the Spokesman (1998) 'Recall of Ambassador Speckhard', press release, 22 June.
414 U.S. Department of State, Office of the Spokesman (1998) 'Refutation of Lukashenko Remarks', press release, 24 July.
415 U.S. Department of State, Office of the Spokesman (1999) 'Return of U.S. Ambassador', 14 September.
416 OSCE, Office For Democratic Institutions and Human Rights (2001) 'Belarus Parliamentary Elections – Technical Assessment Mission Final Report', Warsaw, 30 January, p. 1.
417 Cf. Congressional Resolution on Parliamentary Elections in Belarus, 25 October 2000.

concluded.[418] In a White House statement, President Bush subsequently declared that

> [n]ot only did Aleksandr Lukashenko, Europe's last dictator, steal the elections from the Belarusian people — for the moment, he also stole their opportunity to return to a path towards democracy and free market economy.[419]

Four years later, Robert Cooper (then Director General for External and Political-Military Affairs of the Council of the European Union) and Dan Fried (then US Assistant Secretary of State for Europe) planned a common trip to Minsk for the EU and the United States to convey 'their shared concern at developments surrounding forthcoming [2006] Presidential elections'.[420] The Belarusian authorities, however, refused to issue visas so that Cooper and Fried could travel simultaneously, and their trips were cancelled. Despite the setback, both parts reiterated that their objective did not signify an attempt to isolate Belarus, the European Union even promising that democratic elections could open a perspective for Minsk to benefit from its European Neighbourhood Policy initiative.[421] Yet, the presidential "elections" held in March 2006 did not lead to any ameliorations. Both the elections themselves and the West's reactions were reminiscent of 2001 and 2002. Lukashenka was confirmed in a ballot that fell short of all international standards, accompanied by a repression of the opposition, the free media and peaceful demonstrations in its aftermath. Leading opposition politicians, including the former presidential candidates Milinkevich and Kazulin, were arrested and convicted. After revolutions in Georgia and Ukraine, it might now have been Belarus's turn to overthrow a dictatorial regime. This was not the case.

---

418 Cf. OSCE, Office For Democratic Institutions and Human Rights (2001) 'Republic of Belarus Presidential Elections Final Report', Warsaw, 9 September.
419 White House, Office of the Spokesman (2001) 'Statement on Belarus Presidential Elections', Washington D.C., 17 January.
420 U.S. Department of State, Office of the Spokesman (2006) 'Belarus Relations', press release, Washington D.C., 3 February.
421 Cf. the press release at http://ue.eu.int/ueDocs/cms_Data/docs/pressdata/en/sg/88279.pdf.

Official protests were, however, not limited to circumstances surrounding rigged elections. On numerous occasions since the mid-1990s, the United States sent notices of complaint to the Belarusian authorities. These protests concerned the arrest, detention, beating and sometimes even disappearance of members of the opposition and journalists, the harassment of organisations and publishers.[422] On an almost regular basis, the U.S. embassy in Minsk called for freedom of expression, religious freedom and the respect of human rights. Needless to say, the Belarusian authorities displayed essentially no regard for such calls.

V.3.2 The Belarus Democracy Act

The first version of the Belarus Democracy Act was introduced in Congress in 2001 by the late Senator Jesse Helms as the Belarus Democracy Bill, inspired by comparable legislation on Cuba, but failed to become a law. What many perceived as the problem was that the 2001 version reflected the very conservative stance of Senator Helms'. In addition, the bill was strongly opposed by the State Department on the grounds that it did not want Congress to dictate foreign policy. Only after being watered down by a private initiative to save the bill in cooperation with the U.S. Helsinki Commission could the text be passed.[423] The bill eventually became the Belarus Democracy Act in 2004.[424]

The Act was a key document on U.S. Belarusian policies, intended to serve the overall objective of promoting democratisation. Its wording and the accompanying presidential statement left no doubt on the nature of the Belarusian regime as seen from Washington. President George W. Bush wrote:

---

422 For instance, in 1999 alone, five such protests have been voiced.
423 Author's interview with Ethan S. Burger, Washington D.C., 8 November 2007.
424 U.S. House of Representatives, federal law HR 5948.

> At a time when freedom is advancing around the world, Aleksandr Lukashenka and his government are turning Belarus into a regime of repression in the heart of Europe, its government isolated from its neighbors and its people isolated from each other. We will work with our allies and partners to assist those seeking to return Belarus to its rightful place among the Euro-Atlantic community of democracies. There is no place in a Europe whole and free for a regime of this kind.[425]

The text of the law itself was no less clear, e.g., qualifying the 1996 referendum as 'illegal and unconstitutional'. The Act's objectives aimed at supporting civil society, authorising assistance for democratic political parties, NGOs, and independent media. It furthermore stated that it is the sense of Congress 'that the President should continue to seek to coordinate with other countries, particularly European countries, a comprehensive, multilateral strategy' (Sec. 6), in order to take measures similar to 'measures described in this act'.

Congress reauthorized the 2004 Belarus Democracy Act in 2006 (in force from January 2007), albeit without noting progress in Belarus. On the contrary, the new text read, for example, as follows: 'The government of the Republic of Belarus has engaged in a pattern of clear and uncorrected violations of human rights and fundamental freedoms' (Sec. 2, 1). The new version of the act moreover contained a newly introduced section, 'Sec. 3, Statement of Policy', stating that it is the United States' policy to:

- call for the immediate release of all political prisoners in Belarus;
- support the aspirations of the people of the Republic of Belarus for democracy, human rights, the rule of law,
- support the aspirations of the people of the Republic of Belarus to preserve the independence and sovereignty of their country;
- support the growth of democratic movements and institutions in Belarus;
- refuse to accept the results of the March 2006 presidential elections in Belarus and support new presidential elections;

---

[425] The White House, Office of the Press Secretary (2004) 'Statement by the President on the Belarus Democracy Act of 2004', 20 October.

- refuse to recognize any referendum that would affect Belarus' sovereignty; and
- work with other countries and international organizations to promote Belarus' integration into the European community of democracies.

Despite the strong wording, the Belarus Democracy Act contained almost no concrete provisions in either of its versions relevant for the period studied. Congress implicitly called for the circumvention of Belarusian authorities, instead recommending that the U.S. support democratic movements — without, however, explicitly requesting it do so. Rather, the Act was a statement of democratic principles, leaving the administration relatively free to take whatever measure it deems appropriate. And even though the relations between the two countries were anything but friendly, there remained a number of fields involving Belarusian authorities within which cooperation and contacts took place. Most importantly, the United States continues to provide humanitarian aid, with a special focus on relief for the victims of the Chernobyl nuclear disaster.

Straightforward rhetoric nevertheless continued to distinguish the U.S. approach to Belarus. On 16 March 2006, only days before the Belarusian presidential "elections", George Bush sent a "Report on Belarus, the Last Dictatorship in Europe, Including Arms Sales and Leadership Assets"[426] to the House Committee on International Relations and the Senate Committee on Foreign Relations. Among other things, the report stated that

> Mr. Lukashenka has created a repressive dictatorship on the doorstep of the European Union (EU). Unlike any other leader in Europe, his actions impede realization of a Europe whole, free and at peace, and introduce an element of unpredictability and potential instability and insecurity in Europe.[427]

To see any potential for improved relations was thus difficult. The United States had nevertheless made it clear that it first wanted to

---

426 The report was sent in accordance with section 7 of the Belarus Democracy Act, requiring the President to inform Congress about weapon exports from Belarus.
427 U.S. Department of State, Bureau of European and Eurasian Affairs (2006) *Report on Belarus, the Last Dictatorship in Europe, Including Arms Sales and Leadership Assets*, Washington D.C., 16 March, p. 2.

see action on Lukashenka's part, unequivocally placing the ball in his court.

V.3.3 Political Prisoners, Sanctions and *Personae Non Gratae*

In June 2006, George W. Bush issued Executive Order 13405 – "Blocking Property of Certain Persons Undermining Democratic Processes or Institutions in Belarus" – , which imposed economic sanctions on the Lukashenka regime.[428] In the Order, the President of the United States determines that

> the actions and policies of certain members of the Government of Belarus and other persons to undermine Belarus' democratic processes or institutions, manifested most recently in the fundamentally undemocratic March 2006 elections, to commit human rights abuses related to political repression, including detentions and disappearances, and to engage in public corruption, including by diverting or misusing Belarusian public assets or by misusing public authority, constitute an unusual and extraordinary threat to the national security and foreign policy of the United States [...].

The Order blocked Lukashenka's assets as well as those of nine other Belarusian senior officials listed in its annex, a list that was extended to sixteen when another six Belarusian officials were added in February 2007. In November 2007, the U.S. Department of Treasury (in coordination with the State Department) 'designated Belarus's largest petrochemical conglomerate [Belneftekhim] under Executive Order 13405 as being controlled by oppressive Belarusian President Alexander Lukashenko.'[429] Belneftekhim, also known as Belarusian State Concern for Oil and Chemistry, and the entities it owns are in fact the country's major exporting firms. In other words, the sanctions imposed were a targeted move against the Belarusian petro-chemical industry, indispensable for Belarus's eco-

---

428 Cf. Federal Register, Vol. 71, no. 118, Tuesday, 20 June 2006.
429 U.S. Department of Treasury (2007) 'Treasury Targets Lukashenko-controlled Petrochemical Conglomerate', Washington D.C., 13 November (press release HP-676).

nomic well-being. In June 2008, President George W. Bush extended the freeze of Belarusian leaders' assets in time.[430] This extension was a direct reaction to the lack of progress in releasing political prisoners, as Deputy Assistant Secretary for European and Eurasian Affairs David Kramer confirms in an interview with Belapan (Belarus Information Company) on 11 March 2008.[431] In the same interview, Kramer also made clear that '[t]he way to avoid further sanctions from the United States is for Belarus to release Alyaksandr Kazulin', a Belarusian opposition leader in jail on political grounds since July 2006. Kazulin was the last name on a list of originally six political prisoners that the U.S. requested Belarus to release. He was allowed to leave prison in August 2008.[432]

Instead, the diplomatic game went on for several rounds. Not only did the U.S. resort to economic sanctions and the blocking of assets, diplomatic means of "warfare" were taken on both sides. Disputes over sanctions escalated into visa restrictions and expulsions of diplomats. On several occasions, Minsk declared American diplomats *non grata*. As a consequence, the U.S. embassy in Minsk had a staff of merely four people by May 2008, as compared to thirty-five at the beginning of the year. Although Tom Casey, at the time the State Department's deputy spokesman, qualified Lukashenka's acts as 'unwarranted and unjustified action'[433], the U.S. chose not to take any countermeasures such as declaring Belarusian diplomats *personae non gratae* or to end diplomatic relations between the two countries altogether. The reduction of staff at the Belarusian embassy in Washington D.C. and the Belarusian consulate in New York City were the result of unilateral decisions taken by Minsk. In addition to expelling diplomats, Minsk also made attempts at making the U.S. ambassador, Karen B. Stewart, leave the country, while

---

430 Cf. The White House, Office of the Press Secretary (2008) 'Message to the Congress of the United States', Washington D.C., 6 June.
431 Available at the U.S. Department of State webpage, http://www.state.gov/p/eur/rls/rm/102247.htm (accessed 28 July 2008).
432 Cf. BBC News Online (2008) 'Belarus Dissident Leaves Prison', 16 August.
433 Cf. U.S. Department of State, Office of the Spokesman (2008) 'Daily Press Briefing', Washington D.C., 1 May.

nevertheless refraining from officially declaring her *non grata*. Although not giving in immediately, Washington recalled her for consultations when it became clear that she would be declared *non grata* should the United States fail to recall her "voluntarily". Ambassador Stewart left Belarus on 12 March 2008.[434]

V.3.4 "Selective engagement" and foreign policy tools

With President Lukashenka's accession to power, Belarus became an unfriendly state from a Washington perspective. This is not least evident in U.S. characterisations of bilateral relations as 'cool' and 'anything but smooth', an evolution directly linked to the 1996 referendum and the Drosdy affair.

During the time span covered in the above section, U.S. objectives with respect to Belarus exclusively consisted of getting Minsk to respect general principles of democracy, human rights and conduct in international affairs. The very problematic relationship between Washington and Minsk had a major impact on the foreign policy tools to which the United States resorted, which exclusively belong to the negative power categories. It appears that Washington's main foreign policy objective with regard to Belarus involved discrediting the country within the international community, denying it a role as a legitimate actor in order to undermine the country's prestige. The foreign policy tools Washington implemented were to a large extent symbolic in nature.

- Negative material power tools: negative material power measures in U.S. Belarusian policies include economic sanctions such as freezing assets and especially the sanctions imposed on Belneftekhim.
- Negative symbolic power tools: on the symbolic side, the number of foreign policy tools has been important. On numerous occasions, Washington has resorted to declaratory politics, voicing its concern over developments in Belarus. This concern pertained to both abstract principles such as the rule of law and very concrete individual aspects. The

---

434 Cf. U.S. Department of State, Office of the Spokesman (2008) 'Daily Press Briefing', Washington D.C., 12 March.

exchange of statements has been a frequent occurrence. The words chosen by American officials, including at the highest levels, are perfectly unambiguous, qualifying Lukashenka as a "dictator" and his country an "outpost of tyranny". Consequently, travel restrictions have been imposed on prominent Belarusian officials.

Beyond publicly voicing concern, the U.S. also took to highly symbolic measures such as calling back its ambassador on two occasions. A U.S. law was directed at addressing Belarus as a human rights problem, and Belarus was named in connection with other pariah states of current international affairs. Although the usefulness and effectiveness of the Belarus Democracy Act may be questioned, it nevertheless is proof of a particularly strong American stance on Lukashenka's regime. In the same spirit, Washington denied Belarus all kinds of high-level contacts.

In sum, the U.S. was unsuccessful at imposing its will, even on isolated matters. For instance, although Lukashenka eventually agreed to free some political prisoners, he nevertheless refused to release the most "valuable" of them for many months. Moreover, the release of those prisoners cannot be directly linked to U.S. pressure, as it could just as well be seen as an attempt by Minsk to improve its relations with the European Union.[435]

Any measure that could be qualified as positive power used in the Belarusian context was in fact directed towards Belarusian non-state actors or purely humanitarian in nature (mainly aid for Chernobyl accident victims) and cannot, therefore, be considered in the present context, focusing on state-to-state relations. All these foreign policy tools were in essence meant to bypass official Minsk, hence applied with the deliberate intention of undermining the regime and / or providing purely humanitarian assistance to civilians in need.

---

[435] As a matter of fact, relations between Belarus and the European Union have improved in late 2008. Lukashenka for instance permitted the European Commission to open a Delegation in Minsk. Cf. http://www.delblr.ec.europa.eu/home.html (accessed 28 November 2008).

A look into U.S.-Belarusian relations since 1994 thus reveals the lack of any basis for a relationship based on mutual trust and friendship. Instead, suspicion and disagreement over basic principles such as democracy, human rights and constitutionality characterise both countries' relations with each other. Under such circumstances, positive power tools can hardly work, lacking the power base necessary. Consequently, as an unfriendly state, Belarus was exclusively met with negative power tools on the United States' part.

V.4 The wider context: Belarus in international politics

V.4.1 The Bush II era: Belarus as a rogue state?

The 2006 presidential report to Congress (see above) noted that 'Lukashenka is increasingly seeking partners from other states of concern'. Belarus was said to continue exporting 'significant quantities of defense articles, dual-use items and other military equipment and technology'. The exports included sales to so-called 'states of concerns' and 'state sponsors of terrorism', namely Iran, Sudan, and Syria. Suspicions also included money laundering for the Saddam Hussein Regime by a Belarusian bank, which engendered U.S. Treasury Department sanctions in 2004 (see below). In other words, Belarus was on the agenda within the context of the fight against terrorism, rogue states and arms proliferation. When responding to the Senate in order to be confirmed as Secretary of State in 2005, Condoleezza Rice accordingly called Belarus one of six 'outposts of tyranny'[436]. Two years on, in a press release on the so-called 'Captive Nations Week' (15–21 July 2007), the White House explicitly called Belarus an oppressive regime: 'While there is progress in freedom's advance, nations such as Belarus, Burma, Cuba, North

---

[436] Cf. U.S. Department of State, Foreign Press Center (2006) 'Elections in Belarus and Ukraine', briefing by David J. Kramer, Deputy Assistant Secretary of State for European and Eurasian Affairs, Washington D.C., 2 March. See also: BBC News Online (2005) 'Rice names "outposts of tyranny"', 19 January.

Korea, Syria, Iran, Sudan, and Zimbabwe still oppress their citizens.[437]

Given the nature of Lukashenka's regime and the vast conventional arsenal inherited from the Soviet Union, it is not surprising that Belarus was seen in these terms. Belarus is an arms exporting country and had relations with other states considered problematic by Washington. Luskashenka met with Iran's president Ahmadinejad and Venezuela's President Chavez.[438] Iran and Belarus concluded formal agreements in, among others, the fields of customs, security and agriculture. A security cooperation agreement between the two countries was ratified by the Belarusian parliament in May 2005; Belarus publicly supported Iran's position on the nuclear issue. Also Sudan has framework agreements on cooperation signed with Belarus. Most notably, however, Belarus was among the closest allies of Saddam Hussein's Iraq. As Secretary of Defence Donald Rumsfeld declared in a testimony before Congress in 2002, discussing the options Saddam was facing: 'One choice he has is to take his family and key leaders and seek asylum elsewhere. Surely one of the one hundred and eighty plus counties would take his regime — possibly Belarus.'[439] Washington's concern increased even more when high-ranking members of Saddam Hussein's regime — among them his two sons — were arrested in 2003 and turned out to be carrying Belarusian passports.[440]

Belarus's role in proliferation increasingly became a matter of concern for the United States. A January 2002 *Washington Post* article, titled 'Europe's Armory For Terrorism', contained what Senator

---

437 Cf. The White House, Office of the Press Secretary (2007) 'Captive Nations Week, 2007', Washington D.C., 10 July.
438 Cf. for instance 'Venezuela's Chavez, Belarus's Lukashenka Vow Cooperation', Radio Free Europe / Radio Liberty, 29 June 2007.
439 Donald H. Rumsfeld (2002) 'Prepared Testimony of U.S. Secretary of Defense Donald H. Rumsfeld before the House and Senate Armed Services Committees regarding Iraq. As Delivered by Secretary of Defense Donald H. Rumsfeld', Washington D.C., 18 September.
440 Andrei Sannikov and Mark Lenzi (2004) 'Belarus's Terrorist Ties', *The Washington Post,* 12 June.

Ben Campbell called 'troubling allegations'.[441] The article claimed that 'Belarus is quietly acting as a leading supplier of lethal military equipment to Islamic radicals—with terrorists and militant organizations in the Middle East, Balkans and Central Asia often the recipients', urging Washington to pay more attention to the Lukashenka regime and its arms deals.[442] Belarus was accused of transgressing U.N. embargo rules and cooperating with Saddam Hussein in particular. Also the Iraq Survey Group's final report (commonly called the Duelfer Report) of 2004 linked Belarus to the Iraqi regime, accusing Minsk of both money laundering and arms transfers.[443] The Belarusian embassy in Washington denied all charges. In order to investigate the matter of proliferation, a delegation from the U.S. Congress travelled *inter alia* to Belarus in February 2002, with the goal of discussing 'official concerns about that nation's record on human rights and reports of arms sales to terrorists or countries that harbor terrorist organizations.'[444] The delegation, headed by Rep. Jim Saxton, Chairman of the House Special Oversight Panel on Terrorism, met with high-ranking officials. The issue subsequently appeared a number of times on the agenda of the United Nations' Security Council's meetings, without however leading to any further measures.

Yet, despite Belarus's moving closer to these so-called rogue states, the question remained surprisingly low profile. There did not seem to be any widespread willingness in Washington to frame Belarus as part of the "axis of evil". Even Lukashenka's announcement that Belarus wanted to build a nuclear power plant in October 2007[445] received relatively little international attention, especially in

---

441 Senator Ben Campbell (2002) 'Statement in U.S. Senate on Belarus', Washington D.C., 24 January.
442 Mark Lenzi (2003) 'Europe's Armory For Terrorism', *The Washington Post*, 3 January.
443 Cf. The Iraq Survey Group (2004) *Comprehensive Report of the Special Adviser to the DCI on Iraq's WMD* ('Duelfer-Report'), Washington D.C., 30 September.
444 Congressman Jim Saxton (2002) 'Saxton Delegation Back in the U.S.A.—Antiterrorism trip to Holland, Belarus, Russia, Germany complete', press release, Washington D.C., 25 February.
445 Cf. for instance 'Lukaschenko will Atomkraft', *Belarus News*, 12 October 2007, at www.belarusnews.de (accessed 16 October 2007).

the United States. Washington did not offer any official reaction (which might, of course, also be due to limited conviction in Washington that Lukashenka really has the means and the know-how needed.) Despite the country's unedifying human rights record, Minsk in reality never posed any threat to the United States or its interests. Moreover, U.S.-Russian relations continued to be far more important than developments in Belarus. For that reason, Washington was quite unlikely to risk causing annoyance in Moscow over a state (indirectly) supported by the Kremlin.

V.4.2 Belarus and Euro-Atlantic Integration

Given that the general American approach in Central and Eastern Europe mainly consisted of expanding Euro-Atlantic institutions, Belarus's perspectives of Western integration need to be assessed. For more than a decade, however, Aleksandr Lukashenka's focus was on Eastern integration, accompanied by total disinterest in creating ties with either Europe or the United States. A number of Union Treaties were signed between Minsk and Moscow[446]. Although a Russian-Belarusian Union state became more and more unlikely, these developments led to no reassessment of relations with the West on Lukashenka's part in the time period studied here. Belarus's perspective for Euro-Atlantic integration was consequently non-existent until 2008. Minsk's relations with the EU were complicated. Its relations with NATO are not much better. As the Belarusian Ministry of Foreign Affairs declared on its website, 'one of Belarus' foreign policy priorities is strengthening full-scale cooperation with NATO and its individual member states'.[447] The country joined the Partnership for Peace-programme (PfP) in 1995, but was

---

[446] Cf. the Bilateral Agreement 1992; Agreement on the reciprocal use of military facilities in the respective countries and military cooperation 1995; Agreement on Friendship, Good Neighbourliness and Cooperation, and a Customs Union 1995; Union Treaty 1999. Belarus is moreover a founding member of the Eurasian Economic Union.

[447] Cf. 'Belarus and NATO' at the Belarusian Ministry of Foreign Affairs' homepage at http://www.mfa.gov.by/en/foreign-policy/multilateral/c21ec980e0def482.html (accessed 9 November 2007).

among its most inactive members. Yet, some cooperation still took place; as of 2007, there were officially nineteen areas in which Belarus 'would like to cooperate in with both NATO member-countries and partner-states'.[448]

However, the ministry's statement did not reflect the reality of NATO-Belarusian relations. Despite ongoing cooperation between the Alliance and Belarus, relations between the organisation and the Belarusian regime were anything but constructive. Public rhetoric was characterised by Cold War paranoia. For instance, the 'most prominent pro-government newspaper *Sovetskaya Belorussiya* has repeatedly claimed NATO has made detailed plans for a military strike or political subversion'.[449] Statements such as Lukashenka's declaring that NATO is an 'illegal organisation' were certainly not helpful either.[450] In 1997, the NATO Parliamentary Assembly decided to suspend Belarus's status as Associate Member (granted in 1991), 'a result of the increasingly undemocratic activities of the Lukashenka regime'.[451] Some ties were still maintained, however, as the Assembly continued to invite three representatives of the former 13th Supreme Soviet of Belarus until the year 2000. By then, the Assembly felt the need to entirely re-evaluate its relations with Belarus and decided to send a fact-finding mission to Minsk.[452] Moreover, although Lukashenka wanted to attend the 2002 NATO summit in Prague, the Alliance denied him participation in the EAPC meeting. The Czech Republic simply refused to issue a visa for him to enter the country. Rather unsurprisingly, these measures

---

448 Cf. the Belarusian Ministry of Foreign Affairs' homepage at http://www.mfa.gov.by/en/foreign-policy/multilateral/c21ec980e0def482.html (accessed 9 November 2007)
449 Kaare Dahl Martinsen (2002) *The Russian-Belarusian Union and the Near Abroad*, p. 8.
450 Christophe Chatelot (2007) 'Alexandre Loukachenko: "L'OTAN est une organisation illégale"', *Le Monde*, 20 July [my own translation in the text]: 'l'OTAN est une organisation illégale'.
451 Cf. NATO Parliamentary Assembly (2006) 'More Proactive Strategy Towards Belarus Needed', Press Communiqué, Brussels, 17 October.
452 Cf. NATO Parliamentary Assembly, Standing Committee (2001) *Report of an Assembly Fact Finding Mission to Minsk 25–27 March 2001*, Doc. AU 28 SC (01) 8, Brussels, March.

were considered 'an ignominious act' and 'an act of disrespect not only to the Belarusian President but, first of all, to the Belarusian people' in a speech by Lukashenka's plenipotentiary representative at the summit.[453]

In July 2007, Lukashenka had the occasion to explain his points of view in an interview with a major Western newspaper, France's *Le Monde*. As became obvious, there was virtually no basis for trustful relations between the West and Belarus. When asked whether the expansion of NATO was a potential source of conflict, Lukashenka replied:

> I think so. One cannot guarantee that this is not the beginning of a destructive process of destabilisation of our peaceful continent. Other countries could join this conflict, especially when keeping in mind the wars and diplomatic hotspots at Russia's borders. This could lead to a global conflict, of which we know how it would finish.[454]

Belarusian reactions to the then planned missile defence system were reminiscent of the Cold War, and seemed to be catering to Moscow. Seen as yet another American coup, 'the deployment of American missiles on Czech and Polish territory is a matter touching Europe's security, not only that of Belarus'.[455] The Russian ambassador to Minsk, in turn, caused heated debates when he proposed that new nuclear weapons might be stationed in Belarus in response to the missile defence system—which caused outrage in

---

453 NATO, NATO Press Services (2002) 'Statement by the Head of the Delegation of Belarus at the EAPC Meeting at the level of Heads of State and Government', Prague, 22 November.
454 Christophe Chatelot (2007) 'Alexandre Loukachenko: "L'OTAN est une organisation illégale"' [my own translation in the text]: 'Je crois que oui. On ne peut pas garantir que ce ne soit pas le début d'un processus destructeur, de déstabilisation de notre continent tranquille. D'autres pays pourraient se joindre à ce conflit, surtout en tenant compte des guerres et des points chauds diplomatiques aux frontières de la Russie. Cela pourrait aboutir à un conflit global dont on sait comment il se finirait.'
455 Christophe Chatelot (2007) 'Alexandre Loukachenko: "L'OTAN est une organisation illégale"' [my own translation in the text]: 'le déploiement de missiles américains sur les territoires tchèque et polonais est une question pour la sécurité de l'Europe, pas seulement de la Biélorussie'.

Belarus and was considered an act of interference in a sovereign state's internal affairs.[456]

In sum, Belarus's attitude towards NATO was not by any means characterised by trust and a spirit of cooperation. For that reason, one of the driving forces behind reform processes in many Central European countries, i.e., the perspective of joining NATO and / or the European Union, was absent in Belarus throughout the years of Lukashenka's rule.

V.4.3 The wider context and foreign policy tools

As Lukashenka's statements in the *Le Monde* interview quite vividly illustrate, Belarus had no inclinations to consider the world order upheld by the United States — and of which NATO is one product — legitimate. Although Minsk may have had no ambitions to overthrow the international system, the country qualified as non-friend as seen from the U.S. As far as economic aspects were concerned at the time, the U.S. embassy's website in Minsk plainly stated that '[p]resently, the U.S. Government does not encourage American companies to invest in Belarus.'[457] Against that background, it is hardly surprising that the tenor in U.S. descriptions of its relations with Belarus remained constant: the country is seen as an unfriendly state, official relations are 'cool' and 'at a low level'.[458]

Negative power thus continued to be the order of the day. Yet, despite Belarus's "potential" as a so-called rogue state, the U.S. has recurred to a very limited number of foreign policy tools with respect to the country's role and position in international politics. All these reactions are instances of negative power in U.S. Belarusian policies which amount to U.S. efforts at discrediting Belarus at the international level and at undermining Belarus's prestige in the world. No status quo member of the international community has

---

456 Cf. 'Skandal nach Botschafter-Aussage über neue Atomwaffen in Weißrussland' www.belarusnews.de/de/union/skandal-nach-botschafter-aussage-ber-neue-atomwaffen-in-wei-rus.html (accessed 3 January 2008).
457 U.S. Embassy to Belarus (2010) 'U.S.-Belarus relations' (accessed 14 July 2010).
458 Cf. for instance U.S. Department of State (2004) 'Background Note: Belarus, Washington D.C., October.

good relations with Minsk; the company in which Belarus finds itself is composed of other so-called states of concern. Although it is impossible to evaluate the extent to which Belarus's internationally bad standing with third countries is the exclusive result of U.S. diplomacy, it seems fair to say that Washington's stance on the Lukashenka regime at least contributed to its relative isolation.

The above section revealed that the patterns characterising U.S.-Belarusian affairs continued to dominate even beyond the strictly bilateral realm. Not only did the countries have differences over domestic politics (most prominently, human rights issues) and the conduct of diplomatic relations (cf. the Drosdy affair), but also over matters of appropriate state behaviour in international politics. Against that background, it is more than evident that the relationship between Belarus and the United States lacked the prerequisites for positive power bases to function. Positive power tools of foreign policy are thus unlikely to be effective unless the Lukashenka regime changes its attitudes or, for one reason or another, starts feeling compelled to seek alignment with the United States, possibly in a balancing move against Russia (which, to date, seems unlikely to occur).

V.5 Conclusions on U.S. foreign policies towards Belarus 1991–2008

Ever since Aleksandr Lukashenka's accession to power and throughout the period studied here, Belarus qualified as an unfriendly state from a U.S. vantage point. Relations between Washington and Minsk have been under considerable strain, characterised by the fact that disagreement almost invariably lay at the level of basic principles. In other words, Washington and Minsk held diverging views on the very foundations of governance, human rights and practices of international relations. All disputes over concrete matters (e.g., specific imprisoned persons, diplomats declared *non grata,* etc.) are an illustration of this fact, having deeper causes than merely the issue at hand. No proof of positive judgement on Belarus could thus be found in the sources analysed in order to determine the country's status as seen from Washington. For all these reasons, Belarus qualified as a non-friend; the evolution of its relations with the United States leaves no doubt that it deserved the label of "unfriendly state" from a U.S. perspective. The foreign policy tools applied by U.S. administrations targeting Belarus were exclusively based on negative power, both material and symbolic. The Belarusian case hence confirms the assumption that unfriendly states would be met with negative power.

The negative power tools applied did not, however, have much effect. Although, from a normative standpoint, the United States may be praised for taking a tough stance, American policies towards Belarus mainly consisted of issuing declarations using harsh language. There is not much more Washington could do besides, for instance, declaring—jointly with the EU—that

> [t]he European Union and the United States believe that the spread of accountable and representative government, the rule of law, and respect for human rights as enshrined in the Universal Declaration of Human Rights, are a strategic priority as well as a moral necessity. We will continue to work together to advance these priorities around the world.[459]

Moreover, State Department Background Notes explained that

> the United States would respond positively to genuine efforts by Belarusian authorities to improve Belarus' human rights and electoral practices. Belarusian authorities have yet to take such steps to warrant a positive response.[460]

Other than that, there is very little Washington actually was able to do about the situation in the country (short of military measures, of course, which seems a most remote scenario). When asked about the type of leverage the State Department actually had in working with authorities in Belarus, David J. Kramer, Deputy Assistant Secretary of State for European and Eurasian Affairs, replied in 2006:

---

459 The White House, Office of the Press Secretary (2005) 'Joint U.S.-EU Statement: Democracy, Freedom, The Rule of Law and Human Rights', Washington D.C., 20 June.
460 Cf. versions issued October 2004; April 2006; August 2005; January 2007; February, August, October 2008; July 2009.

> Our leverage is not enormous. I'm not going to stand here and pretend that we have the ability to affect the outcome of what happens there. That will largely be in the hands of the people in Belarus. But I think the international community does have a responsibility to do all it can to make sure that people are aware of what's going on.[461]

American stakes in the country were low, if not in fact nonexistent. Belarus did not represent a major threat to European stability, especially since the Union with Russia seemed to be off the agenda according to most observers. Investment by U.S. firms was no major concern for American policymakers, as it almost does not exist. Unlike many other Central and Eastern European nations, Belarus does not have an organised diaspora in the United States. All this allowed Washington to lead "exemplary" policies towards a non-democratic state in a way it could not deal with a country for which it actually must show consideration.[462] The absence of important stakes arguably also opened up for a rather high degree of coordination with partners such as the EU and its individual member states. The Europeans were, however, more cautious in terms of political language, even though they undoubtedly shared Washington's views on the nature of the Belarusian regime.

Yet, the quasi absence of trade relations especially not only means that Belarus missed chances for economic growth, but implies also that the U.S. lacked a tool creating leverage over Minsk, as economic statecraft is hardly an option. The more limited the number of contacts, the lesser obviously the chances to exert power. A country that chooses to isolate itself from Europe, the West and the world will not easily be attracted by the carrots Washington (or Brussels, or the West in general) has to offer. At the same time, a country that does not want anything cannot be punished by withholding something it wishes to obtain.

---

461 U.S. Department of State, Foreign Press Center (2006) 'Elections in Belarus and Ukraine', press briefing by David J. Kramer, Deputy Assistant Secretary of State for European and Eurasian Affairs, Washington D.C., 2 March.
462 For instance, human rights concerns would certainly be as relevant in the Saudi-Arabian case, but given considerable U.S. interest in favourable attitudes on the Saudi regime's part, as tough a stance as on Belarus seems unthinkable.

In the case of Belarus, positive power resources did not come to use; negative symbolic power was to no effect. In other words, its relatively strong economic autarky and independence from the West made Belarus impermeable to Western influence attempts, leaving officials in Washington and Brussels clueless about what to do. The relatively long list of declarations, condemnations and broadcastings from Poland notwithstanding, it is clear that the United States lacked effective policy tools that would allow it to exert decisive influence on the Belarusian leadership. Support for the extremely weak and small civil society was nothing but an admission of that fact: if Washington had known how to exert power over the Lukashenka regime, it would have been superfluous to bypass it. Measures such as United States support for 'external broadcasting and other efforts to bring objective, independent information to Belarus, key to breaking the government's stranglehold over television and radio'[463] were arguably a step in the right direction. Yet, absent a coordinated opposition in Belarus, its efficiency remained insufficient.

US policies towards Belarus in the years 1994 to 2008, therefore, were tantamount to the absence of effective policies towards Belarus. Belarus is a case illustrating the limits of U.S. influence, confirming Zbigniew Brzezinski's assessment that

> [t]he scope of America's global hegemony is admittedly great, but its depth is shallow, limited by both domestic and external constraints. American hegemony involves the exercise of decisive influence but, unlike the empires of the past, not of direct control.[464]

To put it simply, a country that by no means wants to be subject to U.S. power can find ways to elude Washington's might. Not being among the top-priorities of American foreign policy naturally helps, too. Yet, the Belarusian case also illustrates the limited power of the so-called single remaining superpower vis-à-vis Russia. In

---

463 Cf. U.S. Department of State, Bureau of European and Eurasian Affairs (2006) 'Report on Belarus, the Last Dictatorship in Europe, Including Arms Sales and Leadership Assets', Washington D.C., 16 March.
464 Zbigniew Brzezinski (1997) *The Grand Chessboard*, p. 35.

Belarus, a potential 'rogue state' in all aspects the term comprises,[465] especially the second Bush administration would have had an ideal candidate for its declared objective of promoting democracy. The fact that Belarusian democracy obviously was not worth upsetting Russia hints at the fact that *realpolitik* factors remained most relevant even if the contrary was professed. Yet, most observers agree that the one (and only) actor truly able to exert leverage on Belarus is Russia:

> Over the past eight years, two U.S. administrations have half-heartedly tried to convince Russia of the need to change the situation in Belarus. Russia, however, has chosen not to use its overwhelming leverage on Lukashenko to improve his dangerous behavior.[466]

For many years, Belarus had been de facto subsidised by Russia, albeit indirectly. Indeed, Belarus did not have to pay the market price for gas exports from Russia, but was only charged the domestic price. The same used to be valid for Russian crude oil exported to Belarus, which would then be refined and sold to Western Europe at considerable gains. In 2007, however, Russia changed its policy and is now charging market prices even for Belarus, which represents a considerable increase. The altered gas and oil prices are however only the last such measure taken by Russia. In 2001, already, Russia forced Minsk to raise duty levels for transit goods to Russian levels. Back then, the loss was compensated by further loans from Russia, illustrating the Belarusian need for cash with foreign provenience. Still, economic problems could not be avoided:

> In the course of 2001, occasional reports over delays in wage payments, compulsory un-paid holidays, and four-day working weeks surfaced in the press. This usually happened in the larger provincial towns with Minsk relatively unaffected. Judging from newspapers reports, the problems became more widespread from early 2001 and were now affecting enterprises in the

---

465 Cf. The National Security Strategy of the United States (2002)
466 Andrei Sannikov and Mark Lenzi (2004) 'Belarus's Terrorist Ties', *The Washington Post*, 12 June.

> capital. Lukashenka responded in two ways, one was to scold the government in front of television cameras. The other was to arrest an increasing number of enterprise directors.[467]

In the long run, severe economic problems thus seemed unavoidable, albeit not imminent. "Wait-and-see" was hence the predominant approach in both Washington and Brussels. It was, however, also the indirect acknowledgment that, 'the West' did not have any means to exercise significant power on Belarus.

---

467 Kaare Dahl Martinsen (2002) *The Russian-Belarusian Union and the Near Abroad,,* p. 17.

VI Conclusions

VI.1 Returning to the research questions

Why, this study asked, did the United States lead entirely different policies towards three countries under circumstances where realism would predict highly similar approaches? Why, in other words, did Washington's approaches towards Poland, Ukraine and Belarus differ to the extent they did in the years from 1989 to 2008, although systemic conditions were identical for all three? This observation indeed runs counter to expectations derived from (neoclassical) realist core principles: while Washington's quest for preserved (and even expanded) unipolarity confirms its basic assumptions, realism — as an environment-based approach — would also predict similar policies to be led under similar circumstances. Yet, under the exact same circumstances of unipolarity, the exact same state led highly divergent policies towards three neighbouring countries sharing important features. Policy makers' perceptions of systemic conditions alone cannot, therefore, account for the observed differences. Rather, this study has argued, their perception of the state with which they are dealing must also be considered as a part of the equation. On the theoretical side, in order to explain that puzzling observation, this study's objective has sought to develop a theoretical framework which allows for incorporating a bilateral dimension into a neoclassical realist analysis of state behaviour. This framework has been applied in an analysis of the United States' attempts at managing unipolarity through its policies towards Poland, Ukraine and Belarus during the years 1989 to 2008.

Based on the assumption that all acts of foreign policy necessarily occur within the framework of a previously existing bilateral constellation, this study has argued that this relationship and especially perceptions thereof must be included as an important factor into the analysis. It has done so by introducing three categories of ideal-typical relationships, i.e. positions or attitudes states can hold with respect to other states, namely friend, non-friend or undecided statuses. Perceptions of these statuses were expected to have a decisive impact on the foreign policy tools states employ to exert power over other states. Foreign policy tools are defined as any measure state A uses when it wants another state B to act in a specific way (as defined by A). Foreign policy tools are always a vehicle for and an expression of the wielding state's power. This power and the resources upon which it draws can be split into two types, each comprising two sub-types: power resources can either be positive — meaning: based on incentives and rewards — or negative — meaning: based on coercion and threats. Both positive and negative power resources can either take material or symbolic forms.[468] As the underlying base values — i.e., that which makes power work as seen from the recipient's end — for each type are essentially different, it should be expected that the application of these types would be highly circumstantial. This expectation is in fact theoretically grounded, since the prerequisites for the underlying power bases' efficiency vary accordingly.

The sources analysed for this study have been approached in three steps. Firstly, the objective involved determining the United States' perceptions of a country's friend / non-friend / undecided status vis-à-vis Washington by retracing the evolution of its bilateral relationship with the United States through official U.S. resources. Secondly, the foreign policy tools applied by the United States within the framework of that bilateral relationship and the type of power upon which they were built have been identified. Thirdly and finally, the analysis has aimed to establish the correlation between the country's perceived friend / non-friend / undecided status and the type of power underlying the foreign policy tools employed.[469]

The following pages shall be devoted to summing up the findings. The next section (VI.2.) offers a summary of empirical findings, notably an overview of foreign policy tools applied in the

---

[468] Cf. table 1, *Foreign policy tools attributable to positive and negative power resources* for details.
[469] For a detailed discussion of methodological considerations, cf. chapter III of the present study.

three cases. It is followed by a discussion of theoretical findings and implications for theory development in VI.3. Finally, implications for the continued development of a neoclassical realist research agenda are the subject of section VI.4, which concludes this chapter and this study.

VI.2 Empirical findings: U.S. post-Cold War policies towards Poland, Ukraine and Belarus

The empirical chapters contained in this study have dealt with United States policies towards Central and Eastern Europe from 1989 to 2008. They covered three target countries (i.e., Poland, Ukraine and Belarus) and three U.S. presidencies (i.e., George H. W. Bush from 1989 onwards, William J. Clinton and George W. Bush), focusing on the foreign policy tools employed by Washington in the three bilateral contexts. Each of these countries represented one category of ideal-typical attitudes states can hold vis-à-vis each other: from a Washington perspective, Poland qualified as the United States' friend, Lukashenka's Belarus as a non-friend, whilst Ukraine held an undecided attitude towards Washington. Neither state evolved in its status vis-à-vis the United States throughout the period covered in this study. In other words, the independent or background variable has remained constant.

As has been shown in the present study, the United States recurred to foreign policy tools belonging to all four types of power resources in its policies towards Poland, Ukraine and Belarus. These tools range from dinner invitations to the White House and millions of dollars in economic and military aid to embargos and unfriendly statements issued by U.S. embassies. In other words, Washington made use of the entire bandwidth of foreign policy tools short of physical violence, but otherwise including everything from kind words to missiles.[470] The instances in which these foreign policy tools came to use were most of the time very concrete matters

---

[470] Patriot missiles serving as an incentive for Poland to sign the missile defence agreement.

(such as a nuclear power plant to be built in Iran), sometimes considered to be representative of more abstract phenomena (such as general principles of nuclear non-proliferation in the world). Yet, it lies within the nature of foreign policy tools that they are concrete measures, which, as such, can only be applied in concrete situations: foreign policy tools are explicit acts. It is however missing the mark to believe that foreign policy tools are only applied in situations of conflict or differences over proceedings. Rather, foreign policy tools have been used in two different ways: one, to indeed obtain a specific outcome in times of disagreement; two, in order to sustain or in hopes of fostering good relations. The latter two obviously only implies tools attributable to positive power, applied in order to maintain a state's friendship with the United States.

In attempting to retrace the events that, taken together, represent U.S.-relations with the respective countries during the period of time covered, it has clearly been easier to account for relations characterised by differences over specific matters instead of abstract issues. In the context of this study, this means that U.S. relations with Ukraine have proven to be the richest case. Differences over concrete matters cause mentions of these issues and leave traces in documents, allowing the researcher to reconstruct positions and evolutions. Unproblematic and smooth relationships, on the other hand, strangely leave much fewer traces. They receive little attention in the sources, at press and background briefings, and coverage is often contingent on orchestrated events such as state visits or other ceremonies. Ironically, absence of a bilateral relationship from official sources could therefore in itself be considered an indicator of good relations. This has been a challenge in analysing U.S.-Polish relations, whereas the repeated ups and downs in U.S.-Ukrainian relations have led to extensive presence in U.S. administration sources, making the Ukraine chapter the longest one in this study.

As far as information on Washington's perceptions of the respective countries' status is concerned, in turn, it is interesting to note that U.S. appraisals are expressed in a much more straightforward manner in the case of friends and non-friends. For both Poland and Belarus, Background Notes contain unambiguous appraisals of the bilateral relationships' quality. In the Ukrainian — i.e., undecided — case, relevant information on the country's perceived status to a much greater extent figured in transcripts of background briefings — thus in itself reflecting the fact that Kyiv behaved in ambiguous ways throughout the period covered here. Most likely, U.S.-Ukrainian relations were never stable enough to allow for definite judgements expressed in such basic documents like Background Notes. Moreover, it seems fair to assume that Washington refrained from issuing negative appraisals in the Notes in order not to cause any more damage in an already problematic relationship.

The above named difficulties notwithstanding, the analyses carried out allow for answers to the empirical questions asked at the outset of this study. The table on the following page summarises the foreign policy tools applied by the U.S. towards Poland, Ukraine and Belarus in terms of the type of power to which they are attributable. It clearly confirms the assumption that there is a correlation between a country's friend / non-friend / undecided status and the type of power resources applied: foreign policy tools applied towards friends are indeed (predominantly) based on positive power resources; foreign policy tools applied towards non-friends are (predominantly) based on negative power resources, whereas foreign policy tools applied towards undecided states are based on both types. Poland as a very good friend exclusively benefited from positive power measures. Warsaw appears as a recipient of financial and practical aid (ranging from language training to offered warships), a beneficiary of moral support and as 'America's best friend'. The country was allowed to enjoy all the pomp of ostensibly displayed excellent relations and all the prestige this confers (or is intended to confer). Lukashenka's Belarus as a non-friend, in turn, was exclusively met with foreign policy tools pertaining to the realm of negative power. These ranged from harsh words to international "shaming" measures, from travel restrictions to blocked property. Ukraine's undecided status, finally, clearly resulted in the U.S. using foreign policy tools covering almost the entire range from kind words to cruise missiles. Washington pursued denuclearisation using carrots and sticks, agreed to hold meetings between the Presidents at some points and refused to do so at others, spent tremendous amounts of money and offered the Ukrainian space industry a future, publicly condemned Kyiv's democracy record and sent fact finding missions to investigate transgressions of international norms. The U.S. declared a 'strategic partnership', pushed for Ukraine's NATO membership, and had its ambassador state that trust between the countries had been 'eroded' and that the relationship had reached its 'most difficult point' since its beginnings.

Another conclusion to be drawn is that U.S. measures had no effect on any of the countries' long-term attitude towards Washington as seen by U.S. foreign policy makers. Despite its (sometimes costly) attempts and efforts, the United States did not succeed at increasing its number of friends. In other words, Washington has not succeeded in expanding its already dominant power position, at least as far as Central and Eastern Europe is concerned. This, in itself, illustrates the limits of its power. From a global perspective, it may therefore be argued that, as contemporary politics in the post-Soviet sphere illustrate, the post-Cold War era is not over in the sense that the redistribution of spheres of influence remains unfinished. The ongoing war in Ukraine and the annexation of Crimea in 2014 clearly illustrate this. Perhaps more than ever, Russia continues to be a most relevant actor, although Moscow is no match for Washington at a systemic level. The fact that since the Bush II administration and especially under Obama, due to the war against terrorism and what came to be labelled the 'Pacific Pivot', Central and Eastern Europe lost in relevance to Washington certainly also matters. The boundaries of the Western—hence (also) American—sphere of influence may have been pushed eastward with the expansions of NATO and the European Union. Yet, In Central and Eastern Europe, the United States did not succeed in making reluctant states become its friends, inducing them to bandwagon with Washington. The friend / non-friend / undecided attitudes states hold vis-à-vis other states (and perceptions thereof) should therefore be considered rather stable and difficult to change from the outside. The example of Belarus underscores this assessment, as Minsk tellingly is the case which proved to be most problematic for Washington—yet not because the US, with its vast resources, did not have enough potential policy tools at its disposal, but for the much simpler reason that Minsk was not willing to engage in any relationship with Washington. In other words, not a lack of power resources on the United States' part was the problem, but rather the absence of a Belarusian response. This led even U.S. officials to admit that American leverage over the authorities in Minsk was very limited. This finding perhaps is the fact that best supports the claim that power resources on the foreign policy emitting state's side cannot single-handedly account for that state's behaviour.

In sum, the table below thus provides compelling evidence for the assumption that there is a link between a country's perceived friend / non-friend / undecided status and the type of power resources applied towards it:

Table 2: Foreign policy tools applied in U.S. policies towards Poland, Ukraine and Belarus 1989–2008

	Positive power tools		Negative power tools	
	material	symbolic	material	symbolic
Poland	Economic aid programmes / business training / education cooperation; Environmental aid programmes; support for membership in and aid from financial institutions; military cooperation and aid, extremely favourable armament deals	Backing Solidarność; promoting NATO membership (complemented by material power tools), comparably important number of high level contacts; ostentatious display of "friendship"	-	-
Ukraine	Economic aid; Nunn-Lugar; support for membership in and aid from financial institutions; access to U.S. markets (Sea Launch), civil nuclear cooperation	Inviting Ukraine to the international scene; "strategic partnership"; security assurances; high level contacts; engaging Ukraine in NATO	Cutbacks on financial aid	Denied high level contacts; voicing public concern; threats of "consequences"
(Lukashenka's) Belarus	-	-	Economic sanctions	Declarations of "concern", rejection, outrage; travel restrictions; refused high level contacts; The Belarus Democracy Act

The results of the empirical analyses carried out in this study hence clearly allow for the inference that the use of power resources indeed is circumstantial, contingent on the target country's perceived friend / non-friend / undecided status. Whether positive or negative power is employed in influence attempts directed towards other states is linked to perceptions of these other states' attitude towards the foreign policy emitting state. The theoretical implications of these findings shall be discussed in the following sections.

VI.3 Implications for theory building: linking status to power

Neoclassical realists consider perceptions to be an intervening variable between a state's power resources and its behaviour — in other words, perceptions are said to be an element of the so-called missing link. This is an assumption confirmed by the present study. The study's contribution to theory development is, however, not limited to confirming that assumption at an aggregate level. As a matter of fact, 'perception' is a largely underspecified notion in International Relations. By basing the analysis of perceptions' role in explaining state behaviour on the ideal-typical categories of friendly, unfriendly and undecided states, this study also strove to offer a theoretically more elaborated — and indeed operationalisable — approach to the phenomenon of perception. Moreover, by analysing 'state behaviour' in terms of foreign policy tools emitted, it allowed for a firmer grasp of a notion often encompassing the entire range from single acts of foreign policy to balancing moves and Grand Strategy. Somehow as a by-product, this study has hence yielded a pair of notions — i.e., states' friend / non-friend / undecided status and foreign policies based upon positive or negative power — which allow for a more concise handling of the somewhat cloudy phenomena of perception and state behaviour, within and beyond the confines of neoclassical realism.

VI.3.1 Friends, non-friends and undecided states: an element of the missing link

At the most basic level, a first result of this study is that one and the same actor — the United States — has resorted to different combinations of foreign policy tools, based on different types of power, in its policies towards countries to which it attributed different friend

/ non-friend / undecided statuses. As the empirical analysis has shown, there is an obvious correlation between the perceived friend / non-friend / undecided status a country holds and the kind of power employed in foreign policies towards it by another state. That status must therefore be considered an element of the missing link between power resources and foreign policy output. How states perceive a target state's friend / non-friend / undecided attitude is thus an intervening variable between power resources and foreign policy output. What follows is that an update or rather 'bilateralisation' of the traditional realist concepts of revisionist and status quo states as well as perceptions thereof is necessary. Perceptions of the international system may certainly be important, but in states' actual policies on the ground, perceptions of the actors they target with their measures seem at least equally important. As a matter of fact, the system being the same at one given moment, differences in states' behaviour towards different actors are hardly explicable by their perception of systemic conditions alone. This is also valid when states pursue systemic objectives: for instance, even when engaging in balancing moves in order to restore a systemic balance of power, a state's choice of allies will logically depend on its perception of its fellow states.

Yet, when attempting to explain foreign policy beyond balancing and under-balancing, states' perceptions of other states are relevant at an even more fundamental level. As discussed in Chapter II, the very nature of that which makes power work—the so-called base values—vary depending on whether a state is dealing with a friend, a non-friend or an undecided state. The same foreign policy tools—economic aid, for instance—may in fact yield different results in different contexts and constellations, depending on who the recipient is. In other words, the cases studied above indicate that the power resources at a state's disposal vary depending on the targeted state's friend / non-friend / undecided status. This, in turn, is a fact policy makers are highly likely to have in mind when using power. From a realist vantage point, this may be surprising and even run counter to traditional realist assumptions, not least if considering, for instance, that Poland, Ukraine and Belarus should be roughly at the same level when comparing their relative power to that of the United States. Yet, as especially the Belarusian case has illustrated, a mere look at U.S. capabilities does not allow for conclusions on Washington's ability to exert power. The distribution of power resources alone is thus no sufficient explanation of states' ability to exert influence on other states. American power resources being the same in all three cases, reasons for different approaches under identical systemic conditions towards actors similar in terms of their power resources, size and geographical location must lie elsewhere. As this study has argued, the explanation lies in the fact that Poland, Ukraine and Belarus held different attitudes towards Washington, in other words: U.S. perceptions of their respective friend / non-friend / undecided status is the missing link in explaining how the United States translated its power resources into foreign policy behaviour.

VI.3.2 A category of its own: undecided states

Traditional realist conceptualisations of states' attitudes towards the system know no equivalent of undecided states. It is therefore appropriate to ask whether undecided states really qualify as a category in itself. In the Ukrainian case, which has been treated as the undecided example in this study, it is therefore especially interesting to note the changes over time, as the country oscillated between friendly and less friendly attitudes. In other words, it is worth asking in which instances the U.S. resorted to positive and in which instances to negative power. The most logical assumption would arguably be that the more unfriendly Ukraine's attitude, the more the U.S. should likely resort to negative power. This assumption is based on the idea that approaches towards non-friends would essentially be based on negative power tools, an expectation confirmed by the Belarusian case. Yet, if that assumption were correct, a look at the data reveals some sort of paradox: the more unfriendly Ukraine behaved, i.e. the deeper the disagreement, the more Washington's approach towards Kyiv was dominated by positive power measures. In terms of issues, the more Kyiv behaved in an unfriendly way, the more relevant the issues at hand were to the United States' national security, namely the nuclear question and

Ukraine's accession to the MTCR. This is a paradox since it may be expected that disagreement over issues pertaining to national security have the highest potential to engender enmity in the most essential, Schmittean sense of the term.

In reality, however, both in the context of the nuclear question and Ukraine's accession to the MTCR, the United States' approach was clearly dominated by positive material power. At second glance, the United States' policies seem nevertheless much less paradoxical, and for two reasons. First, the Ukrainian case confirms that undecided states indeed are a category distinct from friends and non-friends and not merely oscillating between these two poles. Rather, in approaching undecided states, policy makers tend to avoid (further) alienation, instead trying to preserve a basis for cooperation. Second, U.S. policies towards Ukraine may also be interpreted as acknowledging the fact that international politics is about interests. Accordingly, Ukraine is more likely to comply with U.S. demands if it stands to gain something from its compliance. The following quote by a senior U.S. official on President Kravchuk clearly illustrates that Ukraine's constraints and interests were part of Washington's thinking about foreign policy measures:

> [Kravchuk] said, look, we have to address the concerns of the [Ukrainian] parliament. And he said, I'm willing to do that. Working together with the United States, working together with Russia, we'll deal with — some of their main concerns had to do with compensation, for example. He said, "Then I will be resubmitting the package, the Lisbon Protocol package, which includes START I as well as the NPT part of it, to the Rada. [...] He said he expects to resubmit the package in March or shortly thereafter for another vote. I [senior official] expect, based on what I have been hearing from some Ukrainian parliamentarians, that they will be satisfied with what they have seen emerge from this deal.[471]

In the end, Washington essentially bought Kyiv's getting rid of its nuclear question and adherence to the Missile Technology Control Regime. The foreign policy tools that allowed Washington to obtain the desired outcome were thus based on positive material power. In other words, the measures which allowed the United States to

---

471 The White House, Office of the Press Secretary (1994) 'Background Briefing by Senior Administration Officials', Conrad Hotel, Brussels, 10 January.

actually *shape* its environment made use of positive power foreign policy tools.

VI.3.3 Positive and negative power as means to shape and control the environment

In the case of U.S. policies towards Poland over almost two decades, the sources contained no evidence of negative power being applied. Negative power, however, is the kind of power traditionally considered to be in the realist focus. An analysis limited to a notion of power equalled to capabilities or merely looking at negative power might consequently come to the conclusion that the United States refrained from exerting power over Warsaw. This, in turn, would clearly be an inaccurate assessment. What follows is that for a neoclassical realist analysis of state behaviour in terms of foreign policy, a wider notion than that traditionally associated with political realism becomes mandatory.

As may be deduced from the theoretical considerations discussed at the outset of this study, the prerequisites for states' wielding of power vary depending on whether they deal with friends, non-friends or undecided states. The empirical analyses have shown that the kind of power employed indeed varies depending on the perceived status. And although this study has not been designed to assess the effectiveness of different types of power, its results allow for a number of observations—somehow as a by-product of the empirical analyses. If assuming that it is in any state's interest to have more friends than enemies, it may be concluded that U.S. foreign policies towards Poland, Belarus and Ukraine from 1989 to 2008 have not served to increase the number of friendly states. Rather, the respective countries' status remained unchanged throughout the period analysed. While Poland continued to be a friend, the measures applied towards Ukraine and Belarus had no positive effect on Kyiv's and Minsk's perceived attitude towards Washington. It may therefore be deduced that negative power—at least as applied in those two cases—is not suited to make a country's status evolve. Conversely, it may be argued that this study's findings point to the direction of positive power being more effective and sustainable than negative power (at least as long as war, the ultimate instance of negative material power, is no option). This, however, would have considerable consequences from a realist vantage point, nonetheless for the impressive number of realists essentially concerned with power as capabilities to inflict damage, hence: negative power. Thus, this study only confirms Joseph Nye's appraisal that

> There is no contradiction between realism and soft power. Soft power is not a form of idealism or liberalism. It is simply a form of power, one way of getting desired outcomes.[472]

Negative power may save a state from being attacked or allow it to prevail in case of war. It will allow a state to uphold a balance of power defined in terms of capabilities. As the empirical findings of this study indicate, however, negative power hardly puts a state in the position to effectively control and shape its external environment, the chief state objective according to neoclassical realism. Thus, no proof of negative power tools inciting a target state to actively *do* something could be found in the sources. All negative power tools found could be interpreted as (more or less successful) attempts to make the target state *refrain* from unwanted behaviour, be it human rights abuse, transgression of non-proliferation rules or disregard of international law. In the analyses carried out, foreign policy tools inciting states to take action were, in turn, all based on positive power resources. Put simply, one may therefore argue that negative power serves the purposes of deterrence, whereas 'constructive' power is primarily exerted on the basis of positive power resources. In other words, while negative power may be helpful in *controlling* the external environment, positive power enables states to actually *shape* it. Within the context of the present study, this is nonetheless a valid observation for all matters with systemic implications: Poland's inclusion in the Western sphere of influence and Ukraine's denuclearisation. None of these objectives

---

472 Joseph S. Nye (2005) 'Notes on a soft power research agenda', in: Felix Berenskoetter and Michael J. Williams (eds.) *Power in World Politics*, p. 170.

were attained by means of negative power. For that reason, realists should feel compelled to take a more differentiated stance on their conceptualisations of power and further pursue the path chosen in this study.

This conclusion is linked with another observation to be made on the basis of the empirical results. Quite evidently, there is a link between the nature of the issue at hand and the kind of power used in addressing it. Thus, disagreement over principles and values is exclusively met with negative power tools in all instances it occurs. Both Ukraine's and Belarus's violations of democratic principles, human rights and international code of conducts are "punished" with public statements containing harsh words, cutbacks in aid, frozen assets and the like. The interrelationship between such fundamental disagreement and unfriendly relations is obvious: a state will hardly ever consider another state legitimate under such circumstances. In other words, friends would per definition not disagree over fundamental values at all or, in case of a purely strategic "friendship", circumvent the issue. Disagreement over concrete issues, in turn, is predominantly met with positive power tools: nuclear warheads, membership in non-proliferation regimes, or reactors in Iran were all problems Washington "solved" by offering Ukraine incentives to change its behaviour. Although further research is needed, a tentative conclusion to be drawn from that observation pertains to the efficiency of negative power in international politics, confirming the assessment that negative power serves the purpose of controlling the external environment, whereas positive power allows for shaping it. The Belarusian case clearly illustrates that U.S. efforts evaporated to no effect on Minsk's behaviour. The country's leadership obviously saw no reason to adopt different policies as a consequence of Washington's denouncing statements.

Realists are traditionally more concerned with system disruptions and conflict than with peaceful international cooperation. Consequently, realists taking interest in intra-state influence are prone to study states' relations with their non-friends or even enemies at war. Yet, in the conduct of international affairs, having friends and dealing with them is at least equally important as deterring one's enemies—a fact nonetheless (implicitly) acknowledged by realist approaches focusing on alliances and balances of power, threat or interest. Approaches to friends and positive power are therefore important to include within realist frameworks, in order to depict a more complete international reality. This is nonetheless the case for scholars interested in how states shape their environment beyond merely attempting to control it, be it through incentives for bandwagoning, alliance formation or other forms of inducement for states to behave in a specific way.

VI.4 Final remarks

If states make use of their power resources in order to control and shape their external environment, then the environment itself needs to be a prominent part in explaining state behaviour. This environment being populated by states, elite perceptions of these other states' are indeed most relevant. In the present study, perceptions of these other states' friend / non-friend / undecided attitudes have been introduced as ideal-typical categories in order to make (parts of) this context tangible. As this study has shown, perceptions of the "other actor", i.e., the state at the receiving end of foreign policy, simply are an integral part of the equation. For that reason, they should be considered an element of the missing link. Neoclassical realists' concern with elite perceptions of systemic factors must therefore be widened to also include perceptions of other states. This is an indispensable move for any research programme with the ambition to not only explain recurrent patterns of behaviour in order to attain to a theory of the international system, but which actually seeks to explain foreign policy. Shifting a research agenda's *explanandum* from recurrent patterns of behaviour to foreign policy and the behaviour of specific states indeed comes along with a number of consequences. One of these consequences is the increased need for attention devoted to foreign policy as a necessarily bilateral phenomenon. By expanding the notion of perception—one of the two major categories of intervening variables in neoclassical realism—to explicitly encompass states' perceptions of other states, this study has offered a response to that lacuna. By linking these perceptions to state behaviour, it has contributed to further elucidating the so-called missing link neoclassical realists identified between a state's power resources and the foreign policies it pursues. In sum, the results of this study thus constitute a strong argument for an increased bilateralisation of the analysis of state behaviour.

That said, realism continues to be an 'environment based theory'.[473] For that reason, systemic conditions and perceptions are highly relevant. The above commended bilateralisation is therefore clearly meant to supplement neoclassical realism's concern with systemic factors, not to supplant it. This study has thus argued that a focus on the system is insufficient to explain state behaviour — not least in case of dissimilar state behaviour under identical systemic conditions. A look at systemic conditions may certainly allow for inferences on why states, for instance, choose to balance, but not with whom. A research programme seeking to explain foreign policy, however, must arguably also be able to answer the latter question. It is in this respect neoclassical realism may contribute to reversing the study of international politics' bifurcation into International Relations and Foreign Policy Analysis. After all, both deal with the same phenomena, making the distinction of the two disciplines seem oddly artificial.[474] As a matter of fact, realist strands of International Relations and Foreign Policy Analysis could draw mutual benefit from each other: the strength of realism draws upon its awareness that 'a state's foreign policy cannot transcend the limits and opportunities thrown up by the international environment'[475] — but perhaps sometimes losing sight of levels of analysis other than the international system. Many *innenpolitikers*, in turn,

---

[473] Jennifer Sterling-Folker (1997) 'Realist Environment, Liberal Process, and Domestic Level Variables', p. 4.

[474] On that matter, see also Colin Elman (1996) 'Horses for Courses: Why Not Neorealist Theories of Foreign policy?', Security Studies 6(1), pp. 7-53, as well as the ensuing debate between Elman and Kenneth Waltz. See also Randall L. Schweller (2003) 'The Progressiveness of Neoclassical Realism,' in Miriam Fendius Elman (ed.) *Progress in International Relations Theory: Appraising the Field*, Cambridge: MIT Press, pp. 311-348.

[475] Gideon Rose (1998) 'Neoclassical Realism and Theories of Foreign Policy', p. 151.

privilege the individual and domestic levels at the expense of the international, essentially studying processes of decision-making. Neoclassical realism is thus perhaps also rightly termed, in that it reunites academic strands whose separation was indeed foreign to Hans J. Morgenthau and his fellow classical realists.

Annex

High-level contacts between the U.S. and Poland, Ukraine and Belarus

1) Visits by Polish officials to the United States

Who	Function	Date	Remarks
Tadeusz Mazowiecki	Prime Minister	20–23 March 1990	Working visit
Tadeusz Mazowiecki	Prime Minister	29 September 1990	Met President Bush at UN General Assembly
Lech Wałęsa	President	19–22 March 1991	State visit
Jan Krzysztof Bielecki	Prime Minister	11 September 1991	Met President Bush during a private visit
Jan Olszewski	Prime Minister	13–14 April 1992	Met President Bush during a private visit.
Lech Wałęsa	President	20–22 April 1993	Attended dedication of the Holocaust Memorial Museum and met President Clinton.
Aleksander Kwaśniewski	President	9–10 July 1996	Working visit
Jerzy Buzek	Prime Minister	8–10 July 1998	Met President Clinton during a private visit
Aleksander Kwaśniewski / Jerzy Buzek	President / Prime Minister	23–25 April 1999	Attended NATO's 50th Anniversary Summit
Leszek Miller	Prime Minister	10–11 January 2002	Working visit
Aleksander Kwaśniewski	President	17–18 June 2002	State visit
Aleksander Kwaśniewski	President	12–14 January 2003	Working visit
Leszek Miller	Prime Minister	4–7 February 2003	Working visit
Aleksander Kwaśniewski	President	26–27 January 2004	Working visit
Marek Belka	Prime Minister	7–9 August 2004	Working visit
Aleksander Kwaśniewski	President	8–9 February 2005	Working visit

Aleksander Kwaśniewski	President	12 October 2005	Working visit
Lech Kaczyński	President	8–10 February 2006	Working visit
Lech Kaczyński	President	15–17 July 2007	Working visit

2) Visits by U.S. officials to Poland

Who	Function	Date	Remarks
George H. W. Bush	President	9–11 July 1989	Met government officials and Solidarity leaders. Addressed the Polish National Assembly on July 10. Accompanied by Secretary of State James A. Baker III
James A. Baker III	Secretary of State	6 May 1990	Met Polish officials and Solidarity leaders
George H. W. Bush	President	5 July 1992	Met President Wałęsa and attended a memorial service for former Prime Minister Paderewski. Accompanied by Secretary of State James A. Baker III
William J. Clinton	President	6–7 July 1994	Addressed the Polish Parliament and attended ceremonies commemorating the Warsaw Ghetto revolt. With Secretary of State Warren M. Christopher
William J. Clinton	President	10–11 July 1997	Met President Kwaśniewski and former President Wałęsa. Accompanied by Secretary of State Madeleine K. Albright
Madeleine K. Albright	Secretary of State	24–27 June 2000	Attended the World Forum on Democracy; received honorary degree from the University of Gdansk
George W. Bush	President	15–16 June 2001	State visit. Accompanied by Secretary of State Colin L. Powell
George W. Bush	President	30–31 May 2003	Met President Kwaśniewski and Prime Minister Miller; visited former Nazi concentration camps. Accompanied by Secretary of State Colin L. Powell
Colin L. Powell	Secretary of State	31 July–1 August 2004	Met Foreign Minister Cimoszewicz and attended ceremonies commemorating the Warsaw Uprising.

| Condoleezza Rice | Secretary of State | 5 February 2005 | Met Prime Minister Belka and Foreign Minister Rotfeld. |
| George W. Bush | President | 8 June 2007 | Met President Lech Kaczyński |

3) Visits by Ukrainian officials to the United States

Who	Function	Date	Remarks
Leonid Kravchuk	President	5–7 May 1992	Official working visit
Leonid Kravchuk	President	3–5 March 1994	Working visit
Leonid Kuchma	President	21–23 November 1994	State visit
Leonid Kuchma	President	20–22 February 1996	Met President Clinton during a private visit.
Leonid Kuchma	President	14–16 May 1997	Attended meeting of the U.S.-Ukraine Binational Commission
Leonid Kuchma	President	23–25 April 1999	Attended NATO's 50th Anniversary Summit
Leonid Kuchma	President	7–8 December 1999	Working visit
Viktor Yushchenko	President	4–5 April 2005	Working visit

4) Visits by U.S. officials to Ukraine

Who	Function	Date	Remarks
George H. W. Bush	President	29 July–1 August 1991	Attended U.S.-Soviet Summit Meeting. Signed START. Addressed the Ukrainian Parliament.
James A. Baker III	Secretary of State	18–19 December 1991	Met President Kravchuk
Warren M. Christopher	Secretary of State	24–26 October 1993	Met President Kravchuk and senior Ukrainian officials
William J. Clinton	President	12 January 1994	Met President Kravchuk. With Secretary of State Warren M. Christopher
William J. Clinton	President	11–12 May 1995	State visit. Accompanied by Secretary of State Warren M. Christopher

Warren M. Christopher	Secretary of State	18–19 March 1996	Met President Kuchma and Foreign Minister Udovenko
Madeleine K. Albright	Secretary of State	6 March 1998	Met President Kuchma and signed nuclear cooperation agreement
Madeleine K. Albright	Secretary of State	14–15 April 2000	Met President Kuchma and Foreign Minister Tarasyuk
William J. Clinton	President	5 June 2000	Met President Kuchma
George W. Bush	President	1 April 2008	

5) Visits by Belarusian officials to the United States

Who	Function	Date	Remarks
Stanislav Shushkevich	Chairman	21–23 July 1993	Met with President Clinton during a private visit.

6) Visits by U.S. officials to Belarus

Who	Function	Date	Remarks
James A. Baker III	Secretary of State	18 December 1991	Met Soviet Chairman Shuskevich and Foreign Minister Kravchenko
Warren M. Christopher	Secretary of State	26 October 1993	Met Chairman Shuskevich and senior officials
William J. Clinton	President	15 January 1994	Met Chairman Shushkevich. With Secretary of State Warren M. Christopher

References

Primary Sources

Speeches, Press Releases and Briefings[*]

American Forces Press Service, Fred W. Baker III (2009) 'Obama Announces Changes for European Missile Defense', Washington D.C., 17 September.

Baker, James A. (1989) 'Address to the Berlin Press Club', Berlin, 12 December. Reprinted in: *Berlin Speeches: Secretary of State James A. Baker*, Washington D.C.: U.S. Information Agency, 1991.

Baker, James A. (1990) 'From Revolution to Democracy: Central and Eastern Europe in the New Europe', address at Charles University, Prague, Czechoslovakia, 7 February.

Baker, James A. (1990) 'The Common European Interest: America and the New Politics Among Nations', address before the National Committee on American Foreign Policy, upon receiving the 7th Annual Hans J. Morgenthau Memorial Award, New York, 14 May.

Baker, James A. (1990) 'Statement by Secretary Baker before the Senate Foreign Relations Committee', Washington D.C., 12 June.

Campbell, Ben, Senator, (2002) 'Statement in U.S. Senate on Belarus', Washington D.C., 24 January.

Dobriansky, Paula J., United States Under Secretary for Democracy and Global Affairs (2007) 'Poland as Ukraine's Gateway to the West', remarks at the Heritage Foundation, Washington, D.C., 18 January.

Fotyga, Anna, Polish Minister of Foreign Affairs (2007) 'Annual Address to the Sejm', Warsaw, 11 May.

General Affairs and External Relations Council [European Union] (1997) 'Belarus: Council conclusions', Press Release 269 nr. 10368/97, Brussels, 15 September.

Gore, Al, Vice President of the United States (1993) 'The Principles and Future of U.S.-Polish Relations', address delivered in Warsaw / Poland, 20 April (cf. *U.S. Department of State Dispatch* 4(18), 3 May 1993.)

Grudzinski, Przemysław (2004) 'Poland's Accession to the European Union and Its Impact on United States-Polish Relations', *The Ambassadors Review*, fall 2004.

---

[*] Unless otherwise indicated, the text is available at the respective organisation's web page.

Juster, Kenneth E., Senior Advisor to the Deputy Secretary of State (1990) 'Remarks from a conference sponsored by the RAND Corporation on Supporting East European Democracy and Free Markets', Santa Monica, 21 September.

Küsters, Hans Jürgen and Daniel Hofmann (eds.) (1998) *Dokumente zur Deutschlandpolitik; Deutsche Einheit: Sonderedition aus den Akten des Bundeskanzleramtes 1989/90.* Munich: Oldenbourg.

Kwaśniewski, Aleksander (1996) 'Poland and NATO', remarks at the XIIIth NATO Workshop on Political-Military Decision Making, Warsaw, 19 June.

Lake, Anthony, Assistant to the President for National Security Affairs (1993) 'From Containment to Enlargement', Remarks at the Johns Hopkins University's School of Advanced International Studies, Washington D.C., 21 September.

NATO Parliamentary Assembly (2006) 'More Proactive Strategy Towards Belarus Needed', Press Communiqué, Brussels, 17 October.

NATO Parliamentary Assembly, Standing Committee (2001) 'Report of an Assembly Fact Finding Mission to Minsk 25–27 March 2001', Doc. AU 28 SC (01) 8, Brussels, March.

NATO, NATO Press Services (2002) 'Statement by the Head of the Delegation of Belarus at the EAPC Meeting at the level of Heads of State and Government', Prague, 22 November.

NATO, NATO Press Services (2006) 'Press Point with NATO Secretary General, Jaap de Hoop Scheffer and the Prime Minister of Ukraine, Viktor Yanukovych after the meeting of the NATO-Ukraine Commission at ambassadorial level', NATO Headquarters, Brussels, 14 September.

NATO, NATO Press Services (2008) 'Joint Statement', Meeting of the NATO-Ukraine Commission at the level of Heads of State and Government, Bucharest, 4 April (NATO Press Release (2008)051).

NATO, NATO Press Services (2008) 'Introductory Remarks by Secretary General Jaap de Hoop Scheffer at the meeting of the NATO-Ukraine Commission with Invitees at the Level of Foreign Ministers', Brussels, 3 December.

OSCE, Office For Democratic Institutions and Human Rights (2001) 'Belarus Parliamentary Elections – Technical Assessment Mission Final Report', Warsaw, 30 January.

OSCE, Office For Democratic Institutions and Human Rights (2001) 'Republic of Belarus Presidential Elections Final Report', Warsaw, 9 September.

Pascual, Carlos, U.S. Ambassador to Ukraine (2003) 'U.S.-Ukraine Relations', remarks at the Russia and Eurasia Program Policy Leaders Forum', Center for Strategic and International Studies, Washington D.C., 9 January.

Polish Prime Minister, Press Service (2008) 'Negotiations on the anti-missile shield continue', Press release, Warsaw, 4 July.

Pifer, Steven, Deputy Assistant Secretary for European and Eurasian Affairs (2003) 'The U.S.-Ukraine Relationship: Looking To Move Forward', remarks at the Russia and Eurasia Program Policy Leaders Forum, Center for Strategic and International Studies, Washington, D.C., 13 February.

Rumsfeld, Donald H. (2002) 'Prepared Testimony of U.S. Secretary of Defense Donald H. Rumsfeld before the House and Senate Armed Services Committees regarding Iraq. As Delivered by Secretary of Defense Donald H. Rumsfeld', Washington D.C., 18 September.

Saxton, Jim, Congressman (2002) 'Saxton Delegation Back in the U.S.A. — Anti-terrorism trip to Holland, Belarus, Russia, Germany complete', Press Release, Washington D.C., 25 February.

Talbott, Strobe, Ambassador-at-Large and Special Adviser to the Secretary on the New Independent States (1993) 'The United States and Ukraine: Broadening the Relationship', Statement before the Subcommittee on European Affairs of the Senate Foreign Relations Committee, Washington D.C., June 24, cf. *U.S. Department of State Dispatch* 4(27), 5 July 1993.

Talbott, Strobe (1998) 'The New Ukraine in the New Europe', address at the Workshop on Ukraine-NATO Relations sponsored by the Harvard University Project on Ukrainian Security and the Stanford-Harvard Preventive Defense Project, Brookings Institution. Washington, D.C., 8 April, cf. *U.S. Department of State Dispatch*, May 1998, p. 14 ff.

The White House, Office of the Press Secretary (1989) 'A Europe Whole and Free. Remarks to the Citizens in Mainz by President George Bush', Rheingoldhalle, Mainz, 31 May.

The White House, Office of the Press Secretary (1989) 'Remarks and a Question-and-Answer Session with Reporters on the Relaxation of East German Border Controls', Washington D.C., 9 November.

The White House, Office of the Press Secretary (1990) 'NATO and the U.S. commitment to Europe', address by President George H.W Bush at the Oklahoma State University Commencement Ceremony, Stillwater, 4 May.

The White House, Office of the Press Secretary (1991) 'Speech by President Bush to the Supreme Soviet of Ukraine', Kyiv, 1 August.

The White House, Office of the Press Secretary (1991) 'Ukrainians Vote for Independence', Washington D.C., 2 December, cf. *U.S. Department of State Dispatch* 2(49), 9 December 1991.

The White House, Office of the Press Secretary (1993) 'Press Briefing by Dee Dee Myers', Washington D.C., 29 November.

White House, Office of the Press Secretary (1994) 'Remarks By The President At Intervention for the North Atlantic Council Summit', NATO Headquarters, Brussels, 10 January.

The White House, Office of the Press Secretary (1994) 'Press Briefing by Secretary Warren Christopher', Conrad Hotel, Brussels, 10 January.

The White House, Office of the Press Secretary (1994) 'Background Briefing By Senior Administration Officials', Conrad Hotel, Brussels, 10 January.

The White House, Office of the Press Secretary (1994) 'Remarks by President Clinton and President Kravchuk', Kiev Airport, Kyiv, 12 January.

The White House, Office of the Press Secretary (1994) 'Background Briefing By Senior Administration Officials', Washington D.C., 14 January.

The White House, Office of the Press Secretary (1994) 'Fact Sheet. Ukraine: U.S. Assistance Package', Washington D.C., 4 March.

The White House, Office of the Press Secretary (1994) 'Background on Kravchuk Visit', press briefing, Washington D.C., 4 March.

The White House, Office of the Press Secretary (1994) 'Press Conference by President Clinton and President Kravchuk of Ukraine', Washington D.C., 4 March.

The White House, Office of the Press Secretary (1994) 'Joint Statement on Economic and Commercial Cooperation', Washington D.C., March 4.

The White House, Office of the Press Secretary (1994) 'Speech by President to the Polish Sejm', Warsaw, 7 July.

The White House, Office of the Press Secretary (1999) 'Fact Sheet: NATO-Ukraine Commission', Washington D.C., 24 April.

The White House, Office of the Press Secretary (1994) 'Ukraine's Vote To Accede To The Non-Proliferation Treaty', statement by the Press Secretary, Washington D.C., 17 November.

The White House, Office of the Press Secretary (1994) 'Background Briefing by Senior Administration Officials on Upcoming Visit of President Kuchma of Ukraine', Washington D.C., 21 November.

The White House, Office of the Press Secretary (1994) 'Fact Sheet: State Visit of Ukrainian President Kuchma. U.S. Bilateral Assistance to Ukraine', Washington D.C., 22 November.

The White House, Office of the Press Secretary (1994) 'Joint Summit Statement By President Clinton and President of Ukraine Leonid D. Kuchma', Washington D.C., 22 November.

The White House, Office of the Press Secretary (1994) 'Background Briefing by Senior Administration Officials', Washington D.C., 1 December.

The White House, Office of the Vice President (1997) 'Opening Statement by Vice President Al Gore, First Plenary Session, U.S.-Ukraine Binational Commission', Washington D.C., 16 May.

The White House, Office of the Press Secretary (1998) 'Promoting Democracy and Sovereignty in the Newly Independent States', Washington D.C., 21 May.

The White House, Office of the Press Secretary (2001) 'Statement on Belarus Presidential Elections', Washington, D.C., 17 January.

The White House, Office of the Press Secretary (2001) 'Remarks by the President in Address to Faculty and Students of Warsaw University', Warsaw, 15 June.

The White House, Office of the Press Secretary (2001) 'Statement by the Press Secretary: U.S. and Poland Sign Open Skies Agreement', Presidential Palace, Warsaw, 15 June.

The White House, Office of the Press Secretary (2001) 'President Bush Announces Support for Transfer of Frigate to Poland', Presidential Palace, Warsaw, 15 June.

The White House, Office of the Press Secretary (2001) 'U.S. To Transfer An Additional $20 Million to Polish American Freedom Foundation', Presidential Palace, Warsaw, 15 June.

The White House, Office of the Press Secretary (2001) 'Press Conference of President Bush and President of the Republic of Poland, Aleksander Kwasniewski', Presidential Palace, Warsaw, 15 June.

The White House, Office of the Press Secretary (2002) 'President Bush Delivers Graduation Speech at West Point. Remarks by the President at 2002 Graduation Exercise of the United States Military Academy', West Point, New York, 1 June.

The White House, Office of the Press Secretary (2002) 'Press Briefing by Ari Fleischer', Washington D.C., 19 June

The White House, Office of the Press Secretary (2002) 'Fact Sheet: U.S. Poland Military Cooperation Initiative', Washington D.C., July 17.

The White House, Office of the Press Secretary (2002) 'President Bush Welcomes President of Poland for State Visit', Washington D.C., July 17.

The White House, Office of the Press Secretary (2004) 'Statement by the President on the Belarus Democracy Act of 2004', Washington, D.C., 20 October.

The White House, Office of the Press Secretary (2005) 'Joint U.S.-EU Statement: Democracy, Freedom, The Rule of Law and Human Rights', Washington D.C., 20 June.

The White House, Office of the Press Secretary (2006) 'Press Briefing by Tony Snow', Washington D.C., 8 June.

The White House, Office of the Press Secretary (2007) 'Captive Nations Week, 2007', Washington D.C., 10 July.

The White House, Office of the Press Secretary (2008) 'Message to the Congress of the United States', Washington D.C., 6 June.

The White House, Office of the Press Secretary (2008) 'President Bush discusses the Visa Waiver Program', Washington D.C., 17 October.

U.S. Congress (2000), 'Congressional Resolution on Parliamentary Elections in Belarus', 25 October.

U.S. Department of Defense (1997) 'Cooperative Threat Reduction Assistance to Ukraine', Fact Sheet, Washington DC, 16 January.

U.S. Department of State, Office of the Spokesman (1990) 'A New Europe in a New Age: Insular, Itinerant or International? Prospects for an Alliance of Values', address by Robert Zoellick, Counselor of the State Department before the American-European Community Association's International Conference on US / EC Relations, Annapolis, 21 September.

U.S. Department of State, Office of the Spokesman (1990) 'Focus on Central and Eastern Europe 10/1/1990', cf. *U.S. Department of State Dispatch* 1(5), 1 October 1990.

U.S. Department of State (1991) 'Fact Sheet International Cooperation Act of 1991: Background', U.S. Department of State Dispatch 2(16), 22 April.

U.S. Department of State, Office of the Spokesman (1996) 'Press Briefing by Mike McCurry; Bob Bell, Senior Director for Defense and Arms Control Policy at NSC; and Steve Pifer, Director for Russian and Eurasian Affairs at NSC', Washington D.C., 3 June.

U.S. Department of State, Office of the Spokesman (1997) 'New U.S: Policy Toward Belarus', Washington D.C., 28 February.

U.S. Department of State, Office of the Spokesman (1998) 'Recall of Ambassador Speckhard', Washington D.C., 22 June.

U.S. Department of State, Office of the Spokesman (1998) 'Refutation of Lukashenko Remarks', Washington D.C., 24 July.

U.S. Department of State, Office of the Spokesman (1999) 'Return of U.S. Ambassador', Washington D.C., 14 September.

U.S. Department of State, Office of the Spokesman (2002) 'Daily Press Briefing', briefing by Deputy Spokesman Philip T. Reeker, Washington D.C., 2 October.

U.S. Department of State, Office of the Spokesman (2002) 'Daily Press Briefing', briefing by Spokesman Richard Boucher, Washington D.C., 31 October.

U.S. Department of State, Office of the Spokesman (2002) 'Daily Press Briefing', briefing by Spokesman Richard Boucher, Washington D.C., 6 November.

U.S. Department of State, Office of the Spokesman (2004) 'Briefing by Secretary of State Colin L. Powell', Washington D.C., 24 November.

U.S. Department of State, Office of the Spokesman (2004) 'Daily Briefing', briefing by Spokesman Richard Boucher, Washington D.C., 29 November.

U.S. Department of State, Office of the Spokesman (2005) 'Remarks En Route To Kiev', remarks by Secretary Colin L. Powell, Kyiv, 22 January.

U.S. Department of State, Office of the Spokesman (2006) 'Belarus Relations', Washington D.C., 3 February.

U.S. Department of State, Foreign Press Center (2006) 'Elections in Belarus and Ukraine', press briefing by David J. Kramer, Deputy Assistant Secretary of State for European and Eurasian Affairs, Washington D.C., 2 March.

U.S. Department of State, Office of the Spokesman (2008) 'Current State of U.S.-Belarus Relationship', speech by David Kramer, Deputy Assistant Secretary for European and Eurasian Affairs Washington, D.C., 11 March.

U.S. Department of State, Office of the Spokesman (2008) 'Daily Press Briefing', Washington D.C., 12 March.

U.S. Department of State, Office of the Spokesman (2008) 'Daily Press Briefing', Washington D.C., 1 May.

U.S. Department of State, Office of the Spokesman (2008) 'Remarks by Secretary of State Condoleezza Rice With Czech Foreign Minister Karel Schwarzenberg at Ballistic Defense Agreement Signing Ceremony', Prague, 8 July.

U.S. Department of State, Office of the Spokesman (2008) 'Daily Press Briefing', Washington D.C., 2 July.

U.S. Department of State, Office of the Spokesman (2008) 'Daily Press Briefing', Washington D.C., 3 July.

U.S. Department of State, Office of the Spokesman (2008) 'Ballistic Missile Defense Agreement between the United States of America and the Republic of Poland', Media Note, Washington D.C., 20 August.

U.S. Department of State, Secretary Condoleezza Rice (2008) 'Remarks With Polish President Lech Kaczynski', Presidential Palace, Warsaw, 20 August.

U.S. Department of State, Office of the Spokesman (2008) 'Text of the Declaration on Strategic Cooperation Between the United States and the Republic of Poland', Media Note, Washington D.C., 20 August.

U.S. Department of State, Office of the Spokesman (2008) 'Declaration on Strategic Cooperation Between the United States and the Republic of Poland', Media Note, Washington D.C., 20 August.

U.S. Department of State, Office of the Spokesman (2008) 'Remarks on the NATO Foreign Ministers Meeting', remarks by Secretary Condoleezza Rice Washington D.C., November 26.

U.S. Department of Treasury (2007) 'Treasury Targets Lukashenko-controlled Petrochemical Conglomerate', Washington D.C., 13 November.

U.S. Embassy to Poland (2002) 'Poland Chooses the F16 Fighting Falcon', Press release, 27 December.

U.S. Embassy to Ukraine (1998) 'United States and Ukraine Sign Agreement to Develop Peaceful Nuclear Energy', Kyiv, 6 May.

U.S. Embassy to Ukraine (1999) 'Kharkiv Oblast Hospitals To Receive $16.5 Million In Medical Humanitarian Assistance From United States', 25 August.

World Trade Organisation (2008) 'WTO welcomes Ukraine as a New Member', WTO press release 2008/511, Geneva, 5 February.

Robert E. Zoellick, Counselor of the State Department 1990) 'A New Europe in a New Age: Insular, Itinerant or International? Prospects for an Alliance of Values', address before the American-European Community Association's International Conference on US / EC Relations, Annapolis, MD, 21 September, U.S. *Department of State Dispatch* 1(4), 24 September 1990.

Background Notes

U.S. Department of State (1992) 'Background Note: Belarus', Washington, D.C., May.

U.S. Department of State (1996) 'Background Note: Belarus', Washington, D.C., March.

U.S. Department of State (2001) 'Background Note: Belarus', Washington, D.C., November.

U.S. Department of State (2003) 'Background Note: Belarus', Washington, D.C., November.

U.S. Department of State (2004) 'Background Note: Belarus', Washington, D.C., October.

U.S. Department of State (2005) 'Background Note: Belarus', Washington, D.C., August.

U.S. Department of State (2006) 'Background Note: Belarus', Washington, D.C., April.

U.S. Department of State (2007) 'Background Note: Belarus', Washington, D.C., January.

U.S. Department of State (2007) 'Background Note: Belarus', Washington, D.C., August.

U.S. Department of State (2008) 'Background Note: Belarus', Washington, D.C., February.

U.S. Department of State (2008) 'Background Note: Belarus', Washington, D.C., October.

U.S. Department of State (2009) 'Background Note: Belarus', Washington, D.C., July.

U.S. Department of State (1994) 'Background Note: Poland', Washington, D.C., August.

U.S. Department of State (2000) 'Background Note: Poland', Washington, D.C., June.

U.S. Department of State (2002) 'Background Note: Poland', Washington, D.C., April.

U.S. Department of State (2003) 'Background Note: Poland', Washington, D.C., October.

U.S. Department of State (2004) 'Background Note: Poland', Washington, D.C., May.

U.S. Department of State (2004) 'Background Note: Poland', Washington, D.C., November.

U.S. Department of State (2005) 'Background Note: Poland', Washington, D.C., January.

U.S. Department of State (2005) 'Background Note: Poland', Washington, D.C., February.

U.S. Department of State (2005) 'Background Note: Poland', Washington, D.C., April.

U.S. Department of State (2005) 'Background Note: Poland', Washington, D.C., May.

U.S. Department of State (2005) 'Background Note: Poland', Washington, D.C., June.

U.S. Department of State (2005) 'Background Note: Poland', Washington, D.C., August.
U.S. Department of State (2005) 'Background Note: Poland', Washington, D.C., October.
U.S. Department of State (2005) 'Background Note: Poland', Washington, D.C., November.
U.S. Department of State (2006) 'Background Note: Poland', Washington, D.C., August.
U.S. Department of State (2007) 'Background Note: Poland', Washington, D.C., February.
U.S. Department of State (2007) 'Background Note: Poland', Washington, D.C., March.
U.S. Department of State (2007) 'Background Note: Poland', Washington, D.C., August.
U.S. Department of State (2007) 'Background Note: Poland', Washington, D.C., November.
U.S. Department of State (2008) 'Background Note: Poland', Washington, D.C., June.
U.S. Department of State (2009) 'Background Note: Poland', Washington, D.C., January.
U.S. Department of State (1992) 'Background Note: Ukraine', Washington, D.C., August.
U.S. Department of State (1995) 'Background Note: Ukraine', Washington, D.C., April.
U.S. Department of State (1997) 'Background Note: Ukraine', Washington, D.C., June.
U.S. Department of State (2000) 'Background Note: Ukraine', Washington, D.C., May.
U.S. Department of State (2003) 'Background Note: Ukraine', Washington, D.C., January.
U.S. Department of State (2003) 'Background Note: Ukraine', Washington, D.C., December.
U.S. Department of State (2004) 'Background Note: Ukraine', Washington, D.C., December.
U.S. Department of State (2005) 'Background Note: Ukraine', Washington, D.C., January.
U.S. Department of State (2005) 'Background Note: Ukraine', Washington, D.C., February.
U.S. Department of State (2005) 'Background Note: Ukraine', Washington, D.C., August.

U.S. Department of State (2006) 'Background Note: Ukraine', Washington, D.C., April.

U.S. Department of State (2006) 'Background Note: Ukraine', Washington, D.C., May.

U.S. Department of State (2006) 'Background Note: Ukraine', Washington, D.C., August.

U.S. Department of State (2007) 'Background Note: Ukraine', Washington, D.C., March.

U.S. Department of State (2008) 'Background Note: Ukraine', Washington, D.C., March.

Treaties, Laws, Reports and Official Strategies

In chronological order:

Vertrag über die abschließende Regelung in bezug auf Deutschland vom 12. September 1990 (Treaty on the Final Settlement with Respect to Germany), cf. Politisches Archiv des Auswärtigen Amts, Vertragsarchiv, Berlin.

Vertrag zwischen der Bundesrepublik Deutschland und der Republik Polen über die Bestätigung der zwischen ihnen bestehenden Grenze, 14 November 1991 (cf. *Bulletin des Presse- und Informationsamtes der Bundesregierung vom 16.11.1990, Nr. 134, p. 1394*).

Protocol to the treaty between the United States of America and the Union of Soviet Socialist Republics on the Reduction and Limitation of Strategic and Offensive Arms, signed 23 May 1992 in Lisbon by Belarus, Kazakhstan, Russia, Ukraine and the United States.

The Soviet Nuclear Threat Reduction Act of 1991 (United States Public Law No: 102-228).

U.S. Congress, Office of Technology Assessment (1994) *Proliferation and the Former Soviet Union*, U.S. Government Printing Office, Washington D.C., September.

Charter on a Distinctive Partnership between the North Atlantic Treaty Organization and Ukraine, Madrid, 9 July 1997.

The National Security Strategy for a New Century 1997, Washington D.C.

The National Security Strategy of the United States of 2002, Washington D.C.

The Iraq Survey Group (2004) *Comprehensive Report of the Special Adviser to the DCI on Iraq's WMD* ('Duelfer-Report'), Washington D.C., 30 September.

The Belarus Democracy Act of 2004 (United States Public Law No: 108-347)

The Belarus Democracy Reauthorization Act of 2006 (United States Public Law No: 109–480).

The National Security Strategy of the United States of America, March 2006, Washington D.C.

The Comprehensive Immigration Reform Act of 2006

U.S. Department of State, Bureau of European and Eurasian Affairs (2006) *Report on Belarus, the Last Dictatorship in Europe, Including Arms Sales and Leadership Assets*, Washington, D.C., 16 March.

Executive Order 13405 — Blocking Property of Certain Persons Undermining Democratic Processes or Institutions in Belarus, Federal Register, Vol. 71, nº 118, 20 June 2006.

Office of the United States Trade Representative (2008) *Trade and Investment Cooperation Agreement Between the Government of Ukraine and the Government of the United States of America*, Washington 28 March and Kyiv 1 April.

Agreement between the Czech Republic and the United States of America on establishing a United States Ballistic Missile Radar Site in the Czech Republic, 8 July 2008, Prague.

U.S. Department of State, Bureau of European and Eurasian Affairs (2008) *United States-Ukraine Charter on Strategic Partnership*, Washington D.C., 19 December.

European Commission (2009) "What the European Union could bring to Belarus", Non-Paper, Brussels, December.

Websites

The White House: www.whitehouse.gov

U.S. State Department: www.state.gov

U.S. Department of Treasury: www.ustreas.gov

Library of Congress (Thomas): http://thomas.loc.gov/

U.S. Embassy Minsk / Belarus: http://belarus.usembassy.gov/

U.S. Embassy Warsaw / Poland: http://poland.usembassy.gov/

U.S. Embassy Kyiv / Ukraine: http://kiev.usembassy.gov/

NATO: www.nato.int

NATO Parliamentary Assembly: www.nato-pa.int

Mission of Ukraine to NATO: www.ukraine/be [then 'Ukraine-NATO']

George Bush Presidential Library: http://bushlibrary.tamu.edu/index.php

William J. Clinton Presidential Library: http://www.clintonlibrary.gov/

Nuclear Threat Initiative: www.nti.org

The Cooperative Threat Reduction
Program: http://www.dtra.mil/oe/ctr/index.cfm
The Missile Technology Control Regime (MTCR): www.mtcr.info
The Sea Launch consortium: http://www.boeing.com/special/sea-launch
Polish American Freedom Foundation: www.pafw.pl

Books and Articles

Agner, Michael (2009) 'Going Beyond the State?: Applying Neoclassical Realism to the Study of Interstate Security Cooperation', unpublished paper, presented at the 5th ECPR General Conference, Potsdam, 10–12 September.

Albright, Madeleine K. (2003) *Madam Secretary*. New York: Miramax.

Aristotle (1998 [ca. 340 BC]) *Politik*. Munich: DTV.

Aristotle (2006 [ca. 350 BC]) *Die Nikomachische Ethik*. Munich: DTV.

Aron, Raymond (2004 [1962]) *Paix et Guerre entre les Nations*. Paris: Calmann-Lévy.

Aron, Raymond (1967) *Les étapes de la pensée sociologique*. Paris: Gallimard.

Art, Robert J. (1991) 'A Defensible Defense: America's Grand Strategy after the Cold War', *International Security* 15(4): pp. 5–53.

Art, Robert J. (1998) 'Geopolitics Updated: The Strategy of Selective Engagement', *International Security* 23(3): pp. 79–113.

Åslund, Anders and Michael A. McFaul (eds.) (2006) *Revolution in Orange. The Origins of Ukraine's Democratic Breakthrough*. Washington D.C.: Carnegie Endowment for International Peace.

Asmus, Ronald D., Richard L Kugler and F. Stephen Larrabee (1993) 'Building a New NATO', *Foreign Affairs* 72(4): pp. 28–40.

Asmus, Ronald D. (1993) *Future U.S. Defense Policy Toward Europe: The New Politics And Grand Strategy Of European-American Relations*. Santa Monica: RAND paper nº P-7809.

Asmus, Ronald D., Richard L Kugler and F. Stephen Larrabee (1996) 'NATO Expansion: The Next Steps', *Survival* 37(1): pp. 7–33.

Asmus, Ronald D. (2002) *Opening NATO's Door. How the Alliance Remade Itself For A New Era*. New York: Columbia University Press.

Attali, Jacques (1995) *Verbatim, tome III, 1ère partie: Chronique des années 1988 à 1989*. Paris: Le Livre de Poche.

Attali, Jacques (1995) *Verbatim, tome III, 2ème partie: Chronique des années 1990 à 1991*. Paris: Le Livre de Poche.

Axelrod, Robert (ed.) (1976) *Structure of Decision: The Cognitive Maps of Political Elites*. Princeton: Princeton University Press.

Baldwin, David A. (1979) 'Power Analysis and World Politics: New Trends versus Old Tendencies', *World Politics* 31(2): pp. 161–194

Baldwin, David A. (1985) *Economic Statecraft*. Princeton: Princeton University Press.

Baldwin, David A. (1989) *Paradoxes of Power*. New York: Basil Blackwell.

Baldwin, David A. (2002) 'Power and International Relations', pp. 177–191 in: Walter Carlsnaes, Thomas Risse and Beth A. Simmons (eds.) *Handbook of International Relations*. London: Sage.

Barkawi, Tarak (1998) 'Strategy as a Vocation: Weber, Morgenthau and modern strategic studies', *Review of International Studies* 24(2): pp. 159–184.

Berenskoetter, Felix and Michael C. Williams (eds.) *Power in World Politics*. London: Routledge.

Bersch, Gary and Viktor Zaborksy (1997) 'Bringing Ukraine Into the MTCR: Can U.S: Policy Succeed?', *Arms Control Today*, April.

Beschloss, Michael R. and Strobe Talbott (1993) *At the Highest Levels: The Inside Story of the End of the Cold War*. Boston: Little & Brown.

Brooks, Stephen G. and William C. Wohlforth (2008) *World Out Of Balance: International Relations and the Challenge of American Primacy*. Princeton: Princeton University Press.

Brown, Michael E. et al. (eds.) (1995) *The Perils of Anarchy: Contemporary Realism and International Security*. Cambridge, MA: MIT Press.

Brzezinski, Ian (1993) 'Polish-Ukrainian Relations: Europe's Neglected Strategic Axis', *Survival* 35(3): pp. 26–37.

Brzezinski, Zbigniew (1995) 'A Plan for Europe', *Foreign Affairs* 74(1): pp. 26–42.

Brzezinski, Zbigniew (1997) *The Grand Chessboard. American Primacy and its geostrategic imperatives*. New York, NY: Basic Books.

Brzezinski, Zbigniew (2007) *Second Chance. Three Presidents and the Crisis of American Superpower*. New York, NY: Basic Books.

Bugajski, Janusz (2007) *The Eastern Dimension of America's New European Allies*. Washington D.C.: U.S. Army War College.

Burant, Stephen R. (1993) 'International Relations in a Regional Context: Poland and Its Eastern Neighbours. Lithuania, Belarus, Ukraine', *Europe-Asia Studies* 45(3): pp. 395–418.

Burant, Stephen R. (1999) 'Poland, Ukraine, and the Idea of Strategic Partnership', *The Carl Beck Papers in Russian and East European Studies*, no 1308.

Buzan, Barry, Ole Wæver and Jaap de Wilde (1998) *Security: a New Framework for Analysis*. Boulder: Lynne Rienner Publishers.

Carlsnaes, Walter, Thomas Risse and Beth A. Simmons (eds.) (2002) *Handbook of International Relations*. London: Sage.

Carr, Edward H. (1981[1939]) *The Twenty Years' Crisis 1919–1939*, 2nd edition. London: Macmillan.

Christensen, Thomas J. (1998) *Useful Adversaries: Grand Strategy, Domestic Mobilization, and the Sino-American Conflict, 1947–1958*. New York, NY: Columbia University Press.

Davies, Norman (2001) *Heart of Europe. The Past in Poland's Present*. Oxford: Oxford University Press.

Davis, James W. (2000) *Threats and Promises: The Pursuit of International Influence*. Baltimore: Johns Hopkins University Press.

Dahl, Robert A. (1989) *Democracy and its Critics*. New Haven and London: Yale University Press.

Deudney, Daniel and G. John Ikenberry (1992) 'Who Won the Cold War?', *Foreign Policy*, no 87: pp. 123–128.

Diamond, Howard (1998) 'U.S., Ukraine Sign Nuclear Accord, Agree On MTCR Accession', *Arms Control Today*, March.

Dunn, David H. (2003) 'Poland: America's New Model Ally', pp. 63–86 in: Marcin Zaborowski / David H. Dunn (eds.) *Poland. A New Power in Transatlantic Security*. London: Frank Cass.

Elman, Colin (1996) 'Horses for Courses: Why Not Neorealist Theories of Foreign policy?', *Security Studies* 6(1), pp. 7–53.

Fearon, James and Alexander Wendt (2002) 'Rationalism vs. Constructivism: A Skeptical View', pp. 52–72 in: Carlsnaes, Walter, Thomas Risse and Beth A. Simmons (eds.) *Handbook of International Relations*. London: Sage.

Forbrig, Jörg; David R Marples and Pavol Demeš (eds.) (2006) *Prospects for Democracy in Belarus*. Washington, D.C.: Böll-Stiftung / The German Marshall Fund of the United States.

Foucault, Michel (1975) *Surveiller et Punir. Naissance de la Prison*. Paris, Gallimard.

Frei, Christoph (1993) *Hans J. Morgenthau: eine intellektuelle Biographie*. Bern: Haupt.

French, John R.P. and Bertram Raven (1959) 'The bases of social power', pp. 150–167 in: Cartwright, D. (ed.) *Studies in Social Power*. Ann Arbor: Michigan University Press.

Garnett, Sherman W. (1996) 'Poland: Bulwark or Bridge?', *Foreign Policy* n° 102: pp. 66–82.

Garnett, Sherman W. (1997) 'Comments at a Roundtable on "The Future of Ukrainian-Russian Relations"', Conference Roundtable Transcript, 8–9 May 1997. Washington, D.C.: Kennan Institute for Advanced Russian Studies, Occasional Paper n° 268.

Genscher, Hans-Dietrich (1995) *Erinnerungen*. Berlin: Siedler.

George, Alexander L. (1991) *Forceful Persuasion: Coercive Diplomacy as an Alternative to War*. Washington, D.C.: United States Institute of Peace Press.

George, Alexander L. and Andrew Bennett (2004) *Case Studies and Theory Development in the Social Sciences*. Cambridge, MA: MIT Press.

Gheciu, Alexandra (2005) *NATO in the "New Europe". The Politics of International Socialization after the Cold War*. Stanford: Stanford University Press.

Gilpin, Robert (1981) *War and Change in World Politics*. Cambridge: Cambridge University Press.

Goldgeier, James M. (1999) *Not Whether But When. The U.S. Decision to Enlarge NATO*. Washington D.C.: Brookings Institution Press.

Goujon, Alexandra (2005) 'Nationalisme et identité en Biélorussie', in: Dov Lynch (ed.), *Changing Belarus*. Paris: EUISS Chaillot Paper n° 85.

Grawitz, Madeleine and Jean Leca (eds.) (1985) *Traité de Science Politique*. Paris: Presses Universitaires de France.

Gromadzi, Grzegorz and Olaf Osica (unknown) *Pro-European Atlantists: Poland and Other Countries of Central and Eastern Europe After Accession to the European Union*. Warsaw: Centrum Stosunków Międzynarodowych / Fundacja Stefana Batorego.

Guzzini, Stefano (2000) 'The Use and Misuse of Power Analysis in International Theory', pp. 53–66 in: Ronen Palan (ed.) *Global Political Economy: Contemporary Theories*. London: Routledge.

Hadenius, Axel (1992) *Democracy and Development*. Cambridge: Cambridge University Press.

Hagström, Linus (2005) *Japan's China Policy. A Relational Power Analysis*. London: Routledge.

Hamilton, Daniel and Gerhard Mangott (eds.) (2007) *The New Eastern Europe. Ukraine, Belarus and Moldova*. Washington D.C.: Center for Transatlantic Relations.

Hatto, Ronald and Odette Tomescu (2007) *Les Etats Unis et la "nouvelle Europe". La stratégie américaine en Europe centrale et orientale*. Paris: Ceri Autrement.

Hermann, Margaret G. (1980) 'Explaining Foreign Policy Behavior Using Personal Characteristics of Political Leaders', *International Studies Quarterly* 24(1), pp. 7–46.

Hermann, Margaret G. and Charles F. Hermann (1989) 'Who Makes Foreign Policy Decisions and How: A Theoretical Framework', *International Studies Quarterly* 33(4): pp. 361-387.

Hill, Christopher (2003) *The Changing Politics of Foreign Policy.* London: Palgrave Macmillan,

Hobbes, Thomas (1998 [1660]) *Leviathan or the Matter, Forme and Power of a Commonwealth Ecclesiastical and Civil.* Oxford: Oxford University Press.

Holbrooke, Richard M. (1995) 'America, a European Power', *Foreign Affairs* 74(2), pp. 38-51.

Hollis, Martin and Steve Smith (1990) *Explaining and Understanding International Relations.* Oxford: Oxford University Press.

Holsti, Kalevi J. (1995) *International Politics. A Framework for Analysis*, 7th edition. Englewood Cliffs: Prentice Hall.

Huntington, Samuel (2005) 'The Lonely Superpower', in: G. John Ikenberry (ed.) *American Foreign Policy. Theoretical Essays*, 5th edition. Princeton: Pearson Longman.

Hyde-Price, Adrian (1996) *The International Politics of East Central Europe.* Manchester / New York: Manchester University Press.

Ikenberry, G. John (ed.) (2005) *American Foreign Policy. Theoretical Essays*, 5th edition. Princeton: Pearson Longman.

Ikenberry, G. John (2005) 'America's Imperial Ambition', in: id. (ed.) *American Foreign Policy. Theoretical Essays*, 5th edition. Princeton: Pearson Longman.

Ikenberry, G. John (2005) 'America's Liberal Grand Strategy', in: id. (ed.) *American Foreign Policy. Theoretical Essays*, 5th edition. Princeton: Pearson Longman.

Jervis, Robert (1976) *Perception and Misperception in International Politics.* Princeton: Princeton University Press.

Jervis, Robert (1993) 'International Primacy: Is the Game Worth the Candle?', *International Security*, 17(4): pp. 52-67.

Jervis, Robert (2005) 'Understanding the Bush Doctrine', in: G. John Ikenberry (ed.) *American Foreign Policy. Theoretical Essays*, 5th edition. Princeton: Pearson Longman.

Kaplan, Morton A. (1952) 'An Introduction to the Strategy of Statecraft', *World Politics* 4 (4), pp. 548-576.

Kapstein, Ethan B. and Michael Mastanduno (eds.) (1999) *Unipolar Politics. Realism and State Strategies After the Cold War.* New York: Columbia University Press.

Katzenstein, Peter J. (ed.) (1996) *The Culture of National Security. Norms and Identity in World Politics.* New York: Columbia University Press).

Katznelson, Ira and Helen V Milner (eds.) (2002) *Political Science. State of the Discipline.* New York / London: W.W. Norton & Co.

Keane, Michael P. and Eswar S. Prasad (2001) 'Poland: Inequality, Transfers, and Growth in Transition', *Finance and Development* 38(1) (published online at www.imf.org).

Kegley, Charles; Eugene Wittkopf and James M. Scott (2003) *American Foreign Policy: Pattern and Process*, 6th edition. Belmont, CA: Wadsworth / Thomson Learning.

Khong, Yuen Foong (1992) *Analogies At War: Korea, Munich, Dien Bien Phu and the Vietnam Decisions of 1965.* Princeton: Princeton University Press.

Kissinger, Henry (1979) *The White House Years.* London: Weidenfeld & Nicolson.

Knorr, Klaus and Sidney Verba (1967) (eds.) *The International System: Theoretical Essays.* Princeton: Princeton University Press.

Kramer, Mark (1999) 'Neorealism, Nuclear Proliferation, and East-Central European Strategies', in: Kapstein, Ethan B. and Michael Mastanduno (eds.) *Unipolar Politics. Realism and State Strategies After the Cold War.* New York: Columbia University Press

Krauthammer, Charles (2005) 'The Unipolar Moment Revisited', in: G. John Ikenberry (ed.) *American Foreign Policy. Theoretical Essays*, 5th edition. Princeton: Pearson Longman.

Kubalkova, Vendulka (ed.) (2001) *Foreign Policy in a Constructed World.* New York: M.E. Sharpe.

Kunz, Barbara (2008) 'Les relations polono-américaines depuis 1989: Varsovie, cheval de Troie des États-Unis en Europe?', *Le Courrier des Pays de l'Est*, Paris, April 2008 (no 1066), pp. 62–70.

Kunz, Barbara (2010) 'Hans J. Morgenthau's Political Realism, Max Weber, and the Concept of Power', *Max Weber Studies*, forthcoming.

Kuzio, Taras (1998) 'Ukraine and NATO: The Evolving Strategic Partnership', *Journal of Strategic Studies* 21(2): pp. 1–30.

Kuzio, Taras and Jennifer D.P. Moroney (2001) 'Defining Western Interests in Ukraine: Moving From Stability to Strategic Engagement', *European Security* 10(2): pp. 111–126.

Kuzio, Taras (2003) 'Ukraine's Relations With the West: Disinterest, Partnership, Disillusionment', *European Security* 12(2): pp. 21–44.

Kuzio, Taras (2005) 'Neither East nor West: Ukraine's Security Policy Under Kuchma', *Problems of Post-Communism*, 52(5): pp. 59–68.

Kuźniar, Roman (2008) *Droga do wolności. Poityka zagraniczna III Rzeczpospolitej*. Warsaw: Wydawnictwo Naukowe Scholar.

Lang, Kai-Olaf (2003) *Amerikas bester Freund? Polens atlantizistisch-europäischer Kurs*. Berlin: SWP-Aktuell n° 6/03.

Lang, Kai-Olaf (2005) *Polen und der Osten*. Berlin: SWP-Aktuell n° 22/05.

Lasswell, Harold D. and Abraham Kaplan (1950) *Power and Society. A Framework for Political Inquiry*. New Haven: Yale University Press.

Lindner, Rainer (2005) *Selbstisolierung von Belarus. Konflikte mit Polen und anderen Nachbarstaaten als Sicherheitsproblem der EU*. Berlin: SWP-Aktuell n° 43/05.

Lobell, Steven E., Norrin M. Ripsman and Jeffrey W. Taliaferro (eds.) (2009) *Neoclassical Realism, the State, and Foreign Policy*. Cambridge: Cambridge University Press.

Longhurst, Kerry (2003) 'From Security Consumer to Security Provider — Poland and Transatlantic Security in the Twenty-First Century', pp. 50-62, in: Marcin Zaborowski and David H. Dunn (eds.) *Poland. A New Power in Transatlantic Security*. London: Frank Cass.

Lukes, Steven (2004 [1974]) *Power. A Radical View*, 2nd edition. London: Palgrave Macmillan.

Lundestad, Geir (1978) *The American Non-Policy towards Eastern Europe, 1943-1947: Universalism in an Area Not of Essential Interest to the United States*. Oslo: Universitetsforlaget.

Lundestad, Geir (1986) 'Empire by Invitation? The United States and Western Europe, 1945-1952', *Journal of Peace Research* 23(3): pp. 263-277.

Lundestad, Geir (1998) *Empire by Integration. The United States and European Integration, 1945-1997*. Oxford: Oxford University Press.

Lynch, Dov (ed.) (2005) *Changing Belarus*. Paris: European Union Institute for Security Studies, Chaillot Paper n° 85.

Magdziak-Miszewska, Agnieszka (1999) 'Subregionalny kontekst rozszerzenia NATO', *Sprawy Miedzynarodowe* 52(1): pp. 137-146.

Martinsen, Kaare Dahl (2002) *The Russian-Belarusian Union and the Near Abroad*. Oslo: Institutt for Forsvarsstudier.

Mearsheimer, John J. (1994) 'The False Promise of International Institutions', *International Security* 19(3): pp. 5-49.

Mastanduno, Michael (1997) 'Preserving the Unipolar Moment. Realist Theories and U.S. Grand Strategy after the Cold War', *International Strategy* 21(4): pp. 49-88.

Mastanduno, Michael (1998) 'Economics and Security in Statecraft and Scholarship', *International Organization* 52(4): pp. 824-854.

Mendeloff, David and Mira Sucharov (2005) 'Perception and International Security', unpublished paper, presented at the Annual Meeting of the American Political Science Association, Washington D.C., 1–4 September 2005.

Mendelson, Sarah E. and John K. Glenn (2002) (eds.) *The Power and Limits of NGOs. A Critical Look at Building Democracy in Europe and Eurasia*. New York: Columbia University Press.

Mitchell, Wess (2006) *Mending Fences. Repairing U.S.-Central European Relations after Iraq*. Washington, D.C.: CEPA.

Mitchell, Wess (2006) *Tipping the Scales. Why Central Europe Matters to the United States*. Washington. D.C.: CEPA.

Morgenthau, Hans J. (1946) *Scientific Man vs. Power Politics*. Chicago: Chicago University Press.

Morgenthau, Hans J. (2006 [1948]) *Politics among Nations. The Struggle for Power and Peace*, 7th edition. London: Mc Graw Hill.

Morgenthau, Hans J. (1963) *Macht und Frieden. Grundlegung einer Theorie der internationalen Politik*, with an introduction by Gottfried-Karl Kindermann. Gütersloh: Bertelsmann Verlag.

Mouritzen, Hans (1995) 'The Nordic Model as a Foreign Policy Instrument: Its Rise and Fall', *Journal of Peace Research* 32(1): pp. 9–21.

Nagel, Jack H. (1975) *The Descriptive Analysis of Power*. New Haven: Yale University Press.

Nye, Joseph S. Jr. (2004) *Soft Power. The Means to Success in World Politics*. New York: Public Affairs.

Nye, Joseph S. Jr. (2005) 'Notes on a soft-power research agenda', pp. 162–172 in: Felix Berenskoetter and M. J. Williams (eds.) *Power in World Politics*, New York: Routledge.

Organski, A.F.K. and Jacek Kugler (1980) *The War Ledger*. Chicago: Chicago University Press.

Osica, Olaf (2003) 'In Search of a New Role. Poland vis-à-vis Euro-Atlantic Relations', pp. 21–39, in: Marcin Zaborowski and David H. Dunn (eds.) *Poland. A New Power in Transatlantic Security*. London: Frank Cass.

Pichler, Hans-Karl (1998) 'The godfathers of "truth": Max Weber and Carl Schmitt in Morgenthau's theory of power politics', *Review of International Studies* 24(2): pp. 185–200.

Pifer, Steven (2007) 'European Mediators and Ukraine's Orange Revolution', *Problems of Post-Communism* 54(6), pp. 28–42.

Pifer, Steven (2011),'The Trilateral Process: The United States, Ukraine, Russia and Nuclear Weapons', *Brookings Arms Control Series*, Paper 6, May.

Posen, Barry R. and Andrew L. Ross (1996) 'Competing Visions for U.S. Grand Strategy', *International Security* 21(3): pp. 5–53.

Pressman, Jeremy (2009) 'Power without Influence', *International Security* 33(4): pp. 149–179.

Przeworski, Adam and Henry Teune (1970) *The Logic of Comparative Social Inquiry*. Malabar: Krieger Publishing.

Ragin, Charles C. (2000) *Fuzzy-set Social Science*. Chicago: University of Chicago Press.

Rathbun, Brian (2008) 'A Rose by Any Other Name: Neoclassical Realism as the Logical and Necessary Extension of Structural Realism', *Security Studies* 17(2): pp. 294–321.

Rice, Condoleezza (2000) 'Promoting the National Interest', *Foreign Affairs* 79(1): pp. 45–62.

Rose, Gideon (1998) 'Neoclassical Realism and Theories of Foreign Policy', *World Politics* 51(1): pp. 144–172.

Sandner, Karl (1990) *Prozesse der Macht. Zur Entstehung, Stabilisierung und Veränderung der Macht von Akteuren in Unternehmen*. Berlin: Springer.

Schelling, Thomas C. (1980) *The Strategy of Conflict*. Cambridge: Harvard University Press.

Schmidt, Brian C. (2007) 'Realist conceptions of power', pp. 43–64 in: Felix Berenskoetter and Michael C. Williams (eds.) *Power in World Politics*, London: Routledge.

Schmitt, Carl (1987[1932]) *Der Begriff des Politischen*. Berlin: Duncker & Humblot.

Schweller, Randall L. (1994) 'Bandwagoning for Profit. Bringing the Revisionist State Back in', *International Security* 19(1): pp. 72–107.

Schweller, Randall L. (1996) 'Neorealism's status-quo bias: what security dilemma?', *Security Studies* 5(3): pp. 90–121.

Schweller, Randall L. (2003) 'The Progressiveness of Neoclassical Realism', pp. 311–348 in: Colin Elman and Miriam Fendius Elman (eds.) *Progress in International Relations Theory. Appraising the Field*. Cambridge, MA: MIT Press.

Seguin, Barre R. (2007) 'Why did Poland Choose the F-16?', *Occasional Paper Series*, n°11, Garmisch-Partenkirchen: George C. Marshall European Center for Security Studies, June.

Siedschlag, Alexander (ed.) (2001) *Realistische Perspektiven internationaler Politik*. Opladen: Leske & Budrich.

Simon, Jeffrey (2004) *Poland and NATO: A Study in Civil-Military Relations*. Oxford: Rowman & Littlefield.

Singer, J. David (1961) 'The Level-of-Analysis Problem in International Relations', *World Politics* 14(1): pp: 77–92.

Smith, W.Y. (1991) 'Principles of U.S. Grand Strategy: Past and Future', *The Washington Quarterly*, Spring: pp. 67–78.

Smith, Steve (2001) 'Foreign Policy is What States Make of It: Social Construction and International Relations Theory', pp. 38–55 in: Vendulka Kubalkova (ed.) *Foreign Policy in a Constructed World*, New York: M.E. Sharpe.

Skidmore, David (2005) 'Understanding the Unilateralist Turn in U.S. Foreign Policy', *Foreign Policy Analysis* 1(2): pp: 207–228.

Sterling-Folker, Jennifer (1997) 'Realist Environment, Liberal Process, and Domestic Level Variables', *International Studies Quarterly* 41(1): pp. 1–25.

Sullivan, Michael P. (1990) *Power in Contemporary International Politics*. Columbia: University of South Carolina Press.

Swedberg, Richard (with the assistance of Ola Agevall) (2005) *The Max Weber dictionary: key words and central concepts*. Stanford: Stanford University Press.

The Nuclear Threat Initiative (2007) *Belarus Profile*, available online at www.nti.org.

Timmermann, Heinz (2002) *Die widersprüchlichen Beziehungen Rußland-Belarus im europäischen Kontext*. Berlin: SWP-Studie no 37/02.

Toje, Asle (2008) *America, the EU and Strategic Culture. Renegotiating the Transatlantic Bargain*. London: Routledge.

Van Evera, Stephen (1990) 'Why Europe Matters, Why the Third World Doesn't: American Grand Strategy After the Cold War', *Journal of Strategic Studies* 13(2): pp. 1–51.

Védrine, Hubert (2003) *Face à l'hyper-puissance. Textes et discours 1995–2003*. Paris: Fayard.

Wachsmuth, Ralf (2004) *Außenpolitischer Kurswechsel der Ukraine? Kehrtwende in Richtung Rußland oder wahltaktisches Manöver?*. Kyiv: Politischer Kurzbericht der Konrad-Adenauer-Stiftung, Außenstelle Kiew.

Wallimann, Isidor, Howard Rosenbaum, Nicholas Tatsis and George Zito (1980) 'Misreading Weber: The Concept of "Macht"', *Sociology* 12(2): pp. 261–275.

Wallander, Celeste A. (2005) *Challenge and Opportunity: A U.S. Strategy on Ukraine*. Washington, D.C.: Working Paper, Center for Strategic and International Studies.

Walt, Stephen M. (1987) *The Origins of Alliances*. Ithaca: Cornell University Press.

Walt, Stephen M. (1997) 'The Progressive Power of Realism', *The American Political Science Review* 91(4): pp. 931-935.

Walt, Stephen M. (2000) 'Two Cheers for Clinton's Foreign Policy', *Foreign Affairs* 79(2): pp. 63-79.

Walt, Stephen M. (2002) 'The Enduring Relevance of the Realist Tradition', pp. 197-230 in: Ira Katznelson and Helen Milner (eds.) *Political Science, State of the Discipline*. New York: W.W. Norton & Co.

Waltz, Kenneth N. (1979) *Theory of International Politics*. Reading: Addison-Wesley.

Waltz, Kenneth N. (1990) 'Realist Thought and Neorealist Theory', *Journal of International Affairs* 44(1): pp. 21-37.

Weber, Max (1997 [1919]) 'Politik als Beruf", in: *Schriften zur Sozialgeschichte und Politik*. Stuttgart: Reclam.

Weber, Max (1947 [1922]) *Wirtschaft und Gesellschaft*, 3rd edition. Tübingen: Mohr.

Wendt, Alexander (1999) *Social Theory of International Politics*. Cambridge: Cambridge University Press.

Williams, Michael C. (ed.) (2007) *Realism Reconsidered. The Legacy of Hans J. Morgenthau in International Relations*. Oxford: Oxford University Press.

Whimster, Sam (2004) *The Essential Weber: A Reader*. London: Routledge.

Winnerstig, Mike (2000) *A World Reformed? The United States and European Security From Reagan to Clinton*. Stockholm: Stockholm University, Department of Political Science.

Wohlforth, William Curti (1993) *The Elusive Balance: Power and Perceptions during the Cold War*. Ithaca: Cornell University Press.

Wolfers, (Arnold 1962) *Discord and Collaboration. Essays on International Politics*. Baltimore: The Johns Hopkins University Press.

Wolff von Amerongen, Otto (1980) 'Economic Sanctions as a Foreign Policy Tool?', *International Security* 5 (2): pp. 159-167.

Zaborowski, Marcin and David H. Dunn (eds.) (2003) *Poland. A New Power in Transatlantic Security*. London: Frank Cass.

Zaborowski, Marcin (2004) *From America's protégé to constructive European. Polish security policy in the twenty-first century*. Paris: European Union Institute for Security Studies, Occasional Paper n° 56.

Zakaria, Fareed (1998) *From Wealth to Power: The unusual origins of America's world role*. Princeton: Princeton University Press.

Zelikow, Philip and Condoleezza Rice (1997) *Germany Unified and Europe Transformed. A Study in Statecraft*, 2nd edition. Cambridge, MA: Harvard University Press.

Zięba, Ryszard (2002) 'The "Strategic Partnership" between Poland and Ukraine', *The Polish Foreign Affairs Digest* 2(3): pp. 195–226.

Zielonka, Jan (1994) 'Les paradoxes de la politique étrangère polonaise', *Politique Étrangère* 59(1), pp. 99–114.

Media Sources

Achcar, Gilbert (2003) 'Auxiliary Americans: Washington Watches Over EU and NATO expansion', *Le Monde Diplomatique* (English edition), January.

Board, William J. (1998) 'Offering a Cheaper Ride to the Orbit from the Middle of the Ocean', *The New York Times*, 16 June.

Bosacki, Marcin (2007) 'Nie zamykajmy drzwi przed Ukrainą', *Gazeta Wyborcza*, 31 May.

Castle, Stephen (2002) 'Diplomacy in French saves embarrassment for Nato', *The Independent*, 23 November.

Chatelot, Christophe (2007) 'Alexandre Loukachenko: "L'OTAN est une organisation illégale"', *Le Monde,* 20 July.

Dempsey, Judy (2004) 'Poland's Leader Calls for a Pluralistic, Open, and New Europe ... Including Turkey and Ukraine', *The International Herald Tribune,* 2 September.

Dempsey, Judy (2004) 'Take flexible stance, Polish leader urges. A Plea from a Close Friend of U.S.' *The International Herald Tribune,* 2 September.

Duff, Andrew (2008) 'Behold a European foreign policy', *Financial Times*, 9 April.

Finn, Peter (2006) 'Ukraine's Yanukovych Halts NATO Entry Talks', *The Washington Post*, 15 September.

Fitchett, Joseph (1995) 'Poland is the Key / Clinton and a Sense of History: Moving Cautiously On NATO Expansion Eastward', *The International Herald Tribune*, 29 May.

Freedman, Thomas L. (1993) 'At U.S. Urging, Ukraine Retreats on Nuclear Arms', *The New York Times*, 30 November.

Gordon, Michael R. (1993) 'Aspin Meets Russian in Bid to Take Ukraine's A-Arms', *The New York Times,* 6 June.

Gordon, Michael R. (1998), 'Russia Plans To Sell Reactors to Iran Despite U.S. Protests', *The New York Times*, 7 March.

Greenhouse, Steven (1994) 'U.S. Ready to Help Ukraine and Georgia, if They Help Themselves', *The New York Times*, 4 March.

Greenhouse, Steven (1994) 'Ukraine Votes to Become a Nuclear-Free Country', *The New York Times*, 17 November.

Jehl, Douglas (1994) 'Clinton Offers Poland Hope, But Little Aid', *The New York Times*, 8 July.

Knowlton, Brian (2004) 'Powell threatens "consequences" over voting irregularities: U.S. puts Ukraine on guard', *The International Herald Tribune*, 25 November.

Kralev, Nicholas (2008), 'Poland excluded from visa-waiver list', *The Washington Post*, 18 October

Krauss, Clifford (1991) 'Ukraine Chef Faces Hurdles in Quest for U.S. Recognition', *The New York Times*, 30 September.

Lenzi, Mark (2003) 'Europe's Armory For Terrorism', *The Washington Post*, 3 January.

Lenzi, Mark (2005) 'Poles deserve the West's support', *The International Herald Tribune*, 30 July.

Lewis, Neil A. (1989) 'Clamor in the East, Gratitude and a Request; In Talk to Congress, Walesa Urges A Marshall Plan to Revive Poland', *The New York Times*, 16 November.

Puhl, Jan (2009) 'Aus für Atomschild. Kwasniewski beruhigt die Polen', *Der Spiegel*, 20 September

Reiter, Janusz (2007) 'The visa barrier', *The Washington Post*, 29 August.

Safire, William (1991) 'Ukraine Marches Out', *The New York Times*, 18 November.

Sannikov, Andrei and Mark Lenzi (2004) 'Belarus's Terrorist Ties', *The Washington Post*, 12 June.

Schmidt-Heuer, Christian (2003) 'Die freundliche Übernahme. Vor dem EU-Referendum: Wie Polen zu einer amerikanischen Tochterfirma in Europa geworden ist', *Die Zeit*, 5 June.

Swartz, David H. (1997) 'The mess of Belarus, care of the State Department', *The Washington Times*, 5 June.

Tagliabue, John (2003) 'Lockheed Wins Huge Sale to Poland With Complex Deal', *The New York Times*, 19 April.

Thorpe, Nick (2003) 'Why Poland Loves America', *BBC News Online*, 30 May.

Tyler, Patrick E. (2000) 'Deprived Ukraine City Finds U.S. Help No Help', *The New York Times*, 6 June.

Unger, Frank (2007) 'Ein Trojanisches Pferd: Politisch Unkorrektes über mögliche US-Raketen in Polen und Tschechien', *Freitag*, 30 March.

Wayne, Leslie (2003) 'Polish Pride, American Profits', *The New York Times*, 12 January.

Wines, Michael (1991) 'Baker Will Visit Ukraine To Discuss Nuclear Question', *The New York Times*, 3 December.

Unknown author [in chronological order; available at the respective publisher's website]:

The New York Times (1993) 'Ukraine Now Says It May Keep Nuclear Weapons', 20 October.

BBC News Online (2002) 'From West's Favourite to Pariah', 26 September.

BBC News Online (2002) 'U.S.-Ukraine relations in crisis', 8 November.

Dagens Nyheter (2002) 'Polen har tagit ett politiskt beslut', 27 December.

Air & Cosmos (2003) 'Le F-16 et l'Otan l'emportent en Pologne', n° 1872, 10 January.

BBC News Online (2003) 'US punishes Ukraine over Iraq claim', 1 February.

BBC News Online (2005) 'Rice names "outposts of tyranny"', 19 January.

Radio Free Europe (2005) 'Transcript: What Do Melnychenko's Tapes Say About Gongadze Case?', 3 March.

BBC News Online (2008) 'Belarus Dissident Leaves Prison', 16 August.

Radio Free Europe (2005) 'Poland/Belarus: Warsaw Seems To Be Losing Duel With Minsk Over Ethnic Organization', 12 August.

Radio Free Europe (2006) 'Poland to Begin Radio Broadcasts to Belarus', 6 January.

Deutsche Welle (2006) 'Regionalparlament der Krim protestiert gegen NATO-Manover', 8 June.

Radio Free Europe (2007) 'Venezuela's Chavez, Belarus's Lukashenka Vow Cooperation', 29 June.

Belarus News (2007) 'Skandal nach Botschafter-Aussage über neue Atomwaffen in Weißrussland', 28 August.

Belarus News (2007) 'Lukaschenko will Atomkraft', 12 October.

Polskie Radio dla Zagranicy (2008) 'Keine Patriotraketen? Kein Abwehrsystem!', Warsaw, 8 July.

Polskie Radio dla Zagranicy (2008) 'Missile Defense Agreements should be ratified as soon as possible', Warsaw, 31 October.

SOVIET AND POST-SOVIET POLITICS AND SOCIETY

Edited by Dr. Andreas Umland

ISSN 1614-3515

1   *Андреас Умланд (ред.)*
    Воплощение Европейской
    конвенции по правам человека в
    России
    Философские, юридические и
    эмпирические исследования
    ISBN 3-89821-387-0

2   *Christian Wipperfürth*
    Russland – ein vertrauenswürdiger
    Partner?
    Grundlagen, Hintergründe und Praxis
    gegenwärtiger russischer Außenpolitik
    Mit einem Vorwort von Heinz Timmermann
    ISBN 3-89821-401-X

3   *Manja Hussner*
    Die Übernahme internationalen Rechts
    in die russische und deutsche
    Rechtsordnung
    Eine vergleichende Analyse zur
    Völkerrechtsfreundlichkeit der Verfassungen
    der Russländischen Föderation und der
    Bundesrepublik Deutschland
    Mit einem Vorwort von Rainer Arnold
    ISBN 3-89821-438-9

4   *Matthew Tejada*
    Bulgaria's Democratic Consolidation
    and the Kozloduy Nuclear Power Plant
    (KNPP)
    The Unattainability of Closure
    With a foreword by Richard J. Crampton
    ISBN 3-89821-439-7

5   *Марк Григорьевич Меерович*
    Квадратные метры, определяющие
    сознание
    Государственная жилищная политика в
    СССР. 1921 – 1941 гг
    ISBN 3-89821-474-5

6   *Andrei P. Tsygankov, Pavel
    A.Tsygankov (Eds.)*
    New Directions in Russian
    International Studies
    ISBN 3-89821-422-2

7   *Марк Григорьевич Меерович*
    Как власть народ к труду приучала
    Жилище в СССР – средство управления
    людьми. 1917 – 1941 гг.
    С предисловием Елены Осокиной
    ISBN 3-89821-495-8

8   *David J. Galbreath*
    Nation-Building and Minority Politics
    in Post-Socialist States
    Interests, Influence and Identities in Estonia
    and Latvia
    With a foreword by David J. Smith
    ISBN 3-89821-467-2

9   *Алексей Юрьевич Безугольный*
    Народы Кавказа в Вооруженных
    силах СССР в годы Великой
    Отечественной войны 1941-1945 гг.
    С предисловием Николая Бугая
    ISBN 3-89821-475-3

10 *Вячеслав Лихачев и Владимир
    Прибыловский (ред.)*
    Русское Национальное Единство,
    1990-2000. В 2-х томах
    ISBN 3-89821-523-7

11 *Николай Бугай (ред.)*
    Народы стран Балтии в условиях
    сталинизма (1940-е – 1950-е годы)
    Документированная история
    ISBN 3-89821-525-3

12 *Ingmar Bredies (Hrsg.)*
    Zur Anatomie der Orange Revolution
    in der Ukraine
    Wechsel des Elitenregimes oder Triumph des
    Parlamentarismus?
    ISBN 3-89821-524-5

13 *Anastasia V. Mitrofanova*
    The Politicization of Russian
    Orthodoxy
    Actors and Ideas
    With a foreword by William C. Gay
    ISBN 3-89821-481-8

14 Nathan D. Larson
Alexander Solzhenitsyn and the
Russo-Jewish Question
ISBN 3-89821-483-4

15 Guido Houben
Kulturpolitik und Ethnizität
Staatliche Kunstförderung im Russland der
neunziger Jahre
Mit einem Vorwort von Gert Weisskirchen
ISBN 3-89821-542-3

16 Leonid Luks
Der russische „Sonderweg"?
Aufsätze zur neuesten Geschichte Russlands
im europäischen Kontext
ISBN 3-89821-496-6

17 Евгений Мороз
История «Мёртвой воды» – от
страшной сказки к большой
политике
Политическое неоязычество в
постсоветской России
ISBN 3-89821-551-2

18 Александр Верховский и Галина
Кожевникова (ред.)
Этническая и религиозная
интолерантность в российских СМИ
Результаты мониторинга 2001-2004 гг.
ISBN 3-89821-569-5

19 Christian Ganzer
Sowjetisches Erbe und ukrainische
Nation
Das Museum der Geschichte des Zaporoger
Kosakentums auf der Insel Chortycja
Mit einem Vorwort von Frank Golczewski
ISBN 3-89821-504-0

20 Эльза-Баир Гучинова
Помнить нельзя забыть
Антропология депортационной травмы
калмыков
С предисловием Кэролайн Хамфри
ISBN 3-89821-506-7

21 Юлия Лидерман
Мотивы «проверки» и «испытания»
в постсоветской культуре
Советское прошлое в российском
кинематографе 1990-х годов
С предисловием Евгения Марголита
ISBN 3-89821-511-5

22 Tanya Lokshina, Ray Thomas, Mary
Mayer (Eds.)
The Imposition of a Fake Political
Settlement in the Northern Caucasus
The 2003 Chechen Presidential Election
ISBN 3-89821-436-2

23 Timothy McCajor Hall, Rosie Read
(Eds.)
Changes in the Heart of Europe
Recent Ethnographies of Czechs, Slovaks,
Roma, and Sorbs
With an afterword by Zdeněk Salzmann
ISBN 3-89821-606-3

24 Christian Autengruber
Die politischen Parteien in Bulgarien
und Rumänien
Eine vergleichende Analyse seit Beginn der
90er Jahre
Mit einem Vorwort von Dorothée de Nève
ISBN 3-89821-476-1

25 Annette Freyberg-Inan with Radu
Cristescu
The Ghosts in Our Classrooms, or:
John Dewey Meets Ceauşescu
The Promise and the Failures of Civic
Education in Romania
ISBN 3-89821-416-8

26 John B. Dunlop
The 2002 Dubrovka and 2004 Beslan
Hostage Crises
A Critique of Russian Counter-Terrorism
With a foreword by Donald N. Jensen
ISBN 3-89821-608-X

27 Peter Koller
Das touristische Potenzial von
Kam''janec'–Podil's'kyj
Eine fremdenverkehrsgeographische
Untersuchung der Zukunftsperspektiven und
Maßnahmenplanung zur
Destinationsentwicklung des „ukrainischen
Rothenburg"
Mit einem Vorwort von Kristiane Klemm
ISBN 3-89821-640-3

28 Françoise Daucé, Elisabeth Sieca-
Kozlowski (Eds.)
Dedovshchina in the Post-Soviet
Military
Hazing of Russian Army Conscripts in a
Comparative Perspective
With a foreword by Dale Herspring
ISBN 3-89821-616-0

29 *Florian Strasser*
Zivilgesellschaftliche Einflüsse auf die Orange Revolution
Die gewaltlose Massenbewegung und die ukrainische Wahlkrise 2004
Mit einem Vorwort von Egbert Jahn
ISBN 3-89821-648-9

30 *Rebecca S. Katz*
The Georgian Regime Crisis of 2003-2004
A Case Study in Post-Soviet Media Representation of Politics, Crime and Corruption
ISBN 3-89821-413-3

31 *Vladimir Kantor*
Willkür oder Freiheit
Beiträge zur russischen Geschichtsphilosophie
Ediert von Dagmar Herrmann sowie mit einem Vorwort versehen von Leonid Luks
ISBN 3-89821-589-X

32 *Laura A. Victoir*
The Russian Land Estate Today
A Case Study of Cultural Politics in Post-Soviet Russia
With a foreword by Priscilla Roosevelt
ISBN 3-89821-426-5

33 *Ivan Katchanovski*
Cleft Countries
Regional Political Divisions and Cultures in Post-Soviet Ukraine and Moldova
With a foreword by Francis Fukuyama
ISBN 3-89821-558-X

34 *Florian Mühlfried*
Postsowjetische Feiern
Das Georgische Bankett im Wandel
Mit einem Vorwort von Kevin Tuite
ISBN 3-89821-601-2

35 *Roger Griffin, Werner Loh, Andreas Umland (Eds.)*
Fascism Past and Present, West and East
An International Debate on Concepts and Cases in the Comparative Study of the Extreme Right
With an afterword by Walter Laqueur
ISBN 3-89821-674-8

36 *Sebastian Schlegel*
Der „Weiße Archipel"
Sowjetische Atomstädte 1945-1991
Mit einem Geleitwort von Thomas Bohn
ISBN 3-89821-679-9

37 *Vyacheslav Likhachev*
Political Anti-Semitism in Post-Soviet Russia
Actors and Ideas in 1991-2003
Edited and translated from Russian by Eugene Veklerov
ISBN 3-89821-529-6

38 *Josette Baer (Ed.)*
Preparing Liberty in Central Europe
Political Texts from the Spring of Nations 1848 to the Spring of Prague 1968
With a foreword by Zdeněk V. David
ISBN 3-89821-546-6

39 *Михаил Лукьянов*
Российский консерватизм и реформа, 1907-1914
С предисловием Марка Д. Стейнберга
ISBN 3-89821-503-2

40 *Nicola Melloni*
Market Without Economy
The 1998 Russian Financial Crisis
With a foreword by Eiji Furukawa
ISBN 3-89821-407-9

41 *Dmitrij Chmelnizki*
Die Architektur Stalins
Bd. 1: Studien zu Ideologie und Stil
Bd. 2: Bilddokumentation
Mit einem Vorwort von Bruno Flierl
ISBN 3-89821-515-6

42 *Katja Yafimava*
Post-Soviet Russian-Belarussian Relationships
The Role of Gas Transit Pipelines
With a foreword by Jonathan P. Stern
ISBN 3-89821-655-1

43 *Boris Chavkin*
Verflechtungen der deutschen und russischen Zeitgeschichte
Aufsätze und Archivfunde zu den Beziehungen Deutschlands und der Sowjetunion von 1917 bis 1991
Ediert von Markus Edlinger sowie mit einem Vorwort versehen von Leonid Luks
ISBN 3-89821-756-6

44 *Anastasija Grynenko in Zusammenarbeit mit Claudia Dathe*
Die Terminologie des Gerichtswesens der Ukraine und Deutschlands im Vergleich
Eine übersetzungswissenschaftliche Analyse juristischer Fachbegriffe im Deutschen, Ukrainischen und Russischen
Mit einem Vorwort von Ulrich Hartmann
ISBN 3-89821-691-8

45 *Anton Burkov*
The Impact of the European Convention on Human Rights on Russian Law
Legislation and Application in 1996-2006
With a foreword by Françoise Hampson
ISBN 978-3-89821-639-5

46 *Stina Torjesen, Indra Overland (Eds.)*
International Election Observers in Post-Soviet Azerbaijan
Geopolitical Pawns or Agents of Change?
ISBN 978-3-89821-743-9

47 *Taras Kuzio*
Ukraine – Crimea – Russia
Triangle of Conflict
ISBN 978-3-89821-761-3

48 *Claudia Šabić*
"Ich erinnere mich nicht, aber L'viv!"
Zur Funktion kultureller Faktoren für die Institutionalisierung und Entwicklung einer ukrainischen Region
Mit einem Vorwort von Melanie Tatur
ISBN 978-3-89821-752-1

49 *Marlies Bilz*
Tatarstan in der Transformation
Nationaler Diskurs und Politische Praxis 1988-1994
Mit einem Vorwort von Frank Golczewski
ISBN 978-3-89821-722-4

50 *Марлен Ларюэль (ред.)*
Современные интерпретации русского национализма
ISBN 978-3-89821-795-8

51 *Sonja Schüler*
Die ethnische Dimension der Armut
Roma im postsozialistischen Rumänien
Mit einem Vorwort von Anton Sterbling
ISBN 978-3-89821-776-7

52 *Галина Кожевникова*
Радикальный национализм в России и противодействие ему
Сборник докладов Центра «Сова» за 2004-2007 гг.
С предисловием Александра Верховского
ISBN 978-3-89821-721-7

53 *Галина Кожевникова и Владимир Прибыловский*
Российская власть в биографиях I
Высшие должностные лица РФ в 2004 г.
ISBN 978-3-89821-796-5

54 *Галина Кожевникова и Владимир Прибыловский*
Российская власть в биографиях II
Члены Правительства РФ в 2004 г.
ISBN 978-3-89821-797-2

55 *Галина Кожевникова и Владимир Прибыловский*
Российская власть в биографиях III
Руководители федеральных служб и агентств РФ в 2004 г.
ISBN 978-3-89821-798-9

56 *Ileana Petroniu*
Privatisierung in Transformationsökonomien
Determinanten der Restrukturierungs-Bereitschaft am Beispiel Polens, Rumäniens und der Ukraine
Mit einem Vorwort von Rainer W. Schäfer
ISBN 978-3-89821-790-3

57 *Christian Wipperfürth*
Russland und seine GUS-Nachbarn
Hintergründe, aktuelle Entwicklungen und Konflikte in einer ressourcenreichen Region
ISBN 978-3-89821-801-6

58 *Togzhan Kassenova*
From Antagonism to Partnership
The Uneasy Path of the U.S.-Russian Cooperative Threat Reduction
With a foreword by Christoph Bluth
ISBN 978-3-89821-707-1

59 *Alexander Höllwerth*
Das sakrale eurasische Imperium des Aleksandr Dugin
Eine Diskursanalyse zum postsowjetischen russischen Rechtsextremismus
Mit einem Vorwort von Dirk Uffelmann
ISBN 978-3-89821-813-9

60 Олег Рябов
«Россия-Матушка»
Национализм, гендер и война в России XX века
С предисловием Елены Гощило
ISBN 978-3-89821-487-2

61 Ivan Maistrenko
Borot'bism
A Chapter in the History of the Ukrainian Revolution
With a new introduction by Chris Ford
Translated by George S. N. Luckyj with the assistance of Ivan L. Rudnytsky
ISBN 978-3-89821-697-5

62 Maryna Romanets
Anamorphosic Texts and Reconfigured Visions
Improvised Traditions in Contemporary Ukrainian and Irish Literature
ISBN 978-3-89821-576-3

63 Paul D'Anieri and Taras Kuzio (Eds.)
Aspects of the Orange Revolution I
Democratization and Elections in Post-Communist Ukraine
ISBN 978-3-89821-698-2

64 Bohdan Harasymiw in collaboration with Oleh S. Ilnytzkyj (Eds.)
Aspects of the Orange Revolution II
Information and Manipulation Strategies in the 2004 Ukrainian Presidential Elections
ISBN 978-3-89821-699-9

65 Ingmar Bredies, Andreas Umland and Valentin Yakushik (Eds.)
Aspects of the Orange Revolution III
The Context and Dynamics of the 2004 Ukrainian Presidential Elections
ISBN 978-3-89821-803-0

66 Ingmar Bredies, Andreas Umland and Valentin Yakushik (Eds.)
Aspects of the Orange Revolution IV
Foreign Assistance and Civic Action in the 2004 Ukrainian Presidential Elections
ISBN 978-3-89821-808-5

67 Ingmar Bredies, Andreas Umland and Valentin Yakushik (Eds.)
Aspects of the Orange Revolution V
Institutional Observation Reports on the 2004 Ukrainian Presidential Elections
ISBN 978-3-89821-809-2

68 Taras Kuzio (Ed.)
Aspects of the Orange Revolution VI
Post-Communist Democratic Revolutions in Comparative Perspective
ISBN 978-3-89821-820-7

69 Tim Bohse
Autoritarismus statt Selbstverwaltung
Die Transformation der kommunalen Politik in der Stadt Kaliningrad 1990-2005
Mit einem Geleitwort von Stefan Troebst
ISBN 978-3-89821-782-8

70 David Rupp
Die Rußländische Föderation und die russischsprachige Minderheit in Lettland
Eine Fallstudie zur Anwaltspolitik Moskaus gegenüber den russophonen Minderheiten im „Nahen Ausland" von 1991 bis 2002
Mit einem Vorwort von Helmut Wagner
ISBN 978-3-89821-778-1

71 Taras Kuzio
Theoretical and Comparative Perspectives on Nationalism
New Directions in Cross-Cultural and Post-Communist Studies
With a foreword by Paul Robert Magocsi
ISBN 978-3-89821-815-3

72 Christine Teichmann
Die Hochschultransformation im heutigen Osteuropa
Kontinuität und Wandel bei der Entwicklung des postkommunistischen Universitätswesens
Mit einem Vorwort von Oskar Anweiler
ISBN 978-3-89821-842-9

73 Julia Kusznir
Der politische Einfluss von Wirtschaftseliten in russischen Regionen
Eine Analyse am Beispiel der Erdöl- und Erdgasindustrie, 1992-2005
Mit einem Vorwort von Wolfgang Eichwede
ISBN 978-3-89821-821-4

74 Alena Vysotskaya
Russland, Belarus und die EU-Osterweiterung
Zur Minderheitenfrage und zum Problem der Freizügigkeit des Personenverkehrs
Mit einem Vorwort von Katlijn Malfliet
ISBN 978-3-89821-822-1

75 Heiko Pleines (Hrsg.)
    Corporate Governance in post-
    sozialistischen Volkswirtschaften
    ISBN 978-3-89821-766-8

76 Stefan Ihrig
    Wer sind die Moldawier?
    Rumänismus versus Moldowanismus in
    Historiographie und Schulbüchern der
    Republik Moldova, 1991-2006
    Mit einem Vorwort von Holm Sundhaussen
    ISBN 978-3-89821-466-7

77 Galina Kozhevnikova in collaboration
    with Alexander Verkhovsky and
    Eugene Veklerov
    Ultra-Nationalism and Hate Crimes in
    Contemporary Russia
    The 2004-2006 Annual Reports of Moscow's
    SOVA Center
    With a foreword by Stephen D. Shenfield
    ISBN 978-3-89821-868-9

78 Florian Küchler
    The Role of the European Union in
    Moldova's Transnistria Conflict
    With a foreword by Christopher Hill
    ISBN 978-3-89821-850-4

79 Bernd Rechel
    The Long Way Back to Europe
    Minority Protection in Bulgaria
    With a foreword by Richard Crampton
    ISBN 978-3-89821-863-4

80 Peter W. Rodgers
    Nation, Region and History in Post-
    Communist Transitions
    Identity Politics in Ukraine, 1991-2006
    With a foreword by Vera Tolz
    ISBN 978-3-89821-903-7

81 Stephanie Solywoda
    The Life and Work of
    Semen L. Frank
    A Study of Russian Religious Philosophy
    With a foreword by Philip Walters
    ISBN 978-3-89821-457-5

82 Vera Sokolova
    Cultural Politics of Ethnicity
    Discourses on Roma in Communist
    Czechoslovakia
    ISBN 978-3-89821-864-1

83 Natalya Shevchik Ketenci
    Kazakhstani Enterprises in Transition
    The Role of Historical Regional Development
    in Kazakhstan's Post-Soviet Economic
    Transformation
    ISBN 978-3-89821-831-3

84 Martin Malek, Anna Schor-
    Tschudnowskaja (Hrsg.)
    Europa im Tschetschenienkrieg
    Zwischen politischer Ohnmacht und
    Gleichgültigkeit
    Mit einem Vorwort von Lipchan Basajewa
    ISBN 978-3-89821-676-0

85 Stefan Meister
    Das postsowjetische Universitätswesen
    zwischen nationalem und
    internationalem Wandel
    Die Entwicklung der regionalen Hochschule
    in Russland als Gradmesser der
    Systemtransformation
    Mit einem Vorwort von Joan DeBardeleben
    ISBN 978-3-89821-891-7

86 Konstantin Sheiko in collaboration
    with Stephen Brown
    Nationalist Imaginings of the
    Russian Past
    Anatolii Fomenko and the Rise of Alternative
    History in Post-Communist Russia
    With a foreword by Donald Ostrowski
    ISBN 978-3-89821-915-0

87 Sabine Jenni
    Wie stark ist das „Einige Russland"?
    Zur Parteibindung der Eliten und zum
    Wahlerfolg der Machtpartei
    im Dezember 2007
    Mit einem Vorwort von Klaus Armingeon
    ISBN 978-3-89821-961-7

88 Thomas Borén
    Meeting-Places of Transformation
    Urban Identity, Spatial Representations and
    Local Politics in Post-Soviet St Petersburg
    ISBN 978-3-89821-739-2

89 Aygul Ashirova
    Stalinismus und Stalin-Kult in
    Zentralasien
    Turkmenistan 1924-1953
    Mit einem Vorwort von Leonid Luks
    ISBN 978-3-89821-987-7

90   Leonid Luks
      Freiheit oder imperiale Größe?
      Essays zu einem russischen Dilemma
      ISBN 978-3-8382-0011-8

91   Christopher Gilley
      The 'Change of Signposts' in the
      Ukrainian Emigration
      A Contribution to the History of
      Sovietophilism in the 1920s
      With a foreword by Frank Golczewski
      ISBN 978-3-89821-965-5

92   Philipp Casula, Jeronim Perovic
      (Eds.)
      Identities and Politics
      During the Putin Presidency
      The Discursive Foundations of Russia's
      Stability
      With a foreword by Heiko Haumann
      ISBN 978-3-8382-0015-6

93   Marcel Viëtor
      Europa und die Frage
      nach seinen Grenzen im Osten
      Zur Konstruktion ‚europäischer Identität' in
      Geschichte und Gegenwart
      Mit einem Vorwort von Albrecht Lehmann
      ISBN 978-3-8382-0045-3

94   Ben Hellman, Andrei Rogachevskii
      Filming the Unfilmable
      Casper Wrede's 'One Day in the Life
      of Ivan Denisovich'
      Second, Revised and Expanded Edition
      ISBN 978-3-8382-0044-6

95   Eva Fuchslocher
      Vaterland, Sprache, Glaube
      Orthodoxie und Nationenbildung
      am Beispiel Georgiens
      Mit einem Vorwort von Christina von Braun
      ISBN 978-3-89821-884-9

96   Vladimir Kantor
      Das Westlertum und der Weg
      Russlands
      Zur Entwicklung der russischen Literatur und
      Philosophie
      Ediert von Dagmar Herrmann
      Mit einem Beitrag von Nikolaus Lobkowicz
      ISBN 978-3-8382-0102-3

97   Kamran Musayev
      Die postsowjetische Transformation
      im Baltikum und Südkaukasus
      Eine vergleichende Untersuchung der
      politischen Entwicklung Lettlands und
      Aserbaidschans 1985-2009
      Mit einem Vorwort von Leonid Luks
      Ediert von Sandro Henschel
      ISBN 978-3-8382-0103-0

98   Tatiana Zhurzhenko
      Borderlands into Bordered Lands
      Geopolitics of Identity in Post-Soviet Ukraine
      With a foreword by Dieter Segert
      ISBN 978-3-8382-0042-2

99   Кирилл Галушко, Лидия Смола
      (ред.)
      Пределы падения – варианты
      украинского будущего
      Аналитико-прогностические исследования
      ISBN 978-3-8382-0148-1

100   Michael Minkenberg (ed.)
      Historical Legacies and the Radical
      Right in Post-Cold War Central and
      Eastern Europe
      With an afterword by Sabrina P. Ramet
      ISBN 978-3-8382-0124-5

101   David-Emil Wickström
      Rocking St. Petersburg
      Transcultural Flows and Identity Politics in
      the St. Petersburg Popular Music Scene
      With a foreword by Yngvar B. Steinholt
      Second, Revised and Expanded Edition
      ISBN 978-3-8382-0100-9

102   Eva Zabka
      Eine neue „Zeit der Wirren"?
      Der spät- und postsowjetische Systemwandel
      1985-2000 im Spiegel russischer
      gesellschaftspolitischer Diskurse
      Mit einem Vorwort von Margareta Mommsen
      ISBN 978-3-8382-0161-0

103   Ulrike Ziemer
      Ethnic Belonging, Gender and
      Cultural Practices
      Youth Identitites in Contemporary Russia
      With a foreword by Anoop Nayak
      ISBN 978-3-8382-0152-8

104 *Ksenia Chepikova*
‚Einiges Russland' - eine zweite KPdSU?
Aspekte der Identitätskonstruktion einer postsowjetischen „Partei der Macht"
Mit einem Vorwort von Torsten Oppelland
ISBN 978-3-8382-0311-9

105 *Леонид Люкс*
Западничество или евразийство? Демократия или идеократия?
Сборник статей об исторических дилеммах России
С предисловием Владимира Кантора
ISBN 978-3-8382-0211-2

106 *Anna Dost*
Das russische Verfassungsrecht auf dem Weg zum Föderalismus und zurück
Zum Konflikt von Rechtsnormen und -wirklichkeit in der Russländischen Föderation von 1991 bis 2009
Mit einem Vorwort von Alexander Blankenagel
ISBN 978-3-8382-0292-1

107 *Philipp Herzog*
Sozialistische Völkerfreundschaft, nationaler Widerstand oder harmloser Zeitvertreib?
Zur politischen Funktion der Volkskunst im sowjetischen Estland
Mit einem Vorwort von Andreas Kappeler
ISBN 978-3-8382-0216-7

108 *Marlène Laruelle (ed.)*
Russian Nationalism, Foreign Policy, and Identity Debates in Putin's Russia
New Ideological Patterns after the Orange Revolution
ISBN 978-3-8382-0325-6

109 *Michail Logvinov*
Russlands Kampf gegen den internationalen Terrorismus
Eine kritische Bestandsaufnahme des Bekämpfungsansatzes
Mit einem Geleitwort von Hans-Henning Schröder
und einem Vorwort von Eckhard Jesse
ISBN 978-3-8382-0329-4

110 *John B. Dunlop*
The Moscow Bombings of September 1999
Examinations of Russian Terrorist Attacks at the Onset of Vladimir Putin's Rule
Second, Revised and Expanded Edition
ISBN 978-3-8382-0388-1

111 *Андрей А. Ковалёв*
Свидетельство из-за кулис российской политики I
Можно ли делать добро из зла?
(Воспоминания и размышления о последних советских и первых послесоветских годах)
With a foreword by Peter Reddaway
ISBN 978-3-8382-0302-7

112 *Андрей А. Ковалёв*
Свидетельство из-за кулис российской политики II
Угроза для себя и окружающих
(Наблюдения и предостережения относительно происходящего после 2000 г.)
ISBN 978-3-8382-0303-4

113 *Bernd Kappenberg*
Zeichen setzen für Europa
Der Gebrauch europäischer lateinischer Sonderzeichen in der deutschen Öffentlichkeit
Mit einem Vorwort von Peter Schlobinski
ISBN 978-3-89821-749-1

114 *Ivo Mijnssen*
The Quest for an Ideal Youth in Putin's Russia I
Back to Our Future! History, Modernity, and Patriotism according to *Nashi*, 2005-2013
With a foreword by Jeronim Perović
Second, Revised and Expanded Edition
ISBN 978-3-8382-0368-3

115 *Jussi Lassila*
The Quest for an Ideal Youth in Putin's Russia II
The Search for Distinctive Conformism in the Political Communication of *Nashi*, 2005-2009
With a foreword by Kirill Postoutenko
Second, Revised and Expanded Edition
ISBN 978-3-8382-0415-4

116 *Valerio Trabandt*
Neue Nachbarn, gute Nachbarschaft?
Die EU als internationaler Akteur am Beispiel ihrer Demokratieförderung in Belarus und der Ukraine 2004-2009
Mit einem Vorwort von Jutta Joachim
ISBN 978-3-8382-0437-6

117 Fabian Pfeiffer
   Estlands Außen- und Sicherheitspolitik I
   Der estnische Atlantizismus nach der
   wiedererlangten Unabhängigkeit 1991-2004
   Mit einem Vorwort von Helmut Hubel
   ISBN 978-3-8382-0127-6

118 Jana Podßuweit
   Estlands Außen- und Sicherheitspolitik II
   Handlungsoptionen eines Kleinstaates im
   Rahmen seiner EU-Mitgliedschaft (2004-2008)
   Mit einem Vorwort von Helmut Hubel
   ISBN 978-3-8382-0440-6

119 Karin Pointner
   Estlands Außen- und Sicherheitspolitik III
   Eine gedächtnispolitische Analyse estnischer
   Entwicklungskooperation 2006-2010
   Mit einem Vorwort von Karin Liebhart
   ISBN 978-3-8382-0435-2

120 Ruslana Vovk
   Die Offenheit der ukrainischen
   Verfassung für das Völkerrecht und
   die europäische Integration
   Mit einem Vorwort von Alexander
   Blankenagel
   ISBN 978-3-8382-0481-9

121 Mykhaylo Banakh
   Die Relevanz der Zivilgesellschaft
   bei den postkommunistischen
   Transformationsprozessen in mittel-
   und osteuropäischen Ländern
   Das Beispiel der spät- und postsowjetischen
   Ukraine 1986-2009
   Mit einem Vorwort von Gerhard Simon
   ISBN 978-3-8382-0499-4

122 Michael Moser
   Language Policy and the Discourse on
   Languages in Ukraine under President
   Viktor Yanukovych (25 February
   2010–28 October 2012)
   ISBN 978-3-8382-0497-0 (Paperback edition)
   ISBN 978-3-8382-0507-6 (Hardcover edition)

123 Nicole Krome
   Russischer Netzwerkkapitalismus
   Restrukturierungsprozesse in der
   Russischen Föderation am Beispiel des
   Luftfahrtunternehmens "Aviastar"
   Mit einem Vorwort von Petra Stykow
   ISBN 978-3-8382-0534-2

124 David R. Marples
   'Our Glorious Past'
   Lukashenka's Belarus and
   the Great Patriotic War
   ISBN 978-3-8382-0574-8 (Paperback edition)
   ISBN 978-3-8382-0675-2 (Hardcover edition)

125 Ulf Walther
   Russlands "neuer Adel"
   Die Macht des Geheimdienstes von
   Gorbatschow bis Putin
   Mit einem Vorwort von Hans-Georg Wieck
   ISBN 978-3-8382-0584-7

126 Simon Geissbühler (Hrsg.)
   Kiew – Revolution 3.0
   Der Euromaidan 2013/14 und die
   Zukunftsperspektiven der Ukraine
   ISBN 978-3-8382-0581-6 (Paperback edition)
   ISBN 978-3-8382-0681-3 (Hardcover edition)

127 Andrey Makarychev
   Russia and the EU
   in a Multipolar World
   Discourses, Identities, Norms
   With a foreword by Klaus Segbers
   ISBN 978-3-8382-0629-5

128 Roland Scharff
   Kasachstan als postsowjetischer
   Wohlfahrtsstaat
   Die Transformation des sozialen
   Schutzsystems
   Mit einem Vorwort von Joachim Ahrens
   ISBN 978-3-8382-0622-6

129 Katja Grupp
   Bild Lücke Deutschland
   Kaliningrader Studierende sprechen über
   Deutschland
   Mit einem Vorwort von Martin Schulz
   ISBN 978-3-8382-0552-6

130 Konstantin Sheiko, Stephen Brown
   History as Therapy
   Alternative History and Nationalist
   Imaginings in Russia, 1991-2014
   ISBN 978-3-8382-0665-3

131 Elisa Kriza
   Alexander Solzhenitsyn: Cold War
   Icon, Gulag Author, Russian
   Nationalist?
   A Study of the Western Reception of his
   Literary Writings, Historical Interpretations,
   and Political Ideas
   With a foreword by Andrei Rogatchevski
   ISBN 978-3-8382-0589-2 (Paperback edition)
   ISBN 978-3-8382-0690-5 (Hardcover edition)

132   Serghei Golunov
      The Elephant in the Room
      Corruption and Cheating in Russian
      Universities
      ISBN 978-3-8382-0570-0

133   Manja Hussner, Rainer Arnold (Hgg.)
      Verfassungsgerichtsbarkeit in
      Zentralasien I
      Sammlung von Verfassungstexten
      ISBN 978-3-8382-0595-3

134   Nikolay Mitrokhin
      Die "Russische Partei"
      Die Bewegung der russischen Nationalisten in
      der UdSSR 1953-1985
      Aus dem Russischen übertragen von einem
      Übersetzerteam unter der Leitung von Larisa Schippel
      ISBN 978-3-8382-0024-8

135   Manja Hussner, Rainer Arnold (Hgg.)
      Verfassungsgerichtsbarkeit in
      Zentralasien II
      Sammlung von Verfassungstexten
      ISBN 978-3-8382-0597-7

136   Manfred Zeller
      Das sowjetische Fieber
      Fußballfans im poststalinistischen
      Vielvölkerreich
      Mit einem Vorwort von Nikolaus Katzer
      ISBN 978-3-8382-0757-5

137   Kristin Schreiter
      Stellung und Entwicklungspotential
      zivilgesellschaftlicher Gruppen in
      Russland
      Menschenrechtsorganisationen im Vergleich
      ISBN 978-3-8382-0673-8

138   David R. Marples, Frederick V. Mills
      (eds.)
      Ukraine's Euromaidan
      Analyses of a Civil Revolution
      ISBN 978-3-8382-0660-8

139   Bernd Kappenberg
      Setting Signs for Europe
      Why Diacritics Matter for
      European Integration
      With a foreword by Peter Schlobinski
      ISBN 978-3-8382-0663-9

140   René Lenz
      Internationalisierung, Kooperation
      und Transfer
      Externe bildungspolitische Akteure in der
      Russischen Föderation
      Mit einem Vorwort von Frank Ettrich
      ISBN 978-3-8382-0751-3

141   Juri Plusnin, Yana Zausaeva, Natalia
      Zhidkevich, Artemy Pozanenko
      Wandering Workers
      Mores, Behavior, Way of Life, and Political
      Status of Domestic Russian Labor Migrants
      Translated by Julia Kazantseva
      ISBN 978-3-8382-0653-0

142   David J. Smith (eds.)
      Latvia – A Work in Progress?
      100 Years of State- and Nation-Building
      ISBN 978-3-8382-0648-6

143   Инна Чувычкина (ред.)
      Экспортные нефте- и газопроводы
      на постсоветском пространстве
      Анализ трубопроводной политики в свете
      теории международных отношений
      ISBN 978-3-8382-0822-0

144   Johann Zajaczkowski
      Russland – eine pragmatische
      Großmacht?
      Eine rollentheoretische Untersuchung
      russischer Außenpolitik am Beispiel der
      Zusammenarbeit mit den USA nach 9/11 und
      des Georgienkrieges von 2008
      Mit einem Vorwort von Siegfried Schieder
      ISBN 978-3-8382-0837-4

145   Boris Popivanov
      Changing Images of the Left in
      Bulgaria
      The Challenge of Post-Communism in the
      Early 21st Century
      ISBN 978-3-8382-0667-7

146   Lenka Krátká
      A History of the Czechoslovak Ocean
      Shipping Company 1948-1989
      How a Small, Landlocked Country Ran
      Maritime Business During the Cold War
      ISBN 978-3-8382-0666-0

147   Alexander Sergunin
      Explaining Russian Foreign Policy
      Behavior
      Theory and Practice
      ISBN 978-3-8382-0752-0

148 *Darya Malyutina*
    Migrant Friendships in
    a Super-Diverse City
    Russian-Speakers and their Social
    Relationships in London in the 21st Century
    With a foreword by Claire Dwyer
    ISBN 978-3-8382-0652-3

149 *Alexander Sergunin, Valery Konyshev*
    Russia in the Arctic
    Hard or Soft Power?
    ISBN 978-3-8382-0753-7

150 *John J. Maresca*
    Helsinki Revisited
    A Key U.S. Negotiator's Memoirs
    on the Development of the CSCE into the
    OSCE
    With a foreword by Hafiz Pashayev
    ISBN 978-3-8382-0852-7

151 *Jardar Østbø*
    The New Third Rome
    Readings of a Russian Nationalist Myth
    With a foreword by Pål Kolstø
    ISBN 978-3-8382-0870-1

152 *Simon Kordonsky*
    Socio-Economic Foundations of the
    Russian Post-Soviet Regime
    The Resource-Based Economy and Estate-
    Based Social Structure of Contemporary
    Russia
    With a foreword by Svetlana Barsukova
    ISBN 978-3-8382-0775-9

153 *Duncan Leitch*
    Assisting Reform in Post-Communist
    Ukraine 2000–2012
    The Illusions of Donors and the Disillusion of
    Beneficiaries
    With a foreword by Kataryna Wolczuk
    ISBN 978-3-8382-0844-2

154 *Abel Polese*
    Limits of a Post-Soviet State
    How Informality Replaces, Renegotiates, and
    Reshapes Governance in Contemporary
    Ukraine
    With a foreword by Colin Williams
    ISBN 978-3-8382-0845-9

155 *Mikhail Suslov (ed.)*
    Digital Orthodoxy in the Post-Soviet
    World
    The Russian Orthodox Church and Web 2.0
    With a foreword by Father Cyril Hovorun
    ISBN 978-3-8382-0871-8

156 *Leonid Luks*
    Zwei „Sonderwege"? Russisch-
    deutsche Parallelen und Kontraste
    (1917-2014)
    Vergleichende Essays
    ISBN 978-3-8382-0823-7

157 *Vladimir V. Karacharovskiy, Ovsey I.
    Shkaratan, Gordey A. Yastrebov*
    Towards a New Russian Work Culture
    Can Western Companies and Expatriates
    Change Russian Society?
    With a foreword by Elena N. Danilova
    Translated by Julia Kazantseva
    ISBN 978-3-8382-0902-9

158 *Edmund Griffiths*
    Aleksandr Prokhanov and Post-Soviet
    Esotericism
    ISBN 978-3-8382-0903-6

159 *Timm Beichelt, Susann Worschech
    (eds.)*
    Transnational Ukraine?
    Networks and Ties that Influence(d)
    Contemporary Ukraine
    ISBN 978-3-8382-0944-9

160 *Mieste Hotopp-Riecke*
    Die Tataren der Krim zwischen
    Assimilation und Selbstbehauptung
    Der Aufbau des krimtatarischen
    Bildungswesens nach Deportation und
    Heimkehr (1990-2005)
    Mit einem Vorwort von Swetlana
    Czerwonnaja
    ISBN 978-3-89821-940-2

161 *Olga Bertelsen (ed.)*
    Revolution and War in
    Contemporary Ukraine
    The Challenge of Change
    ISBN 978-3-8382-1016-2

162 *Natalya Ryabinska*
    Ukraine's Post-Communist
    Mass Media
    Between Capture and Commercialization
    With a foreword by Marta Dyczok
    ISBN 978-3-8382-1011-7

163 Alexandra Cotofana,
 James M. Nyce (eds.)
 Religion and Magic in Socialist and
 Post-Socialist Contexts I
 Historic and Ethnographic Case Studies of
 Orthodoxy, Heterodoxy, and Alternative
 Spirituality
 With a foreword by Patrick L. Michelson
 ISBN 978-3-8382-0989-0

164 Nozima Akhrarkhodjaeva
 The Instrumentalisation of Mass
 Media in Electoral Authoritarian
 Regimes
 Evidence from Russia's Presidential Election
 Campaigns of 2000 and 2008
 ISBN 978-3-8382-1013-1

165 Yulia Krasheninnikova
 Informal Healthcare in Contemporary
 Russia
 Sociographic Essays on the Post-Soviet
 Infrastructure for Alternative Healing
 Practices
 ISBN 978-3-8382-0970-8

166 Peter Kaiser
 Das Schachbrett der Macht
 Die Handlungsspielräume eines sowjetischen
 Funktionärs unter Stalin am Beispiel des
 Generalsekretärs des Komsomol
 Aleksandr Kosarev (1929-1938)
 Mit einem Vorwort von Dietmar Neutatz
 ISBN 978-3-8382-1052-0

167 Oksana Kim
 The Effects and Implications of
 Kazakhstan's Adoption of
 International Financial Reporting
 Standards
 A Resource Dependence Perspective
 With a foreword by Svetlana Vlady
 ISBN 978-3-8382-0987-6

168 Anna Sanina
 Patriotic Education in
 Contemporary Russia
 Sociological Studies in the Making of the
 Post-Soviet Citizen
 With a foreword by Anna Oldfield
 ISBN 978-3-8382-0993-7

169 Rudolf Wolters
 Spezialist in Sibirien
 Faksimile der 1933 erschienenen
 ersten Ausgabe
 Mit einem Vorwort von Dmitrij Chmelnizki
 ISBN 978-3-8382-0515-1

170 Michal Vít,
 Magdalena M. Baran (eds.)
 Transregional versus National
 Perspectives on Contemporary Central
 European History
 Studies on the Building of Nation-States and
 Their Cooperation in the 20th and 21st Century
 With a foreword by Petr Vágner
 ISBN 978-3-8382-1015-5

171 Philip Gamaghelyan
 Conflict Resolution Beyond the
 International Relations Paradigm
 Evolving Designs as a Transformative
 Practice in Nagorno-Karabakh and Syria
 With a foreword by Susan Allen
 ISBN 978-3-8382-1057-5

172 Maria Shagina
 Joining a Prestigious Club
 Cooperation with Europarties and Its Impact
 on Party Development in Georgia, Moldova,
 and Ukraine 2004–2015
 With a foreword by Kataryna Wolczuk
 ISBN 978-3-8382-1084-1

173 Alexandra Cotofana,
 James M. Nyce (eds.)
 Religion and Magic in Socialist and
 Post-Socialist Contexts II
 Baltic, Eastern European, and Post-USSR
 Case Studies
 ISBN 978-3-8382-0990-6

174 Barbara Kunz
 Kind Words, Cruise Missiles, and
 Everything in Between
 The Use of Power Resources in U.S. Policies
 towards Poland, Ukraine, and Belarus
 1989–2008
 With a foreword by William Hill
 ISBN 978-3-8382-1065-0

ibidem-Verlag

Melchiorstr. 15

D-70439 Stuttgart

info@ibidem-verlag.de

www.ibidem-verlag.de
www.ibidem.eu
www.edition-noema.de
www.autorenbetreuung.de